MANAGING YOUR MONEY

WITH
MANAGING YOUR MONEY®
SECOND EDITION

MANAGING YOUR MONEY

WITH
MANAGING YOUR MONEY®
SECOND EDITION

JIM BARTIMO

PUBLISHED BY
Microsoft Press
A Division of Microsoft Corporation
16011 N.E. 36th Way, Box 97017, Redmond, Washington 98073-9717

Library of Congress Cataloging in Publication Data
Bartimo, Jim, 1956-
Managing your Money with Managing Your Money
Includes index.
1. Finance, Personal—Data processing.   2. Managing Your Money
(Computer program)   I. Title.
HG179.B339   1989   332.024'0028'55369   88-27347
ISBN 1-55615-190-X

Printed and bound in the United States of America.
1 2 3 4 5 6 7 8 9 MLML 3 2 1 0 9 8

Distributed to the book trade in the United States by Harper & Row.

Distributed to the book trade in Canada by General Publishing Company, Ltd.

Distributed to the book trade outside the United States and Canada
by Penguin Books Ltd.

Penguin Books Ltd., Harmondsworth, Middlesex, England
Penguin Books Australia Ltd., Ringwood, Victoria, Australia
Penguin Books N.Z. Ltd., 182-190 Wairau Road, Auckland 10, New Zealand

British Cataloging in Publication Data available

Project editor: Nancy Siadek
Technical editor: Dail Magee, Jr.

This book is dedicated to Lisa

CONTENTS

CHAPTER 3

Managing Your Budget and Checkbook   49

CHAPTER 4

Managing Your Taxes   105

CHAPTER 5

Managing Your Insurance   145

PREFACE

Welcome to the second edition of the book *Managing Your Money with Managing Your Money* and version 5.0 of the program Managing Your Money. Much has changed since the book *Managing Your Money with Managing Your Money* was published in January of 1987. The stock-market crash added excitement to our lives, the tax laws changed considerably, and the program Managing Your Money saw two upgrades. Version 5.0 of Managing Your Money now includes a built-in word processor and several new features that make it an even more powerful personal-finance tool than it was two years ago.

The second edition of *Managing Your Money with Managing Your Money* includes updated strategies for using the program under the new tax laws and, of course, complete discussions of the program's newest features, particularly the Write on the Money word processor. Those of you who have struggled with Starting A New Year and the best ways to back up your files will be glad to find thorough discussions of these important issues here.

So start up version 5.0 of the program and see what's new. To those of you who are using the program for the first time, welcome to a new world of convenience in personal financial management.

ACKNOWLEDGMENTS

The completion of this edition would not have been possible without the understanding of the editors at the *San Jose Mercury News*. Also invaluable to the completion of this project were my financial adviser Bud Sanders and the editors at Microsoft Press.

INTRODUCTION

Managing Your Money is about to change the way you manage your personal finances, from balancing your checkbook to planning your retirement. Instead of writing the same checks to the same people month after month, you'll print checks for those monthly bills and record the payments automatically in budget categories.

Managing Your Money will also help you plan for your taxes well before the end of the tax year. You won't be surprised, shocked, or hassled at tax time; you'll be prepared and, because you planned ahead, perhaps pay less in taxes.

Managing Your Money will help you determine how much insurance you need and will store your policy information so that it is readily available when you need it.

If you are an investor—beginner or seasoned—Managing Your Money will help you track and analyze your investments. You might want to create a hypothetical portfolio and test the market before you take any risks.

Managing Your Money will help you plan savings for your child's college education and for your retirement. It might even change the way you mail your Christmas cards! But you might need some help.

When Andrew Tobias released his software program for money management in 1984, I began using it immediately. I was impressed with what I saw: a powerful program organized in an easy-to-use format. I soon realized, however, that the program's power could be difficult to tap. The program lacked a comprehensive printed manual, so I wasn't always sure of exactly what I could—or should—do. And the more I talked to other people who used the program, the more I found I was not alone.

After five years of mapping the uncharted regions of Managing Your Money, I saw how the program's power could be used simply and effectively. I discovered how all the pieces fit together and how I had to change some of my habits to really benefit from the program. The following pages show what I learned.

HOW THE PROGRAM IS ORGANIZED

Managing Your Money is organized like a book with nine chapters, each of which helps you with a different set of financial tasks.

Chapter 1, "Utilities," contains a mini-tutorial in which Andrew Tobias explains how the program works. Although this section does not cover everything, it gives worthwhile hands-on practice in entering data. The Utilities chapter also offers help with system setup. From the System Setup menu, you can configure your printer, monitor, hard disk, and other components to work most efficiently with the program.

Chapter 2, "Reminder Pad," organizes your personal schedule. You can list tasks to do and important dates, such as birthdays, graduations, or a loan payment date. Because you always enter the current date when you start the program, Managing Your Money keeps track of important dates that are approaching and reminds you of them each time you use the program.

Chapter 3, "Budget and Checkbook," is the hub of the program. Here you enter financial data—checks, deposits, charge accounts, and loan payments. You can create a budget for meeting your financial goals and then record all your expenses and income in budget categories to determine how well you are meeting those goals. You can then project your cash flow over the coming year, calculate loan payments, and even set up accounts-receivable and accounts-payable ledgers for a small business. Even if you use only this chapter, your finances will be far more organized than before you used the program.

Chapter 4 is the "Income Tax Estimator." With it you can calculate the amount you are likely to pay at tax time. If you know in advance the amount of your tax bill, you can better plan the year's ventures.

Chapter 5, "Insurance Planning," helps you answer the question "Do I have enough insurance?" It also helps you organize your insurance policy information and, in the course of your planning, calculates your life expectancy.

Chapter 6, the "Financial Calculator," is really a handy collection of financial formulas that help you plan for retirement, for paying for your child's college education, for analyzing investments, and for making decisions about refinancing or buying versus renting. You can also calculate the monthly payment of a loan if you know the term, interest rate, and amount of the loan.

Chapter 7, the "Portfolio Manager," is the second most important chapter in the program. With it, you record and monitor the performance of your investments, from mutual funds to blue-chip stocks. Using the sophisticated analysis tools in this chapter, you can see how much your investments yield and decide whether you should sell them.

Chapter 8, "Your Net Worth," is where all your financial information comes together. This chapter collects information from other chapters and calculates exactly how much you are worth financially. And the next time you visit a loan officer or a financial planner, you can take along your own personal balance sheet.

Chapter 9, the "Card File," is a file manager designed specifically to keep a list of telephone numbers and addresses of business contacts, friends, and relatives. From this list, you can create mailing lists and print mailing labels. You can even use it to dial your telephone automatically if you have an auto-dialing modem. Also, when you record birthdays and anniversaries on someone's card, you can send that information to Chapter 2, and you'll be reminded that the special day is coming up.

You can reach the Write on the Money word-processing feature from almost any point in the program by pressing Ctrl-W. Write on the Money lets you create, edit, store, and print documents. You can use Write to edit reports or to create simple letters and memos. You can also use Write in combination with the Card File to create form letters and to create pop-up notes to explain your financial transactions.

HOW THE BOOK IS ORGANIZED

Managing Your Money with Managing Your Money contains two parts. Part I, "The Program," is organized much like the program itself, with each chapter corresponding to a program chapter. So Chapter 3 of this book, called "Managing Your Budget and Checkbook," explains how to use Chapter 3 of the program.

Read each chapter here before you use the corresponding chapter in the program. Each chapter suggests a strategy for using the program. Note that although the program is flexible, it is also powerful, and you can get lost in it if you don't follow a strategy. As I mentioned, I've spent five years trying out different strategies, and I think those I propose will minimize time-consuming sidetracks and mistakes.

Part II, "People Who Manage Their Money," presents four hypothetical examples of individuals who use Managing Your Money. Each user has different financial resources and financial goals, and each uses the program differently to manage those resources and meet those goals.

You might want to read through these cases before you begin to work with the program. They can give you a quick look at how Managing Your Money changes the way you handle your finances. You might also want to choose the case that most closely resembles your own situation and use it as a guide to decide which parts of the program can be most useful.

WHICH VERSION? WHICH MACHINE?

This book was written primarily for users of the IBM version 5.0 of Managing Your Money. However, Apple users can also use this book as a guide. The Apple II version of the program is usually one year behind the IBM version, but for the most part, the most current Apple II version is very similar to the most current IBM version. The major difference in the Apple II version, aside from the absence of new features, is that it does not use function keys. (The Apple II doesn't have them.) Instead, the user must press the Apple key in combination with a number key to mimic the IBM PC function keys. So, when the book instructs to "Press F1," Apple users should instead hold down the Open Apple key and press the 1 key.

The features of the Macintosh version of Managing Your Money differ in the same way. Because the Macintosh operates in a fashion that is unlike the IBM or Apple II computers, the strategies presented here are useful for Macintosh users, but the ''how-to'' instructions for operating the program are not.

GETTING WHAT YOU WANT

No two people will use Managing Your Money in the same way. You might want only to automate your monthly bill payments, whereas your neighbor might want to manage his stock portfolio and the investments of everyone he knows. The key to using Managing Your Money successfully is to use it only as much as you want and need to. Managing Your Money will organize your finances. When you see where your money is, you should be able to make more intelligent decisions about how to save it, spend it, and invest it. But don't feel obligated to use any part of the program that won't make your life a little easier or a little more profitable—or both.

I suggest you start with Chapter 3 and get your checkbook and budget in the best possible shape. Then, if you already have investments, turn to Chapter 7 and set up your electronic portfolio. You might have the most fun with Chapter 8, where you add up your assets and liabilities to find your exact net worth.

One word of caution: This book is not a complete guide to managing your finances. It is a guide for using Managing Your Money to help you manage your finances.

Finally, don't be threatened by any financial terms you don't yet understand. After only a few hours with the program and this book, you will be almost an expert at managing your money with Managing Your Money.

PART I:
THE PROGRAM

CHAPTER 1

MANAGING YOUR COMPUTER

Managing Your Money is a tool that helps you manage your financial life more efficiently in less time. If you are familiar with computers, the program won't create any problems for you. If you're not familiar with computers, you may need a little help with managing your machine before you begin managing your money. That's what this chapter is for—to get you started working with disks, setting up your computer, running the program, saving your information in files, and solving problems when they come up.

You'll find that Managing Your Money does as much as possible to shield you from complicated computer commands. Each screen of the program has clearly labeled choices, and most screens have help screens that are called up by pressing the Escape key. You never have to design your own screens in Managing Your Money, and you never have to write a line of programming code.

To make the program work your way, however, and to get out of inevitable computer jams, you should know how the program operates on a computing level as well as on a financial level. So read this chapter carefully. It will explain everything you must know to use the rest of the chapters.

WORKING WITH THE PROGRAM

Before you start setting up accounts and budgets, you may find it helpful to see first how the program is organized and then how to perform operations, make choices, and enter information. In many ways, Managing Your Money is a list processor. In the reminder pad in Chapter 2, for example, you create lists of important dates and a list of chores to do. In the checkbook in Chapter 3, you create lists of bank accounts, with lists of transactions in each account. In Chapter 7, you create lists of portfolios and lists of assets within each portfolio.

To create the individual entries in these lists, you often use forms. For example, in Chapter 3, you use a Spend Money form to record expense transactions in your checking account. You use a Receive Money form to record deposits in your account. You simply fill in the blanks in these forms and then press a function key to add the entry to the list.

Managing Your Money Screens

Most Managing Your Money screens have two parts: an information box at the top of the screen and an action box at the bottom. You enter financial information in the information box and refer to the action box for the operations that you can perform using function keys. Additional helpful information appears at the bottom of the screen. (See Figure 1-1.)

Menus help you find your way around the program. They list all chapters and all sections within chapters. In fact, the options in the action boxes also form menus for a particular screen. Think of these menus as trees, each branch of which may have several more branches. This design minimizes the need for special computer commands; you can, however, enter information in several other ways.

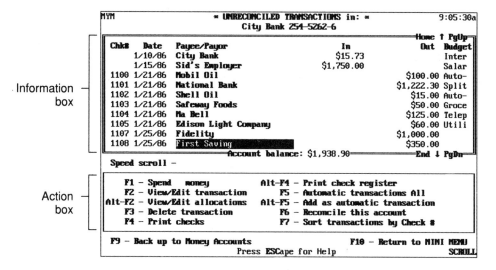

Information box

Action box

Figure 1-1. *A typical Managing Your Money screen.*

Using the Function Keys

The function keys do most of the work in Managing Your Money. You use the rest of the keyboard to enter names, dates, and figures, but you use the function keys to move about on the menu trees.

Be aware that the function keys perform different operations from screen to screen. No one function key will always delete an item from a list; F3 and F4, however, are commonly used for this task. Usually you add to a list by pressing the F1 key. You can almost always use the F9 key to back up to the previous screen. Often, you highlight a list item within an information box and then press a function key to perform an operation on the highlighted item. For example, if you want to work with a particular account, highlight the account in the list of your accounts and press the F1 key to display the list of transactions in the account. You can then highlight one of those transactions and press another key to display detailed information about it.

Many of your lists grow quickly, until they are too long to fit in the information box. You can scroll through these lists with the Down arrow or Up arrow key until you find the item you want. Once you become so familiar with the program that you know the sequence of function keys to move through several screens, you can save time by entering the entire sequence without waiting for the individual screens to appear. The program remembers the keystrokes you make and skips the interim screens.

Saving time can be important because sometimes the program can be downright slow. When you press a function key, a "Wait" sign blinks in the lower-right corner of the screen. The wait is usually, but not always, short. The longest waits occur when you change chapters, back up your files, or archive information. As long as the "Wait" sign is blinking, though, the program is working.

Entering Information

Most of the chapters in the Managing Your Money program consist of lists to which you add information. You usually enter information into a form that has several blanks, such as the form in Chapter 3 for entering information about a deposit in your bank account.

To display the form, press a function key; then you enter the information. Press another function key to add the entry to the list. Sometimes you add information to a list directly by using an ''add-a-new-item'' line at the bottom of the list. First you fill in all the blanks in this line, and then you press a function key to add it to the list.

Blanks appear in action boxes as well as in information boxes. Here, you enter information that the program needs before it can perform the operation you want. For example, if you want to sort the list of transactions in your account, you must tell the program whether you want to sort by date, by check number, by payee, or by amount of the check.

Whether you are entering information in forms, in new lines for lists, or in function-key blanks, you will always do it in the same way.

To enter information, highlight the blank and type the correct information.

To highlight a blank, you can use the Tab, Enter, or arrow keys to move the cursor. A blank becomes highlighted when the cursor reaches that blank. The Tab and Enter keys move sequentially through every blank on the screen. The arrow keys move up and down columns or across rows. If you want to use the arrow keys to move from the information box to the action box or move to the end of the information box, you can turn off scrolling by pressing the Scroll Lock key.

When you highlight a blank, an underline cursor blinks. The next character you type appears at this cursor. Sometimes the program limits your choices by giving you possibilities of what you can type in a blank. For example, when you are sorting your list of transactions, you have only four choices available. The program displays these choices at the bottom of the screen when you highlight the blank. (See Figure 1-2 on the following page.)

For these limited-choice blanks, you type a code in place of the entire choice. The code is the first letter of the choice. If several choices start with the same first letter, you type the number of letters that will distinguish the choice. For example, if you are trying to distinguish a checking account from a charge account, you must type CHE.

```
MYM                  * UNRECONCILED TRANSACTIONS in: *              9:05:49a
                          City Bank 254-5262-6
                                                          ┌Home ↑ PgUp┐
 Chk#    Date    Payee/Payor                    In         Out  Budget│
         1/10/86  City Bank                    $15.73            Inter│
         1/15/86  Sid's Employer             $1,750.00           Salar│
 1100 1/21/86  Mobil Oil                              $100.00 Auto-│
 1101 1/21/86  National Bank                        $1,222.30 Split│
 1102 1/21/86  Shell Oil                              $15.00 Auto-│
 1103 1/21/86  Safeway Foods                          $50.00 Groce│
 1104 1/21/86  Ma Bell                               $125.00 Telep│
 1105 1/21/86  Edison Light Company                   $60.00 Utili│
 1107 1/25/86  Fidelity                            $1,000.00       │
 1108 1/25/86  First Saving                          $350.00       │
               └Account balance: $1,938.90══════════════End ↓ PgDn┘
  Speed scroll -

 ┌─────────────────────────────────────────────────────────────────┐
 │   F1 - Spend    money          Alt-F4 - Print check register     │
 │   F2 - View/Edit transaction       F5 - Automatic transactions All│
 │Alt-F2 - View/Edit allocations   Alt-F5 - Add as automatic transaction│
 │   F3 - Delete transaction          F6 - Reconcile this account   │
 │   F4 - Print checks                F7 - Sort transactions by Check #│
 └─────────────────────────────────────────────────────────────────┘
   F9 - Back up to Money Accounts           F10 - Return to MINI MENU
 Choose one: Date, Check #, Payee or Amount.
```

Figure 1-2. *Entering information in a limited-choice blank.*

Understanding Status Boxes

Managing Your Money lets you know what it is doing by using status boxes. The program's status boxes pop up in the middle of the screen and display messages. For instance, when you leave Chapter 3, a status box pops up to tell you that the program is passing the appropriate information to Chapters 4, 7, and 8 (which use this information to help you with your taxes, portfolio, and net worth). The program even counts how many pieces of information are being passed along. Status boxes are useful because they tell you exactly what's happening while the computer is working.

Even when there are no status boxes, Managing Your Money tells you what kind of file it's saving to disk when you leave a chapter. So, when you leave Chapter 5, you get a little message at the bottom of the screen that says "Saving insure.db...."

Leaving Chapters and Storing Information

Whenever you leave a chapter—usually by pressing F10—you are almost always presented with three options: You can save all changes you made while you were working in the chapter, abandon all changes you made, or return to the chapter you were about to leave. It's almost always best to save your changes before you exit.

Press F1 to save your changes and exit.

If you try to leave a chapter without saving to disk first, the program asks, "Are you sure?" and beeps. You can press **Y** for yes or **N** for no. This feature prevents you from accidentally leaving a chapter after two hours of work and then losing your work because you forgot to save it.

Press F5 to leave the chapter without saving your work.

Press F10 to return to the same chapter.

**Deleting
Information**

Deleting information is just as important as saving information. In fact, if you are using Managing Your Money for the first time, you're going to spend a lot of time deleting information before you enter any of your own material—thanks to Sid and Sara Sample.

Sid and Sara Sample are an imaginary couple who supposedly used your copy of Managing Your Money before you did. They filled in their bank accounts, checks, investments, and even their net worth. Although their information is useful to illustrate how the program works, you will need to take a minute or two to delete it each time you enter a new chapter. You may want to play around with their information as you begin using this book. That way, you can experiment with their figures without making errors with your own. When you are finished using their information, however, be sure to delete it. Otherwise, you may find that your net worth is unexpectedly high, thanks to a windfall Sid and Sara experienced in Chapter 7.

You delete items in a list with a function key—usually, but not always, the F3 key. Sometimes deleting an item in a list deletes an entire account. Sometimes the only way to delete information is to erase the contents of a blank and type your new information in its place.

To delete information from a blank, highlight the blank, position the blinking cursor at the beginning of the blank, and press the spacebar. The blank is now empty, and you can type the new entry.

Using the Help Screens

You will find a Help screen to explain almost every working screen in Managing Your Money. In fact, often you will find several. These Help screens were written by Tobias to take the place of a manual, and they are indeed helpful.

To get help for the current screen, press the Escape key.

The program displays the Help screen and perhaps leads you to others.

Press the spacebar to move forward through the screens.

Press F9 to move backward.

While the Help screen is displayed, you cannot do anything else in the program; you must first return to the program.

To return to the program, press the Escape key again.

Keep in mind that the Help screens monopolize the Escape key, which is usually reserved for "escaping" from the current screen or function. Because you can't use the Escape key to escape, you must use the function keys, which have taken over this duty. Each screen tells you which key or keys to use to move to a different screen.

Responding to Error Messages

When entering information, you may make a mistake. The program can't help you if you typed $10 when you meant to type $100, but it can help you if you entered the wrong type of information in a blank or if you entered information in a blank that you should have left empty. In these cases, it displays error messages that tell you what you have done wrong. For example, if you typed $10 using a lowercase "L" for a 1 when you meant to type $10, the program displays a message on the screen. In this case, the error message is "Number not properly formed. Try again." It indicates that the program doesn't recognize a character you typed.

10

An error message may also warn you if you are using the program incorrectly. For example, you can use the compound calculator in Chapter 6 to calculate the terms of a loan. Fill in any three of the four blanks, and the program calculates the value for the remaining blank. If you fill in all four, however, the program responds "Leave ONE line blank."

When you make an error, the error message blinks and you cannot perform any other operation until you correct the mistake. You can delete an entry by positioning the cursor at the beginning of the blank and pressing the spacebar.

Printing

In many chapters, you can produce reports of your information. You can choose to print the report on a printer or save it in a file on a disk (sometimes called "printing to disk").

The advantage of saving the report in a file before you print it is that the information is stored in ASCII format, which almost any word processor can read. You can open the file with your word processor and add headings and explanations or change the format of the report. You can delete any information you don't want to include. Then you can print it with your word processor.

To save a report in a file, select the print option.

The program lets you send the file to a printer or asks you to name the file in which you want to save the report. Give the file a name that you can remember. For example, if you are printing your personal balance sheet from Chapter 8, you might name the file B:BALANCE.

Type the name of the file, including the drive specification.

After leaving Managing Your Money, you can run a word-processing program and open the file or call up the file with Write on the Money. (See "Write on the Money" later in this chapter.)

You often can choose between normal, compressed, letter-quality, emphasized, or daisy-wheel modes if your printer handles these features. Compressing print is useful when report formats are too wide for your printer carriage. You can also print to the screen so that you can review how your report looks before committing it to paper. After your report is printed on the screen, a touch of any key returns you to Managing Your Money.

HARDWARE REQUIREMENTS AND OPTIONS

The IBM PC version of Managing Your Money runs on any 100 percent–compatible computer, including the COMPAQ Portable, the Epson Equity, the AT&T PC6300, and a host of others. You must use DOS version 2.0 or later. Most computers currently use version 2.0 or later, but check your disk to be sure. (If the version number is not printed on the disk, enter **VER** at the system prompt to display the DOS version number.) You can run the program easily if you have a hard-disk drive or two floppy-disk drives. A one-drive system is less desirable.

These days, most PC-compatible computers come with 640 KB of memory, but you shouldn't have any trouble using the program on a 256 KB system. Memory can become a problem when you enter a large number of transactions in the budget and checkbook chapter or in the portfolio chapter where you record most of your financial information. By the year's end, you could use up all your memory.

To avoid this, you can archive your information. Archived information is removed from memory and stored permanently on a disk. Once archived, it cannot be restored to the copy of your unarchived information—it can only be edited, viewed, and reported on separately.

A hardware option to consider is the 8087 math coprocessor from Intel Corporation. This computer chip speeds up the performance of all mathematical calculations the program makes. You install it by removing your computer's casing and plugging the chip directly into the computer's main circuit board. On most PC-compatible computers, the

8087 fits snugly into an empty socket next to the main processor chip. Note, however, that although this chip can pep up any Managing Your Money operations that involve calculations, it cannot speed up the delay that occurs when you switch between chapters or when you archive information.

No matter what kind of hardware configuration you are using, you can tailor the program to your needs by setting up several software options: customizing your hard disk; setting up a printer, modem, and monitor; and enabling graphics printing. These options are presented in the Utilities chapter and the first time you use the program.

INSTALLING THE PROGRAM

Managing Your Money comes with several disks that contain the main Managing Your Money program as well as several files that store your personal financial information. Before you install the program, you must let Managing Your Money know who its new owner is.

Insert Disk 1 of Managing Your Money in drive A and close the drive door. Type **A:** and press Enter; then type **MYM** and press the Enter key again.

The screen that appears asks you for three items: your name, your customer identification number, and the type of monitor you are using. You can find your customer identification number on the registration card packed with your copy of Managing Your Money.

Type your name in the Name blank and press the Enter key. Type your identification number in the Customer ID# blank and press Enter again. Answer the question, "Do you have a color monitor?" by typing **Y** for Yes or **N** for No. Press F1 to continue.

If you have a color monitor, the next screen will appear in color; otherwise, it will remain black and white. Take a good look at the information displayed, because it will be stored permanently on your copy of Managing Your Money.

If you make a mistake, press F9 to go back and make corrections; otherwise, press F1 to record the information. Read the screen that appears; then press F1 again to leave the program and return to DOS.

Your next task is to create a subdirectory for Managing Your Money and copy the files from the floppy disks onto your hard disk. (If you do not have a hard disk, skip this section and read the next one, ''If You Do Not Have a Hard Disk.'')

At the C> prompt, enter **CD **. Then enter **MD \MYM**. Finally, enter **CD \MYM**.

Insert Disk 1 into drive A, if it isn't already there, and enter **COPY A:*.***.

DOS displays the name of each file it copies from Disk 1 onto your hard disk.

When the C> prompt reappears, remove Disk 1, insert Disk 2, and enter **COPY A: *.*** again. Repeat for each of the remaining disks (Disks 3 through 5 for 5¼-inch disks; Disk 3 if you have 3½-inch disks).

Store the original floppy disks in a safe place. If you lose the files on your hard disk—for example, if you accidentally erase them—you will need the original disks to reinstall the program.

If You Do Not Have a Hard Disk

If you have only floppy-disk drives, you must make working copies of your original disks. You will need five blank floppy disks (three if you have 3½-inch disks).

Insert your DOS disk in drive A and one of the blank disks in drive B. If you have 5¼-inch disks, enter **FORMAT B:**. If you have 3½-inch disks, enter **FORMAT B: /S**. Then press Enter again to begin formatting the blank disk.

When asked if you want to format another disk, enter **Y**. Remove the disk from drive B, label it Disk 1, and insert another blank disk in drive B. Press Enter to format the second disk.

If you have 3½-inch disks, enter **N** after the second disk is formatted. At the A> prompt, enter **FORMAT B:**.

Remove the second disk from drive B, label it Disk 2, insert another blank disk, and press Enter. If you have 5¼-inch disks, format the remaining two disks in the same manner. Then enter **N** to let the FORMAT program know you are finished.

After you have formatted and labeled all the disks, copy the DOS file COMMAND.COM onto Disks 1 and 2.

Insert Disk 1 in drive B. Enter **COPY COMMAND.COM B:** at the A> prompt. Repeat the process with Disk 2.

Now you can install Managing Your Money on your floppy disks.

Remove your DOS disk from drive A and insert the original Disk 1 of Managing Your Money. Insert the newly formatted Disk 1 in drive B. Enter **COPY A:*.* B:**.

DOS displays the name of each file it copies from the original Disk 1 to your working copy of Disk 1.

When the A> prompt reappears, remove both disks. Insert the original Disk 2 in drive A and your new Disk 2 in drive B. Enter **COPY A:*.* B:** again. Repeat for each of the remaining disks (Disks 3 through 5 for 5¼-inch disks; Disk 3 if you have 3½-inch disks).

Store the original floppy disks in a safe place where they are not likely to be damaged and use your working copies whenever you run Managing Your Money. If one of your disks does get damaged, you can use the original disks to make a new copy.

STARTING THE PROGRAM
The main Managing Your Money program is called ''MYM.'' Here's how you start it:

If you have a hard-disk system, enter **CD\MYM** at the C> prompt. Then enter **MYM**.

If you have a two-floppy system, insert Disk 1 in drive A and Disk 2 in drive B. Then enter **MYM** at the DOS A> prompt.

The word "Wait" blinks in the lower-right corner. After a moment, the program's opening screen welcomes you to Managing Your Money with a warning from Andrew Tobias. (See Figure 1-3.)

It's probably a good idea to heed the warning. Managing Your Money is a great program for recording, watching, and analyzing various aspects of your financial life, but it can't give you the advice that a tax accountant or a qualified financial adviser can. However, the program can help you lower the cost of those professional fees when you provide your accountant with organized printouts of your expenses, instead of a shoe box filled with receipts.

Be sure to check the date, which is highlighted, to be certain it is correct. If you entered today's date when you switched on your system or if you have a built-in clock/calendar, it should be correct. Otherwise, correct it before you go on.

Type today's date in the format mm/dd/yy.

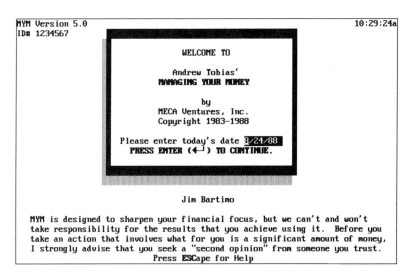

Figure 1-3. *The opening screen.*

If you read only one sentence of this book, read the next one. *Don't ever start the program with a date that isn't today's date.* If you type a date from next year, the program assumes a year has passed and asks you if you are ready to archive all of last year's information. You will have several chances to correct your mistake before the program removes all of your information from the working files on the disk.

If you type a date several months into the future, you run the risk of losing reminders in your reminder pad. This will create even more trouble if you start the program with the real date next time.

The only other option on the opening screen is to change the screen colors (if you have a color monitor). You can change both the lettering and background colors with the function keys.

> Press F1 through F10 and Alt-F1 through Alt-F10 to view different screen color combinations.

Although some of the color combinations are quite exotic, I suggest the F10 colors: white lettering on a blue background. Different colors appear on other screens, but the predominant colors are those on the opening screen.

Once changed, the new colors remain even after you leave the program and then start it again. If you don't want to change the screen colors now, you can always change them by using System Setup in the Utilities chapter.

> Press the Enter key to display the next screen.

The "Hello, New User" Tutorial

If you are using the program for the first time, you go immediately to a built-in tutorial called "Hello, New User," written by Andrew Tobias. This tutorial provides you with both general information and hands-on practice, and it is well worth your time even if you are an old hand at computers. You can go through the tutorial now or press F10 to go back to the program. If you want to return to "Hello, New User" later, you can do so from the Utilities menu.

Press F10 to leave the "Hello, New User" tutorial. Press F10 again to reach the Main menu.

USING THE MAIN MENU

Each chapter in Managing Your Money is really a separate program connected to the others by paths of information. You select the chapter you want to use from the Main menu by pressing the corresponding function key. (See Figure 1-4.) To enter another chapter, you must first return to the Main menu.

Figure 1-4. *The Main menu screen.*

USING THE UTILITIES CHAPTER

The first choice on the Main menu is Utilities. The Utilities chapter lets you return to "Hello, New User," configure your computer setup to work with Managing Your Money, test your printer, register your program, and shop for computer products through the mail. (See Figure 1-5 on the following page.)

Press F1 to go to the Utilities chapter.

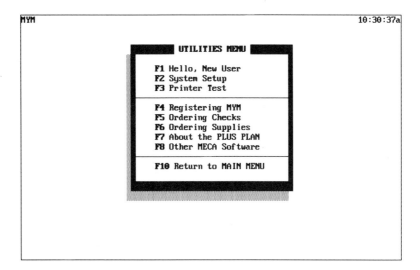

Figure 1-5. *The Utilities menu screen.*

Returning to "Hello, New User"

The first option on the Utilities menu is ''Hello, New User.'' You can return to the ''Hello, New User'' tutorial at any time by pressing F1 at the Utilities menu.

Setting Up Your System

The second option on the Utilities menu, System Setup, lets you configure the program to work best with your computer hardware. (See Figure 1-6 on the following page.)

Press F2 to enter System Setup.

Change Screen Colors

The first option on the System Setup screen, Change Screen Colors, lets you change the screen colors exactly as you did on the opening screen of the program. The second option, Monochrome Monitors, lets you adjust the program to eliminate the screen flicker that some monitors display.

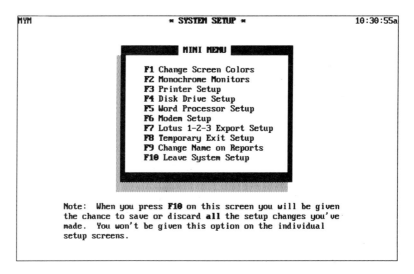

Figure 1-6. *The System Setup mini menu.*

Printer Setup

The third option, Printer Setup, lets you either tell the program what kind of printer you're using or customize the program for a printer not listed. (See Figure 1-7.)

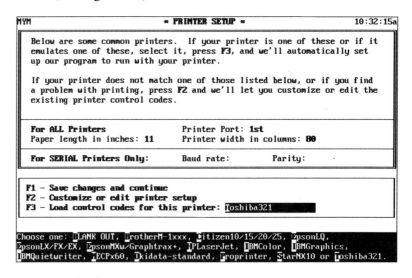

Figure 1-7. *The Printer Setup screen.*

Disk Drive Setup The fourth choice in System Setup, Disk Drive Setup, lets you tell the program whether you are using one floppy disk, two floppy disks, a hard disk, or some other special combination of disks. (See Figure 1-8.) It is almost impossible to use Managing Your Money with only one floppy-disk drive and somewhat inconvenient with two. A hard disk relieves you from having to frequently swap floppy disks in and out of drives.

Managing Your Money uses several different files. If you have a hard-disk system, the program normally looks for these files on drive C. If you have a two-floppy system, it looks first on drive A and then on drive B. You can customize the program by telling it to look on any combination of hard disks, RAM disks, or additional floppy drives for either program files or your financial information.

For example, you can copy the program onto drive C but tell the program to look only on drive A for financial information files. Then each member of your family who uses the program can keep his or her information on a separate disk. When you use the program, you simply insert your information disk into drive A.

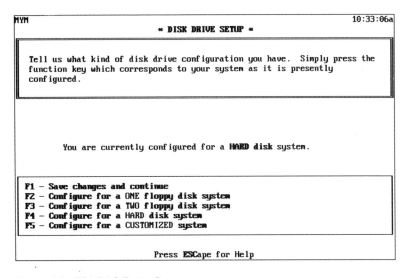

Figure 1-8. *The Disk Drive Setup screen.*

21

If you have at least 512 KB of memory, you can set up a 360 KB RAM disk and copy your information, or .DB, files into it. Then tell the SETUP program to look in the RAM disk for information files. Doing this, you will swap disks much less frequently; but remember to copy the .DB in the RAM disk back onto your working floppy disks, or you will lose your information when you shut down the computer.

> Press F2 for one floppy-disk drive, F3 for two floppy-disk drives, or F4 for a hard disk. Press F5 to customize your disk setup.

> When you've completed your disk-drive setup, press F1 to save the choices you made.

Word Processor Setup

Managing Your Money's newest feature is a built-in word processor and pop-up note pad called Write on the Money. It is explained in more detail later in this chapter. What follows is a discussion of the fifth option on the Setup menu, Word Processor Setup.

You can train Write on the Money to act like WordPerfect, IBM's DisplayWrite 3 or Writing Assistant, Microsoft Word, MultiMate, WordStar, or PFS: Write (limited to Write on the Money's features, of course). To do this, you must select F5 from the System Setup menu.

A screen containing the Keystroke Setup appears and lets you tell Write on the Money to act like one of the word processors listed. Type in the name of the word processor in the F3 blank, and Write will mimic that program. (See Figure 1-9.)

If your favorite word processor isn't listed, you can customize each key so that it functions as it does in your word processor.

> Select a word processor from the list that works in a similar manner to yours and press F2, Customize or Edit Keystroke Setup.

The keystroke chart lists 30 different key commands for moving the cursor, editing, searching and replacing, defining blocks of text, setting margins, and getting help. You can change each command to match your own word processor.

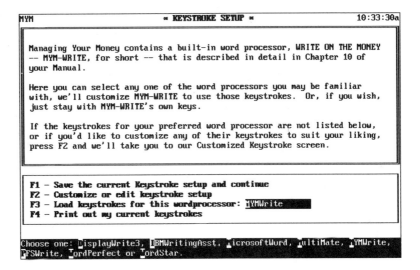

Figure 1-9. *The Keystroke Setup screen.*

> Place the cursor on the particular command you want to change and press F1.

The "Wait" prompt flashes to let you know you are in the process of redefining a key command. Press the two keys, one after the other, that will define the command. The chart changes to reflect your new choice. To define a command with only one keystroke, press that key and then press the spacebar. The chart, with all your changes, appears when you press the Escape key to ask for help.

> Make all your keystroke changes permanent by pressing F1 at the previous screen of Keystroke Setup.

Modem Setup   Setting up your modem is important if you plan to use the card file in Chapter 9 of the program to dial your telephone automatically. To dial automatically, you should have a Hayes-compatible modem (that is, one that is compatible with the Smartmodem 1200 made by Hayes Microcomputer Products of Norcross, Georgia).

> Press F6, Modem Setup, at the System Setup menu to set up your computer's modem.

23

Type **1** at the Modem Port blank if the modem is attached to the first serial port. Or type **2** if it is attached to the second serial port.

The screen also asks if you are using a long-distance service, such as MCI or Sprint. If your long-distance service requires you call a special telephone number or if you must dial 1 before you dial a long-distance number, type that number in the indicated field. If your service uses an access code, type that number in the proper field. This information is now available to the automatic dialing program in Chapter 9. When you call a long-distance number, you do not have to provide special information about the long-distance carrier.

Lotus 1-2-3
Export Setup

On screens that display numeric information, you can choose to send the information to a file in one of three formats: Report, Export, and 1-2-3. Report gives you standard ASCII text that can be read by most word processors. Export lets you create a file that can be read by many spreadsheet and database programs. The 1-2-3 choice produces a file that can be read by the Lotus 1-2-3 spreadsheet program.

Press F7 at the System Setup menu to set up the Lotus 1-2-3 export function.

Type the drive and pathname where you want to store exported 1-2-3 files. The program saves those files with a .PRN extension, such as BALANCE.PRN.

After you send information to a .PRN file, leave Managing Your Money and run Lotus 1-2-3. Select the /File Import Numbers command and then name your file. The file is read directly into 1-2-3 as if you had created it there. This function relieves you from reformatting your print files with all the quotation marks required by 1-2-3.

Press F1 to save the Lotus 1-2-3 information and return to System Setup.

Temporary
Exit Setup

The Temporary Exit feature in Managing Your Money allows you to temporarily leave the program and run a second program while the first remains in the computer's memory. After the initial setup, you can exit to DOS at any point in the program.

Press F8, Temporary Exit Setup, at the System Setup menu to set up the Temporary Exit.

From the screen that appears you can then enable the Temporary Exit feature by indicating where the program should store Managing Your Money information while you're using DOS. If you have a hard disk, type **C**; if not, type **A**.

Press F1 to save your decision to enable the Temporary Exit.

Once it's set up, you can temporarily exit to DOS by pressing and holding the Control key and pressing D at any point in the program. Managing Your Money disappears and the DOS prompt appears. (See Figure 1-10.) From the DOS prompt you can run any other program that fits into the remaining memory. You might run your word processor to edit your reports, or you can use Managing the Market to download some stock prices.

To exit from DOS, type **EXIT** at the prompt to return to Managing Your Money at the point you left it. If you do not have a hard disk, be sure the file COMMAND.COM is on one of your disks, or the Temporary Exit won't work.

```
While in DOS, be sure not to install any new resident programs.
If you do, we'll be hopelessly confused when you return.

Remember to type "exit" to come back to MYM.


Microsoft(R) MS-DOS(R)   Version 3.30
            (C)Copyright Microsoft Corp 1981-1987


C>_
```

Figure 1-10. *Temporary Exit to DOS.*

Always type **EXIT** and not **MYM** when leaving DOS; otherwise, you'll run the program again and probably use up all remaining memory.

A word of warning about temporary exits: Don't try to load a RAM-resident program like SideKick or GRAPHICS.COM on top of the first program. It's like building the basement on the third floor, and the results will be as disastrous to your information; however, you can still run these programs before you load Managing Your Money.

Change Name on Reports

Managing Your Money personalizes your reports by printing your name (and sometimes your address) on them. You're asked to enter your name when you start the program for the first time, but you can always change it by pressing F9, Change Name on Reports, at the System Setup menu. You can then type the new information and press F1 to save it. Your name also appears on the Main menu.

Leave System Setup

Press F10 to leave System Setup and save the information on disk. Confirm that you want to save your information by pressing F1. You then return to the Utilities menu. (See Figure 1-11.)

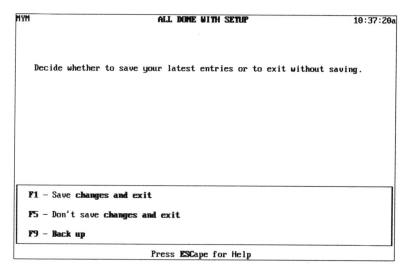

Figure 1-11. *Leaving System Setup.*

Testing Your Printer

After you set up your system, you can test your printer by pressing F3, Printer Test, at the Utilities menu.

Press F1 to test your printer.

Press F10 to return to the Utilities menu.

Registering the Program

The fourth item on the Utilities menu, Registering MYM, explains the importance of registering software and contains information for registering your program.

Press F4 to view the information. At the final screen, press F1, and the program prints a registration card for you to send to MECA Ventures, Inc.

If you register your program, you can order new disks for $15 when you send in a damaged disk (or for free during the first 90 days).

Computerized Advertising

Utilities menu selections F5 through F8 provide an opportunity for you to buy products from printer-ready checks to software.

Press F5, Ordering Checks, to print out an order form for the printer-ready checks that work best with the program.

Press F6 to get instructions on how to order the Deluxe Computer Supply catalog.

Another option is to enroll in MECA's Plus Plan. Subscribing buys you a quarterly newsletter from Andrew Tobias called "Managing Your Money Better" and an upgrade to the following year's program. It also gives you access to telephone support lines, which you can call to ask questions about the program.

Press F7 to learn about MECA's Plus Plan.

For $49.95, you receive the newsletter and next year's upgrade. For $59.95, you receive the newsletter, the upgrade, and a new manual.

Press F8 to see a list of other software products from MECA Ventures, Inc.

Leaving Utilities   The last option on the Utilities menu lets you return to the Main menu.

Press F10 at the Utilities menu to return to the Main menu.

WORKING WITH POP-UP PROGRAMS   Managing Your Money includes two pop-up programs that you can call up from anywhere in the program: the calculator and Write on the Money, the word processor. The pop-up feature works much like the DOS Window—when you call up a program, the main program is suspended and the pop-up program starts working. When you leave the pop-up program, the main program reappears exactly as you left it.

The Calculator   With the pop-up calculator, you can stop what you're doing at any time and make a calculation.

To display the calculator, press Ctrl-N.

The calculator appears at the bottom of the screen (Figure 1-12). It looks like anything but a calculator, but it performs all the basic functions of a desk calculator.

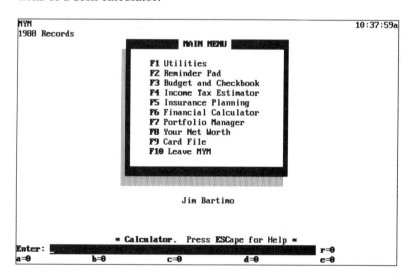

Figure 1-12. *The calculator.*

To perform a calculation, type the numbers, separated by appropriate operator signs, in the Enter blank. Then press the Enter key.

For example, if you want to add 54 and 63, type 54 + 63 in the Enter blank and then press the Enter key. The result—117—appears in the r = blank. You can save the result of a calculation in one of the five blanks labeled a =, b =, c =, d =, and e =. For example, if you want to save the result of the previous example in the a = blank, type a = 54 + 63 when you perform the calculation. The result appears in the a = blank and remains there until you save another calculation in this blank.

You may want to use the result of your calculation elsewhere in Managing Your Money—for instance, to fill in the amount of a check. You can transfer the number in the r = blank to a blank on the screen.

Highlight the blank on the screen in which you want the result of the calculation to appear. Then press Ctrl-N to display the calculator.

Type your calculation in the Enter blank and press the Enter key to display the result in the r = blank. Then press the Enter key again.

The value in the r = blank now appears in the highlighted blank on the screen.

You can also use a number from the screen in a calculation.

Highlight the number on the screen that you want to use in a calculation and press Ctrl-N to display the calculator. Then press F1.

The number in the highlighted blank on the screen appears in the Enter field. You can then complete the calculation by typing other numbers and operators. For example, suppose you want to figure out how much a monthly expense adds up to annually. You can copy the check amount into the Enter blank and multiply by 12.

Write on the Money

Write on the Money is Managing Your Money's built-in word processor and pop-up notepad. Write is a handy little word processor for writing one-page memos and letters—it even performs mail merge. (See "Mail Merge" in Chapter 9.) Write works best, however, as a notepad, and I would not suggest you use it as your primary word processor unless your writing is limited to small jobs.

When working as a notepad, Write can attach very long pop-up notes to transactions in the program. In Chapter 8, for instance, you can point to an asset listing, press F2, and attach an explanation about that asset. The note might explain that your diamond ring was appraised at $7,000 in 1976 but has appreciated each year.

In Chapter 7, you can point to an E.F. Hutton portfolio, press Ctrl-E, and attach a note to remind you who your broker was before Shearson Lehman bought out E.F. Hutton. Even the checks in Chapter 3 use the pop-up notes for the memo field. The pop-up version of Write works best, however, in the Chapter 2 Reminder screen, where you can attach histories, phone numbers, and any notes to your list of To-Dos, Reminders, Appointments, Birthdays, and Anniversaries. Simply move the highlight to one of these items and press F2.

When working in notepad mode, Write leaves an asterisk next to the item that has a pop-up note attached to it. So, whenever you see an asterisk on a Managing Your Money list, you can call up the notepad and look for more text.

Write also acts as a word processor, called up at any time while you're using Managing Your Money. It is technically not a pop-up word processor because you must store a Write document before you can return to Managing Your Money. It is more like running a low-end word processor through the temporary exit to DOS.

To call up Write, press Ctrl-W.

A Write on the Money screen appears that lets you either open a new document or look at a list of Write documents. You can qualify the request for a list with a different drive, a subdirectory, and a DOS wild-card character. (See Figure 1-13.)

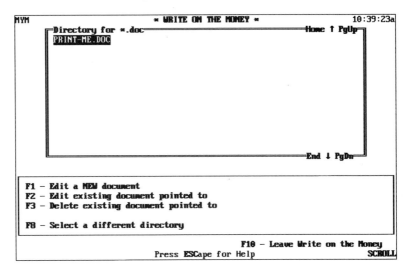

MYM	* WRITE ON THE MONEY *	10:39:23a

Figure 1-13. *Selecting a document in Write on the Money.*

Press F8 to view a list of files in the specified directory. Move the cursor to the desired file and press F2 to open it.

Press F3 to delete a document.

Press F8 to select a different list of files.

Press F10 to return to Managing Your Money.

When you open a document, you can move and delete blocks of text, change the margins, and search or replace strings of text. Write lets you create letters, memos, and even reports of about 5000 words or less. (See Figure 1-14 on the following page.) You can store, retrieve, erase, or print. You can even create form letters and merge them with the names and addresses from your Chapter 9 Card File.

When you finish writing or editing a document, press F10. You are given the choice of going back to edit it again by pressing F2, leaving the document as it was by pressing F3, or printing the document by

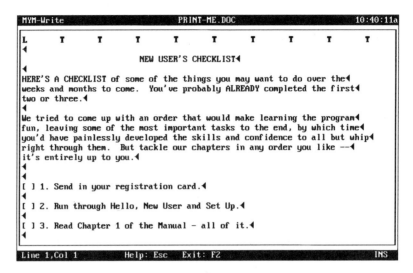

Figure 1-14. *A memo created with Write on the Money.*

pressing F4. (Before printing, Managing Your Money gives you the standard Print menu asking whether to print the document to printer, screen, or disk.) Pressing F5 saves the document.

> Type a filename in the F5 blank.

If you give the document a filename already used by another document, the program asks you if you want to replace the old document with the new one or to rename the new document.

Write has two different modes in which the document can be stored: Document mode is Write's own special format, and ASCII mode is understood by almost all other word processors. (See Figure 1-15.)

> Select either Document or ASCII; then press F5 to save the document.

As mentioned earlier in this chapter, Write on the Money can emulate the standard functions and operations of other word processors. Write does, however, use a special type of command called the ''dot'' command, which lets you fine-tune the printing of your documents. You must type a dot command alone on a single line and press Enter.

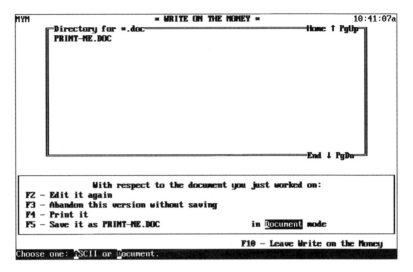

Figure 1-15. *Saving a document in Write on the Money.*

The following is a list of Write's most useful dot commands:

.ds	Prints in double spacing starting with the next line.
.ss	Prints in single spacing starting with the next line.
.pa	Begins printing on the next page.
.ce	Centers the next line horizontally.
.ch	Prints in compressed characters; a second .ch returns to regular printing.
.qp	Produces higher-quality printing; a second .qp returns to regular printing.
.ul	Underlines text; a second .ul returns to regular text.
.ep	Emphasizes (boldfaces) text; a second .ep returns to regular text.
.dp	Prints double-width characters (if your printer supports this); a second .dp returns to regular printing.
.h1	Places a "header" word or phrase at the top of a page; type the word or phrase immediately following the dot command.
.h1[pa]	Prints page numbers at the head (top) of each page.
.fo[pa]	Prints page numbers at the foot (bottom) of each page.

UNDERSTANDING FILES

All Managing Your Money files and all information you enter with the program are stored in several different types of files. The file's extension—the characters following the period in the filename —identifies the type. Four of the file extensions used by Managing Your Money are .EXE, .CHP, .DB, and .ARK.

A .EXE extension indicates a program file. You can run a program by typing its filename at the DOS prompt. (You do not need to type the extension .EXE.) The main Managing Your Money program, MYM.EXE, is an example of a program file.

Each .CHP (chapter) file is numbered and corresponds to a Managing Your Money chapter. The MYM.EXE program uses these files to open new chapters when you turn to the chapter from the Main menu. If you do not have a hard disk, note that different .CHP files appear on each Managing Your Money disk. If you try to turn to a chapter whose .CHP file is on a disk that is not in a drive, the program tells you to insert that disk before you proceed.

A .DB file is an information file. When you enter a chapter, the information you type in that chapter is stored in a .DB file. Later, when you enter a chapter, the information in its .DB file is loaded into memory.

A .ARK file contains information that you archive. Because .DB files are automatically loaded into memory, you will run out of memory as your .DB file grows. When you archive information from a .DB file, the program moves it into a .ARK file, and it is no longer loaded into memory. Although you can no longer use .ARK information in the Managing Your Money program, you can use this information with Chapters 3 and 7 to produce reports.

Finding a File

In order to open a file, Managing Your Money must be able to find the file on a disk in one of the disk drives. If the file is on another disk, it tells you to insert that disk. If you reorganize your files or customize your hard disk, you need to tell the program where to look for the file you requested. To find the file's location, you can display the directory of files on a disk.

To display the files in the current directory of your fixed disk, enter **DIR C:** at the DOS prompt.

To display the files on a floppy disk, insert the disk in drive A and enter **DIR A:** at the DOS prompt.

**Making Backup
Copies of Files**

You should make backup copies of your .DB files whenever you modify them. Make backups of your .ARK files in case one is damaged. If something does happen to your files and you don't have a backup copy, you can lose an entire year's information.

The easiest way to make a backup copy of your files is to let Managing Your Money do the work. When you press F10 from the Main menu to leave the program, the Assistance Backing Up screen appears. (See Figure 1-16.) You can, and *should,* back up your information files at this point. First, enter the name of the floppy-disk drive or the hard-disk subdirectory to which you will copy your information files.

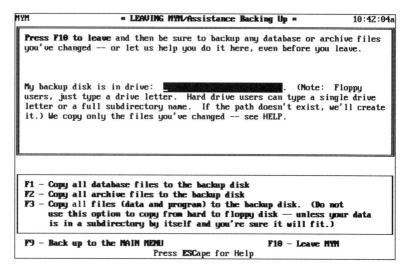

Figure 1-16. *Backing up your files.*

If you have a hard-disk drive, insert your backup disk in drive A and type **A**.

If you have two floppy-disk drives, insert your backup disk in drive B and type **B**.

Press F3 to copy all your .DB files.

Press F4 to copy all your .ARK files.

Press F5 to copy both program and information files. (Don't use this option if you store all Managing Your Money files in one subdirectory on your hard disk—you'll run out of room on the backup disk.)

Always be sure to make backup copies. I've heard too many stories from Managing Your Money users who lost all their information in a hard-disk crash or through simple carelessness and then couldn't get a year's worth of valuable information back.

Remember: Back up your files each and every time you leave Managing Your Money!

Upgrading Files   If you have been using an earlier version of Managing Your Money, carefully follow the instructions included with version 5.0. Don't simply copy all the files from the new disks—if you do, you will lose the information stored in your .DB and .ARK files.

Upgrading is a one-way street: You can upgrade from an earlier version to a later version, but you cannot take files from a later version and use them with an earlier version.

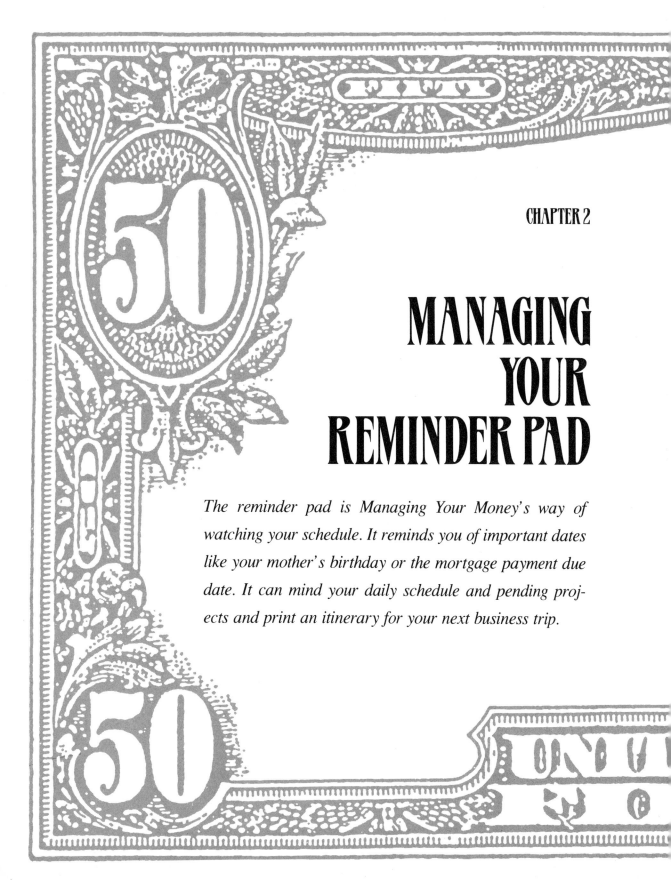

CHAPTER 2

MANAGING YOUR REMINDER PAD

The reminder pad is Managing Your Money's way of watching your schedule. It reminds you of important dates like your mother's birthday or the mortgage payment due date. It can mind your daily schedule and pending projects and print an itinerary for your next business trip.

Managing Your Money sends you to the Reminder Pad chapter the first time each day you enter the program. Later, you'll see how to bypass this feature. You can also view the reminder pad by pressing F2, Reminder Pad, at the Main menu. No matter how you enter the chapter, the first screen you see indicates "Reminders for..." and lists the day and date. I'll refer to this as the Today's Reminders screen. (See Figure 2-1.)

Today's Reminders lists up to four categories of reminders: appointments, reminders, to-do's, and birthdays and anniversaries. These reminders are drawn from different places in Managing Your Money. Appointments, reminders, and to-do's come from lists created within the Reminder Pad chapter. Information in the birthdays and anniversaries category is imported from Chapter 9, "Card File."

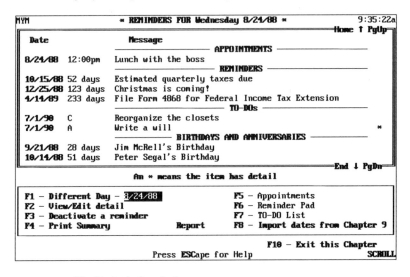

Figure 2-1. *The Today's Reminders screen.*

APPOINTMENTS You can reach the Appointments screen from almost anywhere in the Reminder Pad chapter by pressing F5. (See Figure 2-2.) Appointment listings differ from other reminders in that they monitor activities that take place at a specific time and date.

Creating Appointments

To create an appointment, move the cursor to the New Appointment Line and enter the date and time of the appointment; you must enter both the beginning and ending times of the appointment. In the Message field, give the appointment a descriptive title, such as "Meeting with Ted."

Press F1 to add the appointment to the information box.

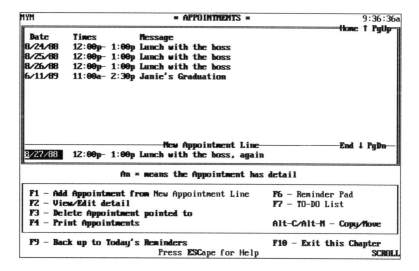

Figure 2-2. *The Appointments screen.*

Deleting and Printing Appointments

As you create appointment reminders, they begin to stack up in the information box. You can delete an entry you no longer need by moving the cursor to the reminder and pressing F3. Follow up by pressing F1 to confirm its deletion.

Press F4 to view the Print screen and mark the appointments you want to print.

You can mark individual appointments by typing **X** in the Mark blank; you can mark all appointments for a range of dates by entering the dates in the F2 blanks and pressing F2; and you can mark all the appointments by pressing F3.

Press F1 to print the marked items.

Press F9 to return to the Appointments screen.

REMINDERS   You can reach the Reminder Pad screen from almost anywhere in the Reminder Pad chapter by pressing F6. (See Figure 2-3.) With Managing Your Money, you can set up one-time, weekly, biweekly, half-monthly, monthly, quarterly, semiannual, and annual reminders, thus ensuring that you will be reminded of all important dates.

To use the reminder pad effectively, you need a strategy for organizing your reminders. For example, some reminders alert you to one-time events—such as a dinner date with your old college roommate. A reminder to contribute to an individual retirement account (IRA), however, is an annual event. Annual reminders come back every year, but a one-time reminder does not return after the date passes.

A notable feature of the reminder pad is its ability to alert you to an important date before that date arrives. You can specify the number of warning days before the event when you want to begin receiving the daily reminder. For example, if April 15 is the date your IRA contribution is due and you want to begin receiving daily reminders ten days

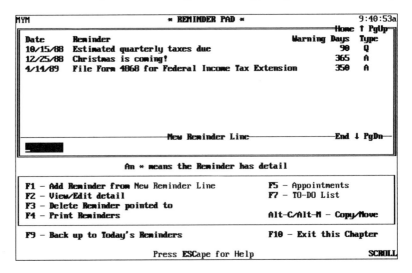

Figure 2-3. *The Reminder Pad screen.*

before, you can set up the reminder with ten warning days. You then will receive the reminder every time you use Managing Your Money between April 5 and April 15. In this way, you'll have enough time to collect the funds from other accounts and send the check.

The number of warning days you need depends on how often you use the program. If you use it only on the first day of the month and you have only ten warning days, you will miss your reminder for March 30 completely. So, if you are a once-a-month user, it is a good idea to specify 30 warning days with all reminders. Making a reminder an annual reminder and typing 365 for the number of warning days makes the reminder appear every day.

It is also important to coordinate the frequency of the reminders with the number of warning days. For instance, don't give a 30-day warning notice to a weekly reminder; the reminders will overlap one another.

Creating Reminders

To add a reminder to the reminder pad, move the cursor to the New Reminder Line. Include the date, a descriptive message, the number of warning days, and the type of reminder (weekly, monthly, or annual).

Type a letter code for the frequency of the reminder in the Type blank. Then press the Enter key.

When you highlight the Type blank, a pop-up menu at the bottom of the screen displays your options. The biweekly option will provide reminders every other week; half-monthly will remind you every 15 or 16 days, depending on the length of the month.

Press F1 to add the reminder to the reminder pad.

Deleting and Printing Reminders

One-time reminders are automatically deleted from the reminder pad when the reminder date has passed. Any other reminders that you no longer need must be deleted by you.

Use the arrow keys to highlight the reminder you want to delete. Press F3 to delete the reminder and press F1 to confirm its deletion.

41

Press the F4 key to view the Print Reminders screen and mark the reminders you want to print.

TO-DO'S

You can reach the To-Do List screen from almost anywhere in the Reminder Pad chapter by pressing F7. (See Figure 2-4.) You can add, delete, and print a list of your projects. In addition, you can prioritize your projects and sort them by different criteria.

Suppose you want to sell all your portfolio investments by July, when you expect another stock-market crash. You can create a project for selling your mutual funds and give the project a due date of 4/1/89. Then you can create another project with a due date of 5/1/89 to sell your blue-chip stocks. For June, you might create a project that includes turning all that cash into gold bullion and, finally, flying to Bolivia before July 1. The to-do's you create will appear on Today's Reminders (depending on how many warning days you give them) and then stop appearing when you mark each project completed.

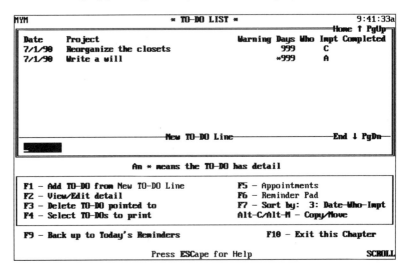

Figure 2-4. *The To-Do List screen.*

**Creating a
To-Do List**

The to-do list has six column headings: "Date," "Project," "Warning Days," "Who," "Impt" (importance), and "Completed." To add a new listing to the information box, move the cursor to the New To-Do Line. Type the due date, project name, number of warning days, initials of the person responsible for completing the project, and one of three letter codes to indicate the level of importance of the project. (A is most important and C least important.)

Press F1 to add the new project to the list.

Sorting To-Do's

Use the F7 key to sort the to-do list by any one of six criteria combinations. Indicate which combination you want from the pop-up menu that appears when you enter the F7 field.

If the sort selection you choose is Date-Impt-Who, the to-do list is re-arranged so that the to-do with the earliest date is at the top of the list. If two dates are the same, the to-do with the highest importance is listed first. If both the date and the importance are the same, the to-do is sorted by the *last* initial in the Who field.

**Marking To-Do's
as Completed**

When a project is completed, move the cursor to the "Completed" column in the information box and type in the date. Once you do so, the to-do will no longer show up on Today's Reminders, but it will stay on the to-do list until you delete it.

**Deleting and
Printing To-Do's**

To delete any item on the To-Do List screen, move the cursor to the item and press F3. Press F1 to confirm its deletion.

Press the F4 key to view the Print To-Do List screen and mark the items you want to print. You can mark them by date, initials, level of importance, or completion status by pressing F2, and then print the marked items by pressing F1. Return to the To-Do List screen by pressing F9.

BIRTHDAYS AND ANNIVERSARIES

You can't create birthday and anniversary reminders through the Reminder Pad chapter. The only way to create them is to enter Chapter 9 in the program and list those dates in the Birthday and Anniversary fields of the card file. When you press F10 to exit Chapter 9, you are asked if you want to send all the dates in Chapter 9 to the reminder pad in Chapter 2. Choosing "Export" instead of "Don't Export" will transfer the reminders when you press F1 to save your changes and exit. When you enter Chapter 2, you must then press F8 at Today's Reminders to bring those dates into Chapter 2 and onto the Today's Reminders screen.

TRANSFERRING ITEMS AMONG SCREENS

In the lower-right corner of the Appointments, Reminder Pad, and To-Do List screens appears the following: Alt-C/Alt-M - Copy/Move. This cryptic little message indicates that you can copy or move an item from any one of these screens to any other.

Suppose you want to copy an item from the to-do list to the reminder pad. Position the cursor over the to-do listing you want to copy and press Alt-C. The item moves from the information box to the New To-Do Line. When you press F6 to enter the reminder pad, the To-Do Line is plugged into the New Reminder Line. Then press F1 to copy the to-do listing into the reminder pad's information box. The MOVE command works like the COPY command, except that the to-do listing disappears from the to-do list when it appears on the New To-Do Line.

Be aware that moving from one list to another sometimes leaves the listing incomplete. Moving an appointment listing to the to-do list, for instance, leaves the new to-do reminder without an entry in the Who field. To fix this, enter the missing information while the item is still in the New Item Line.

**CHANGING
ITEM DATES**

You may notice that you can change most information for an item when it's in the information box, but you can't change the date. The MOVE command can also change the date of an item even if you don't want to move it to another screen.

> Press Alt-M to bring the item to the New Item Line. Change the date and press F1 to put the item back in the information box with the new date.

**TODAY'S
REMINDERS**

Now that you've created some appointment notes, reminders, to-do's, and important dates, the Today's Reminders screen should be filled with entries.

> Press F9 from most places in the Reminder Pad chapter to return to Today's Reminders.

Today's Reminders is now a very useful schedule and project manager. The information box lists the items in each of the categories you created, but this list is useful only if you're sitting at your computer. You might want to print Today's Reminders and use the printout as your daily itinerary and list of upcoming events.

You can view the Today's Reminders screen for any other day by moving the cursor to the F1 field and typing in the desired date. Press F1, and the reminders for that particular day appear.

**Printing an
Itinerary**

You can use Today's Reminders to print a summary of your upcoming activities, much like an itinerary. A summary list prints everything in the Today's Reminders information box, plus a handy mini-calendar. The calendar shows the current, previous, and following months. (See Figure 2-5 on the following page.)

> Move the cursor to the F4 field in the action box and type **S** for Summary Report; then press F4. The Summary Report screen asks which dates are to be included in your itinerary. Enter the dates and press F1 to print.

The F4 printing function uses times from the appointment calendar to create an hour-by-hour report, complete with 15-minute intervals.

Move the cursor to the F4 field in the action box and type **A** for Appointment Schedule; then press F4. The Summary Report screen asks which dates are to be included in your appointment schedule. Enter the dates and press F1 to print.

```
8/24/88                        The Overview Report                      Page 1
Jim Bartimo

          July                    August                    September
   S  M  T  W  T  F  S      S  M  T  W  T  F  S      S  M  T  W  T  F  S
                  1  2         1  2  3  4  5  6                     1  2  3
   3  4  5  6  7  8  9      7  8  9 10 11 12 13      4  5  6  7  8  9 10
  10 11 12 13 14 15 16     14 15 16 17 18 19 20     11 12 13 14 15 16 17
  17 18 19 20 21 22 23     21 22 23 24 25 26 27     18 19 20 21 22 23 24
  24 25 26 27 28 29 30     28 29 30 31             25 26 27 28 29 30
  31


Wednesday  8/24/88

APPOINTMENTS:
12:00pm- 1:00pm   Lunch with the boss

REMINDERS:
10/15/88   52 days    Estimated quarterly taxes due
12/25/88  123 days    Christmas is coming!
4/14/89   233 days    File Form 4868 for Federal Income Tax Extension

TO-DOs:
7/1/90    676 days        Reorganize the closets
7/1/90    676 days        Write a will
                          This is just a sample TO-DO item (we use "999" warning days to make sure it
                          stays on the screen no matter when you buy the program).

                                    But it's true!

                              If you can afford a computer,
                          you should almost certainly have a simple will.


BIRTHDAYS & ANNIVERSARIES:
9/21/88    28 days    Jim McRell's Birthday
10/14/88   51 days    Peter Segal's Birthday
```

Figure 2-5. *The overview report.*

Deactivating Reminders

You may want to deactivate a reminder on the Today's Reminders screen when the need for the reminder goes away before the warning days run out. You can deactivate only reminders—not appointments, to-do's, or birthdays and anniversaries.

For example, suppose you have a monthly reminder that says "Pay the mortgage." The mortgage is due on the fifteenth of the month, and you have given it five warning days. On March 11 you get the first reminder, and you pay the mortgage immediately; but, unless you delete it, the daily reminder will continue to appear for the next four days. Of course, you do not want to delete it from the reminder screen because you want to be reminded next month as well. So you deactivate for this month only.

Place the cursor over the reminder and press F3. The reminder disappears from the screen.

LEAVING THE REMINDER PAD

Whenever you leave the reminder pad, you are asked two questions. The first asks how old an appointment must be before the program archives it. You can archive appointments that are as new as 1 month or as old as 99 months. The second question asks if you want to view the reminder pad the first time you enter the program each day.

Archiving Appointments

Move the cursor to the Archive Appointments question and enter the number of months for which you want to keep an appointment on the Appointments screen. When you press F1 to save the changes in the reminder pad, the program archives the appointments that are older than the number of months you indicated. If you indicated one month and the date is August 15, all the June appointments are archived. When you reenter the reminder pad, the program tells you that there are old appointments.

Press F1 to create a text file that contains the old appointments and then delete them from the Appointments screen.

The program creates a file called JUN88.ARK (if the appointment listings are from June) and then places the archived appointments in that file. You can call up this file with Write on the Money and most other word processors and print it.

Press F5 to delete the old appointments from the Appointments screen without archiving them.

Press F10 in order to leave the archived appointments on the Appointments screen but receive the same reminder each time you enter the Reminder Pad chapter.

Archiving appointments is a handy feature if you like to keep a record of all the places you've gone and people you've met over the course of the year. If you want to keep a file of all your old appointments, you can print your archives and then erase the files, thus not filling up the computer's disk space. If you don't want to keep a record of your appointments, simply delete the archive files. If you want to keep the appointments in the program forever, type **99** in the field that asks how old appointments must be before the program archives them.

Turning Off the Automatic Display   To set the program so that the Reminder Pad chapter doesn't appear the first time you run the program each day, type **N** after the second question as you leave the Reminder Pad chapter. Be sure to press F1 to save your changes and make your decision permanent.

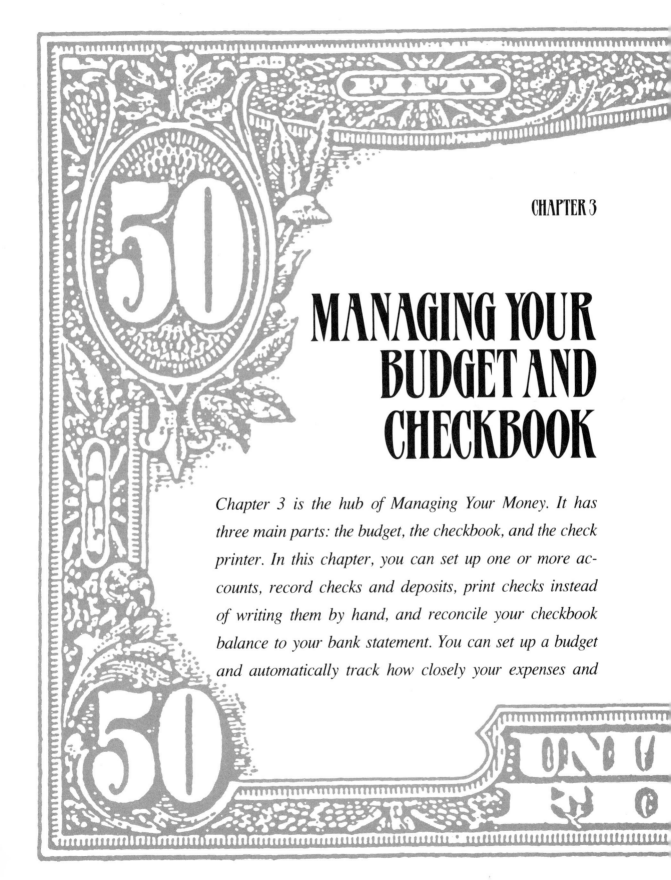

MANAGING YOUR BUDGET AND CHECKBOOK

Chapter 3 is the hub of Managing Your Money. It has three main parts: the budget, the checkbook, and the check printer. In this chapter, you can set up one or more accounts, record checks and deposits, print checks instead of writing them by hand, and reconcile your checkbook balance to your bank statement. You can set up a budget and automatically track how closely your expenses and income follow it. You can calculate loan payments, manage your credit-card accounts, and forecast your cash position. You can even manage a small business.

Although each individual step in setting up a checkbook and budget is simple, all the steps combined can be complex. Each screen in the program leads to other screens, which can be overwhelming. You need a strategy for getting your checkbook and budgets started.

In this chapter I suggest a strategy for starting out. Think of it as a road map. You can explore on your own after you follow it, but stick to the map once you've started; otherwise, you'll find yourself, as I did, going down several wrong roads and not accomplishing what you want right away. Following the map will give you an overview.

SETTING UP AN ACCOUNT

In Chapter 3 of Managing Your Money, you can manage several different types of accounts, from a basic checking account to a money-market or cash-management account. (See "What Kind of Account?") I suggest you start with a checking account, but first delete the sample accounts that come with the program.

The way you first set up your money accounts depends on how you plan to use the program. If you plan to use Managing Your Money mainly as an electronic checkbook, start your account from the current month and use your balance at the beginning of the month as your starting balance. Enter the checks and deposits that you have written for this month as your account data.

If you plan to go beyond a simple recording of your checking-account transactions—to use the budget features of the program—you need to begin the account on January 1 and enter all your transactions since January 1 or since the beginning of your own fiscal year. If today is January 2, this won't be a problem; but if today is June 18, you will have a lot of information to enter all at once.

What Kind of Account?

Managing Your Money offers you seven types of accounts. You probably already know about savings and checking accounts, but you may need some explanation for the other types. Here are some brief definitions and suggestions:

Charge accounts. In Managing Your Money, you can set up a separate account to track your charge-account transactions for each credit-card account. Select this type of account if you plan to keep your credit-card accounts separate from your checking account. (See "Managing Your Credit Cards" later in this chapter.)

Money-market accounts. Even though a money-market account is a form of investment, you treat it like a checking or savings account in this chapter. Note that you probably won't write as many checks against a money-market account, and a money-market account pays dividends instead of interest.

Cash accounts. If you plan to track your finances very systematically, you should set up a petty-cash fund to account for small expenditures, such as the soda you bought from the machine at work. If you set up such an account, identify it as a cash account, but I don't recommend that you go into too much detail.

Noncash accounts. A noncash account represents assets you own but can neither spend nor invest. A trust fund is a good example. Use a noncash account when you cannot include an asset as cash in your net worth. (See Chapter 8, "Managing Your Net Worth.")

Cash-management accounts (CMAs). This type of account is a popular savings vehicle. Like the money-market account, it's a form of investment. Unlike the money-market account, your CMA is linked directly to the portfolio-management sections in Chapter 7. (See Chapter 7, "Managing Your Portfolio.") You can set up as many as nine cash-management accounts.

This is the point at which some people bail out and promise themselves to pick up the program again next year. If it is late in the year when you begin, that is probably the right approach. If it is still somewhat early in the year, you should accept the hard fact that you will have to record each check since January 1. On the positive side, doing this will help you learn more about how the program works.

You are now ready to set up an account. This task takes some time and requires a bit of concentration, so set aside a few hours when you won't be interrupted. You need your account number and at least a month's worth of checks, deposits, automatic transactions, and automated teller machine (ATM) records.

Opening an Account

Before you can enter transactions in your electronic checkbook, you must open your electronic account. You can open as many accounts as your computer's memory can hold when you select the Money Accounts function from the Chapter 3 mini menu. (See Figure 3-1.) If you and your spouse keep two separate checking accounts and one joint account, you can open a different account for each and then work on them separately. The information you enter in an account appears only in that account unless you transfer a transaction.

From the Main menu, press F3 to enter Chapter 3.

From the mini menu, press F3 to work with your money accounts.

The Money Accounts screen appears with the action box listing several choices. You'll select the basic choices now and explore the others later.

Press F2 to add a new account.

A simple form appears which you can use to enter information about your account. (See Figure 3-2.)

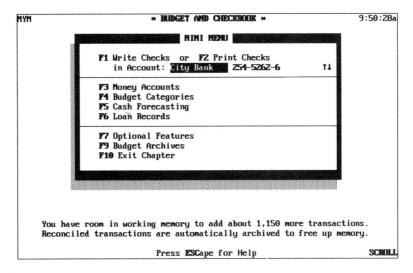

Figure 3-1. *The Chapter 3 mini menu.*

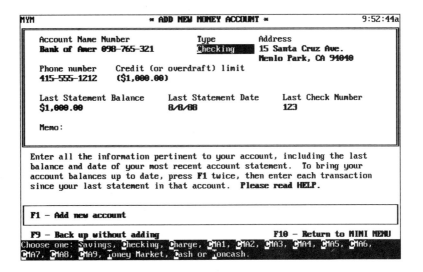

Figure 3-2. *The New Money Account screen.*

Type the name of the financial institution and your account number in the appropriate blanks. Press the Enter key or the Tab key to move from one blank to the next.

Type **CHE** in the Type blank.

When you highlight the Type blank, the program lists the possible types at the bottom of the screen. The code for a checking account is CHE. If you are setting up another kind of account, enter the code of that account.

Type your balance and the number of your last check.

If you are starting with January 1, enter your account balance for January 1. For the last check number, enter the number of the last check you wrote before January 1.

Press F1 to add the account to the list of accounts in the Money Accounts screen.

If you decide against adding an account after you have filled out the New Money Account form, you can press the F9 key to return to the Money Accounts screen without adding the account.

At the Money Accounts screen, highlight the account you want to work with, and press F1.

A new screen lists the unreconciled transactions, those you have entered but have not yet reconciled with your bank statements. Because you just set up your account, you do not have any unreconciled transactions yet.

From this screen, you spend money, receive money, and generally use the program as you would your paper checkbook. You record and write checks and record deposits and other financial transactions that pertain to the account. Unlike your checkbook, however, Managing Your Money gives you a chance to go back and quickly fix something if you make a mistake.

**Recording
Checks**

Begin by recording about a month's worth of checks and other expenses, such as withdrawals from your bank's automated teller. Be sure to select the right account from the Money Accounts screen.

> Position the cursor in the F1 blank. Indicate that you want to spend money by typing **S** and then pressing F1.

The program's version of a check appears on the screen. (See Figure 3-3.) Your current account balance appears below the check. By pressing the arrow keys, the Enter key, or the Tab key, you move the cursor from blank to blank in the check, highlighting each blank as it goes.

Notice the check number and date. The number is the next number in the series following the number you entered when you opened the account. The date is today's date. Be sure to change it to the date on which you actually wrote the check.

> Highlight the date blank, and type the date of the check.

The address is optional. If you plan to use the check-writing feature of the program, you should include the payee's address on the check as

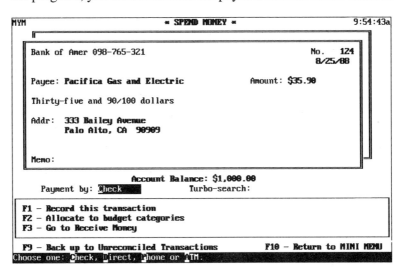

Figure 3-3. *A sample check on the Spend Money screen.*

well. Then you can use an envelope with a window to avoid addressing the envelope by hand. If you are recording a one-time transaction, including the address is not necessary.

> Type the payee's name, the amount of the check, and the payee's address.

You can spend money in four different forms: checks, automatic (direct) payments, phone payments, and withdrawals from an ATM. Identify the type of transaction in the Payment blank that appears below the check.

Checks differ from the other forms in that they are numbered and they can be printed. If an ATM record were entered as a check, the numeric ordering of your checking account would be disrupted, and it would be difficult to reconcile the account. Be sure to enter the correct form of transaction in every item you record.

> Press F1 to record the transaction.

The program records the transaction in the list of unreconciled transactions and displays a new blank check. Your account balance is updated. You can repeat these steps to continue recording checks and other withdrawals. After you enter a month's worth of transactions, return to the Unreconciled Transactions screen by pressing F9. The past month's checks should be listed there now.

If you have made a mistake, highlight the erroneous transaction and press the F2 key to display the check. You can make the necessary changes and press F1 again to record them, or you can press the F3 key at the Unreconciled Transactions screen to delete the transaction completely.

The Chapter 3 mini menu provides a shortcut for writing checks. Press an arrow key, and your list of money accounts scrolls by one line at a time near the top of the menu. When the desired account appears, press F1 to go straight to check writing for that account.

Recording Deposits

Now that you have recorded all your expenses for the month, you should record your income including your paychecks, dividend checks, or profits from a side business. The information about these deposits may come from your checkbook, bank statements, or ATM receipts.

Move the cursor to the F1 field on the Unreconciled Transactions screen and choose the "Receive Money" option by pressing **R** and then F1.

If you are in the Spend Money screen, press F3 to view the Receive Money screen.

When you receive money, the program displays the electronic equivalent of a deposit slip, which is comparable to the electronic checks you use to record withdrawals. (See Figure 3-4.) It doesn't have a check number, and instead of supplying a payee's name and address, you must indicate the source of the income. Note that the deposit slip first appears with today's date. If you are recording deposits for another date, be sure to change the listed date.

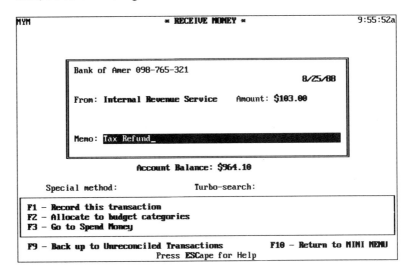

Figure 3-4. *A sample deposit slip on the Receive Money screen.*

Type the correct date, the source of this income, the amount, and a memo. (A memo is not required.)

Press F1 to record the deposit.

When you press the F1 key, the program records the deposit in the list of unreconciled transactions and displays a new blank deposit slip. The account balance is updated.

After you enter a month's worth of deposits, press the F9 key to return to the list of unreconciled transactions. If you make a mistake, highlight the deposit that is in error and press the F2 key to display the slip for that deposit. Then make your changes and press the F1 key again to record them. You can press the F3 key at the Unreconciled Transactions screen to delete the deposit altogether.

Setting Up Automatic Payments

Managing Your Money can save you from the task of writing the same checks month after month. With the automatic-spending feature of the program, you can set up a format for paying the bills you regularly receive. Mortgage payments fall into a special category, however, and you must use the loan-payment section to set them up. (See "Managing Loans" later in this chapter.)

You can also use the automatic transaction feature to record all those past checks, withdrawals, and deposits. Simply handle those transactions as you would any current or future ones. But if you plan to go on to use the budget, don't record all of those items now. You can create a few automatic transactions for practice. When you start working with budgets, you will want to redo the automatic transactions to make budgeting easier.

To set up an automatic payment, enter it as you would a check or other withdrawal. Because you already manually recorded a full month's worth of records, try recording a few new transactions automatically. Don't record transactions that you have already recorded manually.

From the Chapter 3 mini menu, press F3. The Money Accounts screen appears and displays a listing of your accounts.

Highlight the account you want to use for the automatic transaction, and press F5.

Automatic transactions are also reached from the Unreconciled Transactions screen by pressing F5.

The Automatic Transactions screen appears. (See Figure 3-5.) If you had already set up some automatic transactions, they would appear on this screen; because you haven't, it should be empty.

Press F5 to add a spend transaction.

The Automatic Spending screen displays a form that looks like a check except that it doesn't have a number.

Type the payee's name, the amount, and the payee's address.

Press F1 to add the automatic transaction to the list of automatic transactions.

```
MYM                      * AUTOMATIC TRANSACTIONS in: *                    9:56:42a
                              City Bank 254-5262-6
                                                                   Home ↑ PgUp
Payee/Payor            Mark Last Use Type      $ In        $ Out    Chk# Budget
Edison Light Company        1/21/86  U                    $60.00          Utili
I. Magnin                   1/21/86  U                   $100.00          Cloth
Ma Bell                     1/21/86  U                   $125.00          Telep
Mobil Oil                   1/21/86  U                   $100.00          Auto-
National Bank               1/21/86  M                 $1,222.30          IP
Safeway Foods               1/21/86  U                    $50.00          Groce
Shell Oil                   1/21/86  U                    $15.00          Auto-
Sid's Employer              1/21/86  U       $1,750.00                     Salar
                         Account balance: $1,938.90                 End ↓ PgDn

  Speed scroll -
  Mark those transactions you wish to execute by Check    . For recording
  checks, begin with #1110 or alternate number in "Chk#" column.  Execute
  transactions on 8/25/88 or on an alternate date in "Last Use" column.

    F1 - Execute marked transactions      F4 - Print Automatic Transactions
    F2 - View/Edit transaction            F5 - Add a Spend Transaction
Alt-F2 - View/Edit allocations            F6 - Add a Receive Transaction
    F3 - Delete transaction

    F9 - Back up without doing anything    F10 - Return to MINI MENU
Choose one: Check, ATM, Direct or Phone.
```

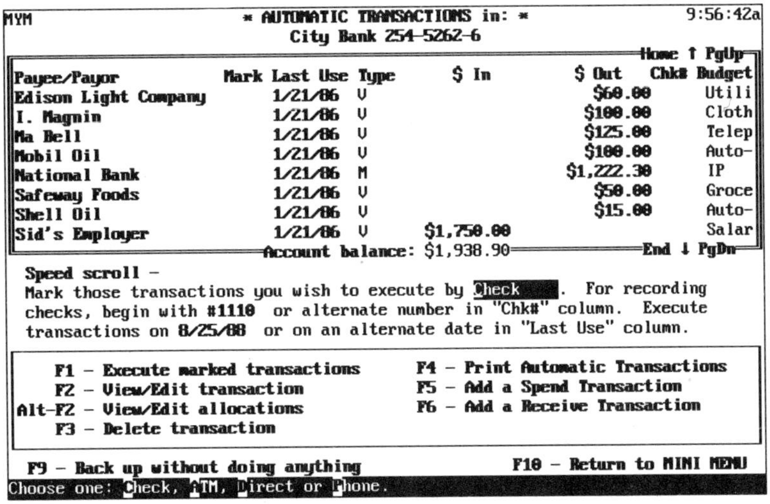

Figure 3-5. *The Automatic Transactions screen.*

The Automatic Transactions screen reappears with the new transaction in the list. You can add as many automatic transactions to the list as you want.

If you no longer have a debt and want to cancel the automatic transaction, bring the cursor to the listing and press F3 to delete it. If the amount of a payment or a payee's information changes, you can modify an entry by highlighting the transaction and pressing the F2 key. The program displays the transaction form on the Automatic Spending screen, where you can make any necessary changes.

Setting Up Automatic Deposits

Not all automatic transactions are debits. You can also record automatic income. A good example of automatic income is your salary.

Setting up automatic deposits is much like setting up automatic payments.

From the Automatic Transactions screen, press F6.

The Automatic Receipts screen appears with a receipt form. (See Figure 3-6.)

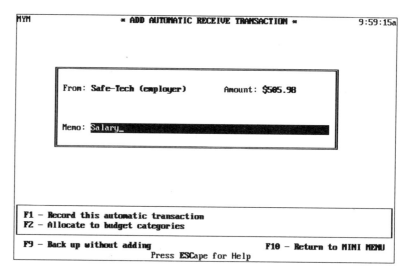

Figure 3-6. *The Automatic Receipts screen.*

Type the source of the income and the amount.

Press the F1 key to add the transaction to the list of automatic transactions.

The transaction now appears on the Automatic Transactions screen. If the amount of an automatic receipt changes, you can use the F2 key to record the change. To delete an automatic receipt altogether, you can use the F3 key.

Invoking Automatic Transactions

Making automatic payments and recording automatic receipts are both two-step processes. Setting up the transactions is only the first step. They do not actually appear as transactions until you invoke them, which you do from the Automatic Transactions screen.

Type an **X** in the "Mark" column for each automatic transaction you want to invoke.

You can invoke one or several transactions at a time. Categorize in your mind all your different types of payments and deposits, and then mark all those that are alike. For example, mark all the checks first.

In the blanks under the information box, type the check number you want to use for the first automatic transaction and the date(s) on which you want the transaction(s) to occur.

The program is set up to date checks with the current date. Verify that the check number shown is the first available check number in your electronic checkbook. You can also specify a particular check number for each payment in the Chk# column of the screen for those you've already written and now want to record.

Type in the appropriate code indicating type of payment.

When you press the F1 key, all transactions marked with an X are recorded in your list of unreconciled transactions. You can then return to the Automatic Transactions screen and invoke all ATM transactions.

Finally, you can record phone payments or home bank payments and then deposits. The Automatic Transactions screen also shows the date you last invoked an automatic transaction. This will prevent you from paying the same bill twice in any one pay period.

Another way to add an automatic transaction is to enter the Unreconciled Transactions screen and place the cursor over any transaction listed there. Press Alt-F5, and the one-time transaction becomes an automatic transaction.

Sorting Transactions

The list of unreconciled transactions is ordered by dates of transaction. You might want to change this organization, perhaps to keep your checks in numerical order or to alphabetize your list of payee names, which can be helpful when you are looking for a check and you don't remember the date or check number. You can sort by check date (from earliest to latest), by check number (from first to last), by payee (alphabetically), or by amount (from smallest to largest). (See Figure 3-7.)

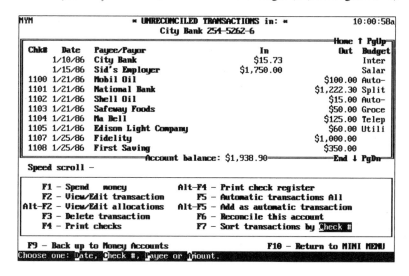

Figure 3-7. *Sorting transactions by check number.*

Use the arrow keys to highlight the F7 blank. Type the code for the sort method you want.

Press F7 to sort the list.

The program sorts the transactions according to your instructions. If you want to print this sorted list of transactions, press Alt-F4.

Transferring Funds Between Accounts

If you have more than one account, perhaps a savings and a checking account, you might need to transfer money between the two. Some couples keep more than one of each account and have to transfer funds quite often. The Managing Your Money program helps you keep track of these transfers.

From the Chapter 3 mini menu, press F3 to display your list of accounts. Then press F6.

The program displays the same list of accounts, this time with blanks for indicating the "from" and "to" accounts. (See Figure 3-8.)

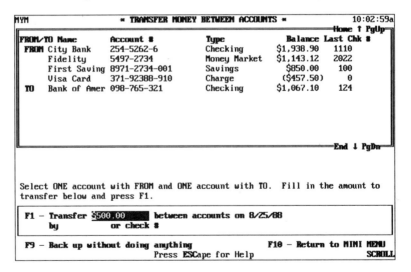

Figure 3-8. *The Transfer Money screen.*

(If you have only one account, the F6 option does not appear on the screen because you can't transfer money from and to the same account. Use the F2 key to add a new account and try this option.)

Highlight the account you want to take money from, and type **F** in the blank. Then highlight the account you want to give money to, and type **T** in the blank.

Now you have identified where the money is coming from and where it is going. Next, tell the program how much money to transfer and what kind of transaction it is. You do this in the action box at the bottom of the screen.

In the F1 blanks, type the amount of money you want to transfer, the date, and the transaction method or the check number.

If you are transferring the money by phone payment or ATM transaction, type the appropriate code in the blank. If you are using a check, type the check number.

Press F1 to record the transaction.

The transaction is recorded in both accounts.

SETTING UP A BUDGET

The Managing Your Money budget is much more than something you may have scratched out once on a piece of lined note paper, with income on one side and expenses on the other. With the program, you can send information about every check you write directly to the budget. You can use budget categories to keep track of transactions that need to be reported at tax time. You can even make graphs to see if you are maintaining your budget; and you will not be as likely to ignore this budget, because every time you exceed your grocery allotment, you'll know it. You can look at your overall budget at any point in the year and project how closely you will meet your budget by December 31.

To set up a budget with Managing Your Money, you begin exactly as you did on paper—by creating a list of budget categories. With Managing Your Money, however, you also assign each budget category to a tax category before you add it to the budget. Then you set your budget amounts for each category and allocate your transactions to budget categories. Before you begin creating your budget categories and apportioning amounts to them, print out a list of your unreconciled transactions. You will need it to build your annual budget. Then clear the existing budget of any existing budget allocations.

Clearing an Old Budget

The hub of budget building is the Budget Categories screen, which contains a list of suggested budget categories, such as interest, dividends, clothing, and groceries. If you have not deleted the Sid and Sara Sample data yet, the screen will include their budget allocations. Clear these existing allocations before you begin.

From the Chapter 3 mini menu, press F4 to display the Budget Categories screen.

Press F5 to clear any values from the budget categories.

Selecting Budget Categories

After you clear the old budget, the built-in list of budget categories appears, along with income or expense category, total annual budget, and tax category headings. (See Figure 3-9 on the following page.) Now you are ready to select your budget categories.

The budget you build should reflect the type of detail you want to keep and the lifestyle you lead. If your month's list of transactions contains many payments for travel expenses, you might want to create more than one travel budget category—one for business travel and one for personal travel, for example. If you own a dog, you might want to create a separate category for veterinary fees. Be sure to create a miscellaneous petty-cash category for both your income and expenses if you don't want to account for every 50 cents you spend.

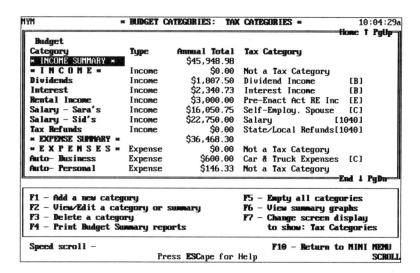

Figure 3-9. *The Budget Categories screen.*

As you create these categories, you can assign each one to a tax category, so keep tax time in mind. You can write off expenditures for your computer and software under the right circumstances, so why not create a special budget category for computer supplies? You can use the printout of your unreconciled transactions to suggest the categories you need, and then delete categories you don't need from the existing list in the Budget Categories screen.

Highlight the category you want to delete, and then press F3 to delete it.

Repeat this step for all categories you do not need—such as mortgage principal if you don't own a house. Then you can start adding categories of your own.

Press F1 to add a new budget category.

The screen for adding a budget category has two blanks. The first is for the name of the category, and the second is for the type of category—income or expense. This screen also lists several tax categories.

> Type the name of the new budget category, and press the Enter key.
> Then type **I** for income or **E** for expense in the Type blank.

If the budget category is not a tax category, highlight "Not a Tax Category" and press F1. Then skip ahead to "Allocating Budget Amounts" later in this chapter.

Choosing Tax Categories

Assigning budget categories to tax categories allows you to sort your transactions by how they are taxed. At tax time, these tax categories let you print a list of all your deductible expenses.

For each category you add, consider what bearing it has on your taxes. Many of your budget categories do not belong to a tax category, but you want to get all your taxable or deductible expenditures in the right tax categories. Also, remember to create budget categories that deal with long-term debts, such as a home loan. If you own a house or condominium, create categories for mortgage principal and mortgage interest. You can create principal and interest categories for each outstanding loan, and then you can assign interest categories to Schedule A so that you remember to deduct them later. The principal budget categories are not tax categories because you can't write them off.

The screen for adding a new budget category lists 14 tax categories. If you need a basic summary of the main tax categories, see "Which Tax Category?" on the following pages.

> Highlight the tax category that applies to your budget category, and
> press F1.

Most of these categories have subcategories; when you choose one, Managing Your Money displays a new screen with the additional categories. If you choose the category for Schedule C items, the program displays a screen that lists the tax categories on Schedule C—income categories, such as sales, and expense categories, such as office expenses. (See Figure 3-10 on page 70.) Because tax categories can be tricky, take a look at all the tax-category screens.

> Highlight the appropriate tax category on the new screen, and press
> F1 again.

Which Tax Category?

When you create a budget category in Managing Your Money, you match it with a tax category. The seven major choices are as follows:

Form 1040: Form 1040 is your yearly balance sheet. As far as your budget is concerned, you should keep track of your salary and any other income for use with this form. You should also track certain expenses, such as federal withholding and estimated tax payments, FICA deductions, contributions to IRA or Keogh accounts, and moving expenses.

Schedule A: Schedule A lists your itemized deductions. Expenditures in this category should have something to do with medical expenses, taxes you paid (other than to the federal government), some kinds of interest you paid on loans, or any charitable contributions.

Schedule B: Schedule B lists your interest and dividend income. Any budget category you label for this schedule is an income category. You are likely to need this form if you have either a savings account or an interest-bearing checking account. Any budget categories that include interest income belong in this tax category, as do any categories that record income from dividends paid by (but not gains from the sale of) stocks, mutual funds, and other income-producing investments.

Schedule C: Use this schedule to report profit or loss from a business or profession. This tax category includes the income and many expenses for a person who is self-employed or runs a business on the side.

Schedule E: Schedule E is where you report supplemental income. This category is something of a miscellaneous category. You might use it for rents collected or losses resulting from rental property you own. Income or loss from a limited partnership also belongs in this category.

Schedule F: Farm income is reported in Schedule F. You need worry about this form only if you own a farm. If you do, use this tax category for profits and losses on livestock and plants as well as other farm income or losses. Expenses for farm equipment and land upkeep also belong here because they are deductible.

Form 2106: Report business expenses and reimbursements from your employer on Form 2106. If your employer doesn't cover all your expenses, you will know exactly how much you can deduct at the end of the year.

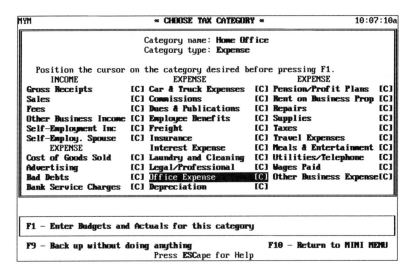

Figure 3-10. *The Tax Category screen.*

Allocating Budget Amounts

After you add a new budget category and assign a tax category, assign a budget amount to the new category using the Budgets and Actuals screen. You can enter a different budget amount for each month of the year. For example, if you are adding a budget category for car repairs, estimate how much your car bills cost each month. The amount you enter here depends on the overall condition of your car. If you have a new car, you might enter only $300 in six-month intervals, because that is the average maintenance cost for a car in good condition. If the car needs more attention, adjust repair and maintenance bills accordingly.

If this budget category is for something more static, such as rent payment, you know that every month you will pay the same amount. In this case, fill in each month of the "Budget" column with that amount. (See Figure 3-11.)

Take another close look at the printout of your transactions list from the checkbook part of the program when you are estimating the budget amounts. You shouldn't be too far from a reasonable budget if you estimate monthly payments based on your transactions for one month, assuming you spend about that much every other month of the year.

```
MYM                    * BUDGETS AND ACTUALS FOR Home Office *        10:08:17a
                      ==Budget==========Actual===
    January            [      $100.00]
    February                $100.00
    March                   $100.00
    April                   $100.00
    May                     $100.00
    June                    $100.00
    July                    $100.00
    August                  $100.00
    September               $100.00
    October                 $100.00
    November                $100.00
    December                $100.00
    Totals              $1,200.00           $0.00


    F1 - Record BUDGETS and ACTUALS as shown and add new Budget Category
    F3 - Divide January's budget over full year
    F4 - Copy January's budget or add $          or      % per month

    F9 - Back up without adding category              F10 - Return to MINI MENU
                          Press ESCape for Help
```

Figure 3-11. *Adding budget amounts.*

Of course, this technique only works within the limits of common sense. If you happen to buy a color television set in your first month, don't assume that you spend $600 on video equipment every month unless you plan on actually buying all that equipment.

At some point, you are simply going to have to estimate how much goes into each category. If you later find your budget is off in some categories, you can go back and change the figures.

> Highlight a blank in the "Budget" column, and type the budget amount for that month. Repeat this for each month that has a budget allocation.

You can speed the process of filling in the "Budget" column if you know the total yearly amount to be entered and want to divide it equally across all 12 months. For example, suppose that you receive an annual gross salary of $42,000, but you are not sure exactly how much that equals per month. Rather than dividing by 12 and entering each figure individually, just type $42,000 in January and press the F3 key. The program automatically divides by 12 and enters the appropriate figure—$3,500 in this case—in each blank in the "Budget" column.

If you know what each monthly entry in the ''Budget'' column should be, as in the case of a loan or monthly condominium payment, enter the figure in the January blank and press the F4 key to duplicate the same figure for the rest of the months. You can even use the F4 key to enter a starting amount and then add a monthly growth amount by filling in the appropriate blank in the action box.

Note that the ''Actual'' column is still empty. This column is automatically filled in as you start to spend money in these budget categories. If you are starting your budget in midyear, there's no need to fill in the ''Actual'' columns yourself. As you enter all your checks for the current year, you can allocate them to budget categories, and the program will fill out the ''Actual'' column. Provided that you enter the correct dates of your checks, they will be assigned to the correct month because the ''Actual'' column is linked to the date listed on the check, not the date you enter the check.

Press F1 to record the new category and its budget allocations.

The program returns to the screen for adding a new budget category. Press the F9 key to return to the list of budget categories if you have no more categories to add. Your new category, its total budget for the year, and its tax category now appear in the list. If you want to change your budget allocation for this category or any other category in the list, highlight it and press F2 to edit the Budgets and Actuals screen.

Allocating Transactions to Budget Categories

In order to analyze your budget and decide how realistic it is, you must allocate each of your month's transactions to a budget category. To do so, you have to leave the budget section and return to the checkbook part of the program.

Return to the Chapter 3 mini menu and press F3 to display your list of accounts. Highlight the account you want, and press F1. The program displays the Unreconciled Transactions screen.

Highlight the transaction you want to allocate, and press F2. Your transaction record appears on the screen.

> Press F2, and the program displays your list of budget categories with a blank for each category.
>
> Highlight the Allocation blank for the appropriate budget category, and then press F2.

If your transaction is a gas bill, for example, scroll through the list of budget categories until you find the one for utilities (or gas bills, if you set up a special category for them). When you highlight that blank and press the F2 key, the amount of your check pops up in the blank. (See Figure 3-12.)

> Press F1 to save your new budget allocation.
>
> Press F2 to record the modified transaction.
>
> Press F9 to return to the transaction.

Deposits are allocated to income categories in the same way that expenses are entered in expense categories. Therefore, you can enter your paycheck in an income category called Salary.

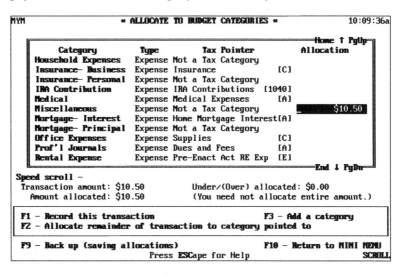

Figure 3-12. *The Allocate to Budget Categories screen.*

If you discover that your list of budget categories is missing a needed category, you can add it now. Simply press F3, and the program displays the screen for adding a budget category. If you recently received a Christmas bonus check from work, for example, but don't have a category for this unexpected income, press the F3 key and add a category called "Bonuses." You can continue this process with the rest of your month's bills.

Allocating Transactions to Multiple Categories

You might want to divide a transaction among several categories. Suppose, for example, that you are recording an ATM deposit that totals $1,500, but the deposit includes a paycheck for $1,000 and a check for $500 to reimburse you for expenses. You can allocate these two checks to two different income categories with one transaction record.

> From the transaction record, press F2. The program displays the list of budget categories.

> Highlight the category for the first amount you want to allocate, and type the amount in the Allocation blank.

In this example, you would highlight the Salary category and type 1000 in the blank.

> Highlight the category for the remaining amount, and press F2.

The program assigns the remaining amount of the transaction to the category. In the above example, you would highlight the Reimbursements category, and the program would assign the remaining $500 of your ATM deposit to Reimbursements.

Turbo-Searching for Budget Categories

Turbo-searching is a shortcut for assigning transactions to budget categories. When you allocate transactions in the Spend Money or Receive Money screens, you press the F2 key to display the list of budget categories and then scroll through the list until you find the right category. With the Turbo-Search feature, you can go directly to the desired category.

From the Spend Money or Receive Money screen, use the arrow keys to highlight the Turbo-Search blank below the check or deposit slip, and then type the category name. For example, if you are recording the purchase of a lawn sprinkler, and you know that you have a budget category called ''Yard Expenses,'' you record the transaction, highlight the Turbo-Search blank, and type the first few letters of the budget category name. You can type ''yard expenses'' or ''yard'' or even ''yar.''

After assigning the category, press F2.

The program displays the Budget Categories screen with the amount of the transaction in the blank for the category you specified. If you select the wrong budget category, use the spacebar to erase the transaction amount. Then scroll through the budget category list to find the correct category and enter it manually.

Press F1 to record the allocation.

Allocating Automatic Transactions

Now you are ready to automate this whole process. Earlier, you set up a few automatic transactions to save time when you were entering checks and deposits. Now you will set up your automatic transactions so that they are allocated to the correct budget categories as well.

From the Chapter 3 mini menu, press F3 to display your list of money accounts. Highlight the desired account and press F5 to display the list of automatic transactions.

If you didn't create any automatic transactions, this screen should be blank. If you have been experimenting with automatic transactions, you can clear each existing transaction by pressing F3.

Reenter your automatic transactions, this time allocating each deposit and withdrawal to a budget category.

Press F5 or F6 to record a spend or receive transaction.

Suppose you are creating an automatic transaction for a rent payment.
Fill in the transaction record with the payee, the amount of your rent,
and the address; but instead of recording the transaction by pressing F1
as you did before, allocate the amount to a budget category.

Press F2 to display the list of budget categories.

Highlight the appropriate category on the screen.

Press F2 to allocate the amount of the automatic transaction to the proper
budget category. The amount you enter appears in the Allocation blank.

Press F1 to save the allocation.

You have now eliminated the need to go through this whole procedure
each month. The only time you need to record checks and deposits individually is when they are unexpected or too infrequent to warrant
their own automatic transactions. You can now begin the task of entering all your year's transactions to date. When you're finished, you can
print the current month's checks, set up the record keeping for your
loans, reconcile your checkbook, monitor your budget with graphs, and
forecast your cash flow.

**PRINTING
YOUR CHECKS**

After you enter all your checks and deposits, Managing Your Money
can print your checks using the information from your check register.
Printing your checks is a simple two-step process. Set up your printer
with checks and then tell the program which of the checks to print and
how to print them.

**Setting Up the
Printer**

It's best to print on check forms that have holes on the sides to catch
the printer's sprockets. You can buy blank sprocket-punched check
forms without magnetic account numbers in most computer stores,
but you can also order preprinted sprocket-punched checks. (See
''Computerized Advertising'' in Chapter 1 or press F4 at the Print
Checks screen.) Whichever type you use, be sure your printer is
properly connected to the computer before you begin.

Insert a blank sprocket-punched check into your printer.

From the Unreconciled Transactions screen, press F4.

Printing options for the Print Checks screen appear in the action box. (See Figure 3-13.) The F2 key prints dummy information so that you can see if your check is lined up properly. If it isn't, try another one until you find the proper alignment.

```
MYM                          * PRINT CHECKS in: *                    10:11:05a
                             City Bank 254-5262-6
                                                                 ┌Home ↑ PgUp┐
  Chk#   Date                                        In              Out
         1/10/86   City Bank                       $15.73
         1/15/86   Sid's Employer                $1,750.00
  1100 1/21/86   Mobil Oil                                         $100.00
  1101 1/21/86   National Bank                                   $1,222.30
  1102 1/21/86   Shell Oil                                          $15.00
  1103 1/21/86   Safeway Foods                                      $50.00
  1104 1/21/86   Ma Bell                                           $125.00
  1105 1/21/86   Edison Light Company                               $60.00
                        ═Account balance: $1,938.90════════════End ↓ PgDn═

  Delete addresses after printing? No   Delete memos after printing? No
  Use pre-numbered checks? Yes          Check size:  Business
    If so, starting number:             Quality print mode? Yes
  Don't pause between checks


 ┌────────────────────────────────────────────────────────────────────────┐
 │ F1 - Print checks 1      thru 1109      F3 - Edit check layouts          │
 │ F2 - Print one line-up check            F4 - To order personalized checks│
 └────────────────────────────────────────────────────────────────────────┘
   F9 - Back up to Unreconciled Transactions         F10 - Return to MINI MENU
 Choose one: Business or Personal.
```

Figure 3-13. *Check-printing options.*

Setting Up the Printing Instructions

In order to print your checks, the program needs to know the range of checks you want to print, whether or not they are prenumbered, and whether to delete addresses and memos when it has finished printing. The F1 blanks in the action box let you indicate the numbers of the first and last checks you want to print. Because you can print many checks in one session, enter all your checks before you go to the check-printing screen.

Fill in the check numbers in the action box. Then press F1 to start printing.

The program prints one check after another until all of the checks you indicated are printed. Of course, you still have to sign your checks and mail them, but if you have included the address of the payee on the check, you can use window envelopes and avoid addressing them. You can print your entire check register (like the one inside a real checkbook) by pressing Alt-F4 from the Unreconciled Transactions screen.

The Chapter 3 mini menu offers a quick way into check printing. Press an arrow key, and your list of money accounts scrolls by one line at a time near the top of the menu. When the desired account appears, press F2 to go straight to check printing for that account.

MANAGING YOUR LOANS

The loan records section of Chapter 3 can help you calculate loan payments for a new or existing loan and later determine its status—how much you have paid, how much you owe, and how much total interest you will pay. You can even print an amortization schedule. The loan records section can send information about a loan to your checkbook register and budget and include loan information when you are calculating your net worth. You don't have to use the loan records section of the program to keep a record of debts and to make loan payments, but you should if you plan to use the budget.

Setting Up a Loan Record

When you set up a loan record, you enter the total amount of the loan (the principal), the term, the interest rate, and the monthly payments. If you already have a loan, you probably know what to enter for each of these. But if you are contemplating a new loan, you can also use the loan record to calculate the loan payments, interest rate, term, or even the principal. You can also use a loan record to track money that *you* lend to someone.

From the Chapter 3 mini menu, press F6 to display the Loan Records screen.

The program displays a list of existing loan records and a New Loan Calculator line. (See Figure 3-14.) If Sid and Sara Sample's loans are still in the list of loan records, you can delete them one at a time with the F3 key.

Highlight the first blank in the New Loan Calculator line; then type the starting date of the loan and press the Enter key.

If you are entering information about an existing loan, type the date you officially received the loan. It should be listed on the original loan document. If you are calculating a new loan, type the anticipated starting date for the loan.

Type the name of the lender, and press the Enter key.

Type **B** if you are the borrower or **L** if you are the lender, and press the Enter key.

Type the amount of the original loan in the Amount blank, and press the Enter key.

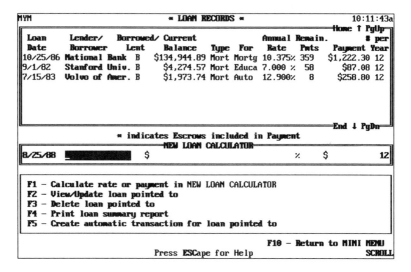

Figure 3-14. *The Loan Records screen.*

Usually you know the amount of money you want to borrow, but if you are trying to determine how much you can afford to borrow, you can leave this blank empty, provided you fill in the remaining blanks.

The four types of loans are mortgages, biweekly mortgages, special loans, and interest-only loans. The most common loan is a mortgage. A mortgage is any loan that has a standard payment schedule like the kind used in most home loans. A special loan does not have a standard payment schedule. A loan to a friend might be a special loan. If you don't plan to set up a payment schedule for such a loan but you want to record the transaction, type **S** in this blank. The program then keeps a record of the loan, but it won't let you calculate interest rates or payment information because there is no set number of payments. Interest-only loans, like special loans, don't follow a standard mortgage amortization schedule.

> Indicate the type of loan in the next blank, and press Enter.

The program designates letters for five categories of loans: automobile (A), education (E), home mortgage (M), personal (P), and other (O).

> Type a letter corresponding to the purpose of the loan, and press the Enter key.

You can calculate the annual interest rate, the loan term, the amount of each payment, or the number of payments by entering three of the four values and the loan amount. For example, if you know you must make 24 monthly payments on an amount of $10,000 at a 10 percent annual interest rate, you can type those values in the appropriate blanks and then press F1 to calculate the monthly payment. The payment—$461.45—appears in the Payment blank.

> Type the annual interest rate, the loan term, the amount of each payment, and the number of payments.

> Press F1 to record the loan or F6 to clear the New Loan Calculator.

The loan now appears in the list of loan records.

Determining the Status of a Loan

After you have set up a loan record, Managing Your Money can track the status of the loan. This includes how many payments you have made, the balance owed, the total principal paid, the total interest paid, the number of payments that remain, and the expected payoff date. You use the Loan Status screen to review and update this information.

Highlight the loan record you want to review and press F2.

The Loan Status screen appears. All status information is based on how many payments you have made. If this is a new loan record, the number of payments is zero. If you are setting up a loan record for an existing loan on which you have already made payments, you need to tell the program how many have been made.

Type the number of payments you have made in the F2 blank in the action box. Then press F2.

The program calculates how much the combined payments (interest and principal) will total over the remaining life of the loan and displays the information in a paragraph in the middle of the screen. (See Figure 3-15 on the following page.) A $75,000 loan paid off at 12.75 percent over 30 years comes to a total of $293,407.17—the original $75,000 plus $218,407.17 in interest. Depressing, isn't it?

Press F1 to record any changes you made to the loan status.

When you press F1, the program records the number of payments in the loan record. The next time you review the loan status, this information appears immediately in the Loan Status screen. If you make an automatic loan payment, the program updates the loan status automatically.

If you do not want to record the number of loan payments—suppose you were only calculating to see how far along you would be after a year of payments—press F9 instead of F1 to return to the Loan Records screen without updating the loan. Practicing calculations before you return to the Loan Records screen can give you a good understanding of how loans work.

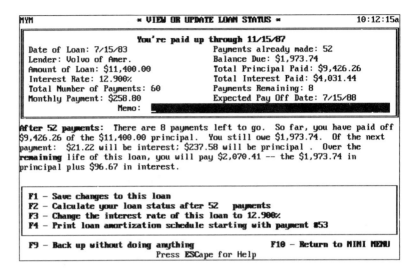

```
MYM                          = VIEW OR UPDATE LOAN STATUS =                    10:12:15a
┌──────────────────────────────────────────────────────────────────────────────────┐
│                         You're paid up through 11/15/87                            │
│  Date of Loan: 7/15/83                    Payments already made: 52                │
│  Lender: Volvo of Amer.                   Balance Due: $1,973.74                   │
│  Amount of Loan: $11,400.00               Total Principal Paid: $9,426.26          │
│  Interest Rate: 12.900%                   Total Interest Paid: $4,031.44           │
│  Total Number of Payments: 60             Payments Remaining: 8                     │
│  Monthly Payment: $258.80                 Expected Pay Off Date: 7/15/88           │
│                          Memo: ██████████████████████████                         │
└──────────────────────────────────────────────────────────────────────────────────┘
After 52 payments:  There are 8 payments left to go.  So far, you have paid off
$9,426.26 of the $11,400.00 principal.  You still owe $1,973.74.  Of the next
payment:  $21.22 will be interest; $237.58 will be principal .  Over the
remaining life of this loan, you will pay $2,070.41 -- the $1,973.74 in
principal plus $96.67 in interest.

┌──────────────────────────────────────────────────────────────────────────────────┐
│  F1 - Save changes to this loan                                                    │
│  F2 - Calculate your loan status after 52    payments                              │
│  F3 - Change the interest rate of this loan to 12.900%                             │
│  F4 - Print loan amortization schedule starting with payment #53                   │
└──────────────────────────────────────────────────────────────────────────────────┘
  F9 - Back up without doing anything                 F10 - Return to MINI MENU
                          Press ESCape for Help
```

Figure 3-15. *The Loan Status screen.*

Printing an Amortization Schedule

A financier almost always gives you an amortization schedule when you take out a loan. No matter how little you know about financial affairs, here is your chance to learn about amortization schedules— and even to print one.

An amortization schedule tells you how much of each monthly payment goes toward the interest and how much goes toward paying off the actual debt (the principal). At first, the payments to the interest are disproportionately high, which may help you at tax time because you can deduct the interest. After the midway point, however, more of the payment goes toward the principal and less to the interest. You pay off your debt more quickly but you have less interest to claim, which is why many people refinance their loans. In addition to the monthly breakdown of payments, the amortization schedule shows you the date of each payment, its chronological number, and the balance due after each monthly payment is made.

> Press F2 to go to the Loan Status screen. Press F4 to print an amortization schedule for the loan.

**Recording a
Change in
Interest Rate**

A problem in the world of loan management is the ''variable-rate mortgage.'' This type of loan includes mortgages that have adjustable rates as well as those that have balloon payments. Such mortgages are most popular when interest rates rise because they often provide the only way for someone who is starting out to buy a piece of property.

The interest rates for a variable-rate mortgage usually start low and rise with inflation, the prime rate, or the blood pressure level of the bank's president—I'm not completely sure which one. When the bank raises or lowers its mortgage rate, you must change the interest rate listed in the program on your loan record. One way to do this is to adjust the interest rate in the Loan Status screen whenever the interest rate changes.

Type the new interest rate in the F3 blank, and press F3.

The remaining payments are adjusted to reflect the new rate. Unfortunately, this simple rate change does not always solve the problem. Rate changes can also affect the principal and interest ratios in variable-rate mortgages and cause ''negative amortization.'' Negative amortization occurs when the remaining balance increases rather than decreases and a borrower owes more after making a number of payments than he or she did previously.

If you find yourself in this situation, you should treat the new rate as a new loan. Make the new loan start at the current balance of your real loan, and set the number of payments equal to the number of remaining payments of your real loan. In the new loan, use the new interest rate, and treat the real loan as if it were simply paid off. You must do this whenever a change in the rate affects your interest and principal ratios—usually only once a year.

Setting Up an Automatic Loan Payment

Although you can choose to enter most expenses manually or as automatic transactions, a loan payment is one type of expense that can only be entered as an automatic transaction through the Loan Records screen. If you set up a loan record and updated its status to reflect the number of payments you made to date, you are ready to create an automatic transaction.

> Position the cursor over the loan for which you want to create an automatic transaction and press F5.

The automatic transaction form appears. (See Figure 3-16.) Usually it is a check, but if you are the lender for a loan, the transaction record is a deposit slip.

> Type the name of the lender and the amount of the check you write each month in the transaction record. You can include an address and a memo.

When you track loan payments in your budget, be sure to track interest and principal separately because your monthly interest payments are tax-deductible, but your principal payments are not. When you

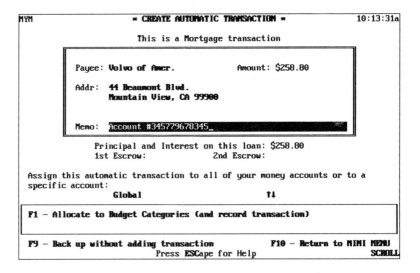

Figure 3-16. *The automatic loan payment screen.*

allocate part of the loan payment to the Interest budget category, that information is stored in the budget under a deductible tax category, and you can use that information for calculating your taxes later.

If you did not set up separate budget categories for principal and interest when you first set up your budget, you can add those categories in the next screen. If you did set up separate categories, you are ready to allocate your automatic loan payment to the proper category.

> Press F1 to display the list of budget categories.
>
> Highlight the Mortgage Principal budget category and type **P** in the "Allocation" column. Then highlight the Interest budget category, and type **I**.

You do not have to specify the amounts of the principal payment and the interest payment. The program automatically allocates the correct portion of your payment to the interest and principal categories because it knows the rate of interest and the number of monthly payments you have made.

> Press F1 to add the loan payment to the "Budget" column in the categories you chose. The Loan Records screen appears.

From now on, each time you use this automatic transaction, the total payment is recorded in the list of unreconciled transactions, and the calculated interest and principal payments are recorded in your budget. Notice that you can tell the program whether you normally pay this monthly debt on time, early, or late by typing a number in the F1 blank before you press F1. To simplify, you may want to leave this blank empty to indicate that you pay zero days late.

MANAGING YOUR CREDIT CARDS

Credit-card payments make up another transaction category that needs special treatment. Depending on your credit-card usage, you may want to treat your charge payments as normal payments from your checking account or open a separate account listing the expenses in detail.

If you pay your entire charge-account balance every month, you really don't need to set up a separate account. You can pay your credit-card bill in one lump sum from your checkbook, either automatically or manually, and then look at your statement and allocate each charge to the appropriate budget category.

For example, if your MasterCard bill has six restaurant charges, two charges from the men's department at Macy's, and a number of other small charges, enter the total of the first six charges in an "Entertainment" category and the next two in a "Clothing" category. Then highlight the Unallocated Expenses category and press F2. The remaining charges appear there.

If you carry a balance on your charge card every month, it's a good idea to create a separate account. Set it up exactly as you would a checking account in which each transaction is recorded as a separate transaction record. You can reconcile the account against your charge-account statement using your purchase receipts in the same way that you reconcile your checking account against your bank statement using your canceled checks. (See "Reconciling Your Checkbook," later in this chapter.) Instead of starting out with a balance of money against which you write checks, you start out with a zero or negative balance. Then each payment you make reduces your outstanding balance.

To set up a new charge account, go to the Chapter 3 mini menu and press F3. The program displays a list of your accounts.

Press F2 to add a new account. Type the name of the account and the account number.

In the Type blank, type **CHA**.

In the Last Statement Balance blank, type your current account balance with a minus sign (unless you have a credit balance).

The Last Check Number blank is not applicable in this case. Do not fill in this blank.

Press F1 to add the account.

Your charge account now appears in your list of accounts. You can treat your charge account much as you do your checking account—record transactions, allocate transactions to budget categories, and reconcile the transactions with your charge-account statement. You can transfer money from your checking account to your charge account whenever you make a payment.

RECONCILING YOUR CHECKBOOK

When you reconcile your checkbook, you verify that all the transactions on your bank statement match the ones in your checkbook and that the bank balance and your balance match. Most people dislike this task because it is time-consuming and often the figure from the checkbook and the figure from the bank statement don't match.

Reconciliation is easier, faster, and more successful with the Managing Your Money program. After you check a transaction against the bank statement and find it was paid, you no longer need to keep the record in your list of unreconciled transactions. The program gives you an opportunity to archive the reconciled transactions.

Matching the Bank Statement

If you entered half a year's worth of data, you have several bank statements to match. If you don't reconcile all the transactions to date, you will not be able to reconcile any future transactions. You are now ready to gather your bank statements and start reconciling. You can reconcile several months' worth of statements in one session, but be aware that the archiving may take 15 minutes or longer.

> From the Chapter 3 mini menu, press F3 to display your list of accounts. Highlight the one you want to reconcile, and press F1. Your list of unreconciled transactions appears. Then press F6.

The program displays a new copy of the transactions with blanks for marking the checks that appear on your statements. The screen also includes blanks for entering the statement balance as well as any fecs or other charges.

Type **X** in the blank for each transaction that appears on your bank statement.

In any month, several transactions will probably remain unreconciled because the bank statement does not include your most recent transactions. For instance, if you wrote a check to the electric company on May 2 and your statement arrives on May 10, the check probably won't appear on the statement. You have to wait until next month to reconcile it. Don't try to account for transactions that are not on your statement or you'll never get your checkbook balanced. It's best to leave them unmarked.

Enter the balance from the bank statement and any other charges in the blanks above the action box. This area includes blanks for entering finance charges, interest earned (if you are reconciling an interest-bearing checking account or savings account), and service charges. Remember to enter this information accurately from the bank statement and include any fees that were subtracted, such as those charged on a check that didn't clear.

Press F1 to compare the balances.

If all goes well, the balances match, and the program displays a new screen and gives you the opportunity to archive the reconciled transactions. If all does not go well, it displays a message that shows the discrepancy in your balance. (See Figure 3-17.)

If your balance is off, you most likely forgot to record a single check or ATM transaction. If the discrepancy is very small, check to see if you recorded all your account charges. After you find the error, press F9 to return to the Unreconciled Transactions screen and add any missing transactions or fix an erroneous one. Then press F6 to return to the list of reconciled transactions. All your information is still there, and you can compare the balances again by pressing F1.

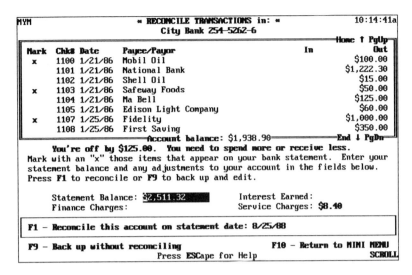

```
MYM                    * RECONCILE TRANSACTIONS in: *              10:14:41a
                          City Bank 254-5262-6
                                                            ┌Home ↑ PgUp┐
   Mark  Chk#  Date    Payee/Payor                    In          Out
    x    1100 1/21/86  Mobil Oil                              $100.00
         1101 1/21/86  National Bank                        $1,222.30
         1102 1/21/86  Shell Oil                                $15.00
    x    1103 1/21/86  Safeway Foods                            $50.00
         1104 1/21/86  Ma Bell                                 $125.00
         1105 1/21/86  Edison Light Company                     $60.00
    x    1107 1/25/86  Fidelity                              $1,000.00
         1108 1/25/86  First Saving                            $350.00
   ─────────────────────── Account balance: $1,938.90══════════End ↓ PgDn┘
       You're off by $125.00.  You need to spend more or receive less.
   Mark with an "x" those items that appear on your bank statement.  Enter your
   statement balance and any adjustments to your account in the fields below.
   Press F1 to reconcile or F9 to back up and edit.

        Statement Balance: $2,511.32          Interest Earned:
        Finance Charges:                      Service Charges: $8.40

   ┌──────────────────────────────────────────────────────────────────────┐
   │ F1 - Reconcile this account on statement date: 8/25/88                │
   └──────────────────────────────────────────────────────────────────────┘

    F9 - Back up without reconciling              F10 - Return to MINI MENU
                        Press ESCape for Help                       SCROLL
```

Figure 3-17. *An unbalanced account screen.*

Archiving Transactions

When you reconcile your checkbook, the program archives reconciled transactions. It removes the transactions from the program and stores them in a file with a .ARK extension. Archiving frees memory in your computer. Each record takes up space in the computer's random-access memory, and a full year's worth of records may exceed your computer's limit. Archiving ensures that you have room for all your current transactions.

You can't archive a transaction until you have reconciled it, which means you must match the bank's balance. After you do, the program displays a Reconciled Account screen. (See Figure 3-18 on the following page.) From here, archiving is a simple process.

Press F1 to archive your reconciled transactions.

You can still reach your archived transactions by pressing F9 at the mini menu. (See Chapter 4 for more detailed information.) If you do not want to archive your transactions but want to delete them from the list, you can press F3, but this is not recommended. Press F10 if you want to cancel what you've done and return to the mini menu. The transactions you worked on will remain in your list of unreconciled transactions.

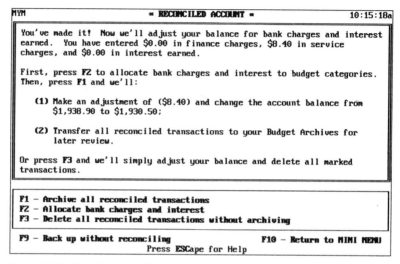

Figure 3-18. *The Reconciled Account screen.*

MONITORING YOUR BUDGET

After time has passed and you have been writing checks and allocating them to budget categories, you may wonder how well you're doing. Are you sticking to your budget? Where is your money going?

Managing Your Money answers these questions with numbers and graphs. You can get a quick visual representation of your budget and actual spending for any individual budget category; you can graph total expenses or total income, comparing actual spending or receipts to the amounts you budgeted; you can see how closely you are sticking to your total budget by graphing income and expenses together; and you can create pie charts that display the distribution of your income and expenses.

From the Chapter 3 mini menu, press F4 to view your list of budget categories.

Reviewing the Numbers

You can compare your monthly budgets with your actual monthly spending or income for any category in your budget. Suppose, for example, that you want to compare your budgeted gas bill with your actual gas bill.

Highlight the budget category you want to review, and press F2.

The program shows a month-by-month breakdown of your budget and actual figures, and the difference between them. (See Figure 3-19.) If the number in the "Difference" column appears in parentheses, it is a negative number, and you are over your budget estimate. If the number is positive, you are under your budget estimate.

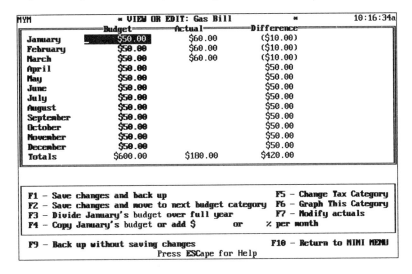

Figure 3-19. *Reviewing a budget screen.*

Graphing a Budget Category

Although the numbers tell you how well you are doing month by month, viewing a graph is the best way to see the relationship between budget and actual figures over several months. If you have already displayed the review of your budget and actuals for a single category, you can graph this information in one step.

91

Press F6 to graph the information for the budget category.

Note that if your computer does not have a graphics card, or if you turned the graphics feature off, the F6 key does not appear in your list of options, and you cannot create a graph. See "Special Options," later in this chapter, for more information on enabling or disabling the graphics feature.

If you do have a graphics card and the graphics feature is turned on, the program displays an easy-to-read bar chart. To illustrate how you can use it, suppose you are graphing your gas-bill expense. If you projected $50 per month in gas bills, but for three months you paid $60 (which was recorded in the unreconciled transactions), the graph of your gas bill looks like Figure 3-20.

For one month, this bar chart may not be particularly helpful. But after three or four months, a quick glance at it will tell you immediately if you are consistently meeting or missing your budget. If you are missing your budget regularly, perhaps it is time to revise your budget to reflect the actuals more closely.

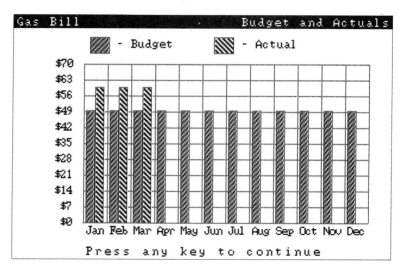

Figure 3-20. *A budget category graph.*

Graphing Total Expenses and Income

Now suppose you want to see how well you are meeting your projections for all your expenses, all your income, or both. You can review combined budgets and actuals for income, expenses, or both, and then graph them exactly as you did a single budget category. The Budget Categories screen displays Income Summary, Expense Summary, and Net Summary in the information box.

Highlight your choice, and press F2.

As before, the program displays a month-by-month report of your budget and actual figures, and the difference between them. But this time the report combines all categories for income, expenses, or both. If you choose Expenses, the "Difference" column tells you how close you come to meeting your budgeted expenses. If you choose Income, the "Difference" column tells you how close you come to meeting your budgeted income.

Press F1 to graph your budget figures.

The program displays a bar chart for the figures you choose.

Graphing Distributions

If you are having trouble spending within your budget and want to get a quick visual picture of which budget categories are consuming most of your money, you can show your budget as a pie chart with each piece of the pie representing a different budget category.

From the budget categories screen, press F6.

A pie chart shows the total amount of money you projected for income this year. The pie has as many slices as you have income categories. For example, a large part of the pie—40 percent—might be your salary. Another slice might be your spouse's salary. If you have savings-account interest, bonuses, or gambling income, these will also appear as slices.

Press any key to display your expenses.

A second pie chart that displays the total amount budgeted for expenses appears. If you're like most people, this pie chart probably has many more slices than the income pie chart.

Press any key to return to your list of budget categories.

If your pie charts have made you reconsider some of your budget categories, you can now review your budget, category by category, to make necessary revisions.

FORECASTING YOUR CASH FLOW

With Chapter 3 of Managing Your Money, you can project how much cash you will have at the end of each month for the next 11 months. This will let you know whether or not you will have enough cash on hand to meet your financial goals.

Suppose, for example, that you are trying to save enough for a down payment on a house, and you know you need to save $1,000 per month in order to do it in one year. Cash forecasting tells you, roughly, whether you are going to have $1,000 per month to save.

Calculating Your End-of-Month Cash

To determine how much money you will have at the end of a given month, you must add the contents of your checking account to any money left over after you entered your salary and paid your bills. The program does this computation for you, using both your projected budget and the actuals you entered. It can calculate your end-of-month cash for the next 11 months.

From the Chapter 3 mini menu, press F5 to calculate your cash figures.

The program displays your current cash position. At the top of the screen, it shows your current cash—the amount available today— and projects your cash for the end of the month. It also summarizes how much you budgeted to have at the end of the month, how much you have yet to spend, or how much you already overspent. The lower half of the screen performs the same mathematics for the remaining months in your annual budget, listing your projected income, expenses, profit or loss, and cash at the end of each month.

Notice that the ''projected ending cash'' figures either increase or decrease progressively, which makes sense. If you save $1,000 in January, you are going to put it in the bank and have $1,000 more at the beginning of February than you did at the beginning of January. If your budget is somewhat stable, you will then save another $1,000 in February and have $2,000 more at the beginning of March than you had at the beginning of January.

On the opposite end, if you owe $1,000 at the end of the month, then you have $1,000 less in February. In March, if you keep overspending, you will have $2,000 less than you had in January. By April, you will have stopped overspending and rearranged your budget—well, let's hope you will have.

Graphing Your Wealth

All figures in the Cash Forecasting screen answer one question: How much richer (or poorer) will I be tomorrow? You can see a graphic representation of the answer.

Press F1 to graph your end-of-month cash.

The projections for your cash at the end of each of the next 11 months appear as a line graph. (See Figure 3-21 on the following page.) If you are making money each month, the line goes up, up, up. During the months in which you lose money, the line drops down. Note again that if you don't have a graphics board, or if you turned off the graphics option, the F1 option is not available.

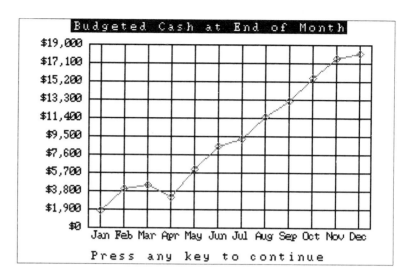

Figure 3-21. *An end-of-month cash graph.*

SPECIAL OPTIONS

Chapter 3 of Managing Your Money includes some special options designed for someone who plans to run a small business or a side business. From the Optional Features screen, you can change the standard checkbook lists of the program into Accounts Payable and Accounts Receivable ledgers. You can even change the calendar year of the program to match the fiscal year of your business and create a five-year plan for your budget. (See Figure 3-22.)

> Press F7 from the Chapter 3 mini menu to view the Optional Features screen.

(Note that this screen is also where you turn the graphics option off and on. When you first display this screen, the Graphs choice is already selected. You should keep it selected, unless you really need to save memory, so that you can use the graph functions in the program.)

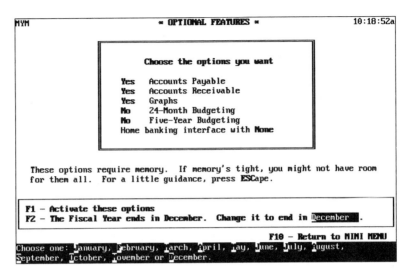

Figure 3-22. *The Optional Features screen.*

Tracking Your Accounts Payable

In the Accounts Payable ledger you can add transactions, allocate them to a budget category, and mark them for tax purposes in a tax category. The resulting income or loss is recorded in a list of unreconciled transactions, exactly as in a checking account. You can print checks to pay your accounts payable.

However, the Accounts Payable ledger accepts expenses only in the form of bills because it keeps track of the money your business owes to people or other businesses. Also, bills you enter in the Accounts Payable ledger are not subtracted from your checking-account balance until you actually pay them. So even though you might not pay a bill until midmonth, you can keep track of it and all your other bills on the Accounts Payable screen.

To set up and use an Accounts Payable ledger, select the Accounts Payable option, add the account to your list of accounts as usual, and enter information about your bills.

Type **Y** in the Accounts Payable blank on the Optional Features screen, and press F1 to activate the option. The program returns you to the mini menu.

Press F3 to display your list of accounts.

Now, when you display your list of accounts, you have a new option: The F8 key displays the accounts payable in the account you select. This will probably be your business checking account.

If you did not already add this account to the list, press F2 to add it now.

Highlight the account with which you want to work, and press F8.

A list of current accounts payable appears. However, because you are only now setting up your accounts payable, you see no accounts listed.

Press F5 to add an account payable.

The program displays a form, which you use to enter information about a single bill.

Type the date of the bill, the date it is due, the payee, the amount, and the address.

Press F2 to allocate the bill to a budget category.

Allocate the account payable to a budget category exactly as you allocate any checkbook transaction.

Press F1 to save the allocation and return to the Accounts Payable screen.

The bill is recorded in the Accounts Payable ledger, and the program displays the ledger. (See Figure 3-23.) If you are not ready to pay the bill, you can stop here. You can, however, record the payment now and print a check.

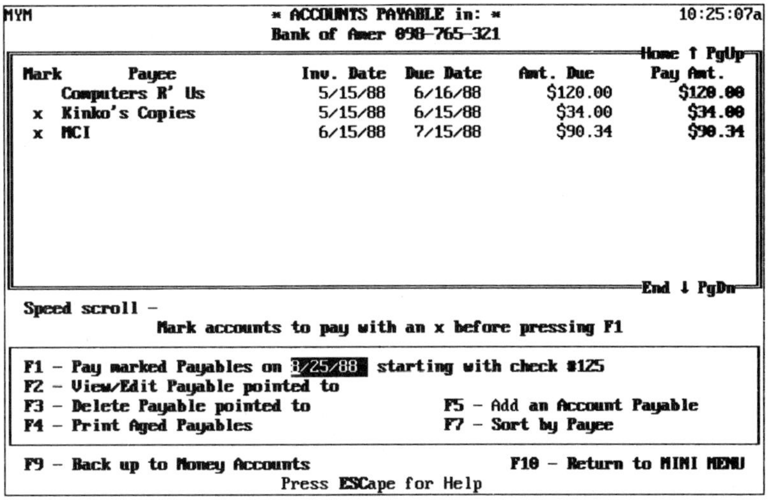

```
MYM                          * ACCOUNTS PAYABLE in: *              10:25:07a
                              Bank of Amer 098-765-321
                                                              ┌Home ↑ PgUp┐
  Mark        Payee           Inv. Date  Due Date    Amt. Due    Pay Amt.
          Computers R' Us       5/15/88   6/16/88    $120.00      $120.00
     x    Kinko's Copies        5/15/88   6/15/88     $34.00       $34.00
     x    MCI                   6/15/88   7/15/88     $90.34       $90.34



                                                              └End ↓ PgDn┘
  Speed scroll -
              Mark accounts to pay with an x before pressing F1
  ┌─────────────────────────────────────────────────────────────────────┐
  │ F1 - Pay marked Payables on ▓7/25/88▓ starting with check #125        │
  │ F2 - View/Edit Payable pointed to                                     │
  │ F3 - Delete Payable pointed to          F5 - Add an Account Payable   │
  │ F4 - Print Aged Payables                F7 - Sort by Payee            │
  └─────────────────────────────────────────────────────────────────────┘
    F9 - Back up to Money Accounts              F10 - Return to MINI MENU
                          Press ESCape for Help
```

Figure 3-23. *An Accounts Payable screen.*

Type an **X** next to the bills you want to pay. Type the correct date and starting check number in the F1 blank.

Press F1 to record the payment.

The program now displays the list of unreconciled transactions for your checking account. The payment appears as a debit in your checkbook. From here, you can print the check by pressing F4 at the Unreconciled Transactions screen. Note also that you can print a list of your unpaid bills by pressing F4 from the Accounts Payable screen. And you can sort the payables by different criteria by pressing F7.

Tracking Your Accounts Receivable

The flip side of your accounts payable is your accounts receivable. Accounts receivable track the money that others owe your business. You set up a separate ledger for your accounts receivable, following the same steps you took to set up your accounts payable.

Type **Y** in the Accounts Receivable blank on the Optional Features screen, and press F1 to activate the option. You return to the Chapter 3 mini menu.

Press F3 to display your list of money accounts.

You now have another new option: The F8 key can access an Accounts Receivable screen.

Place the cursor next to the F8 option and type **R**.

Highlight the account with which you want to work, and press F8. The Accounts Receivable ledger is probably empty.

Press F5 to add an account receivable.

The Accounts Receivable form looks like an invoice. It has blanks for the invoice date and the due date, as well as for the payor, the amount, the payor's address, and the terms. (See Figure 3-24.)

After you fill in the information for the invoice, you can press F2 to allocate the amount to the budget and tax categories. Then press F1 to record the allocation and F1 again to record the transaction.

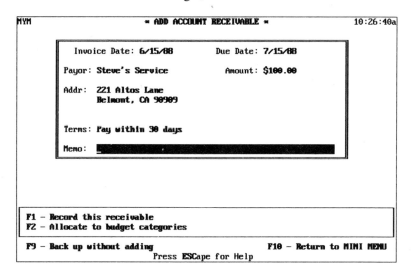

Figure 3-24. *An Accounts Receivable form.*

Although you can allocate accounts receivable to budget categories, they do not take effect until you actually receive the money in payment for an invoice and you mark the invoices paid. Mark them as paid on the Accounts Receivable screen.

Type **X** next to the bills that have been paid, and press F1.

The payment is recorded as income in your checking account, and your balance is adjusted.

One timesaving feature of the Accounts Receivable ledger is the option to print invoices. Rather than typing each invoice, you can create the invoices in your Accounts Receivable ledger and print them automatically. When you print an invoice on standard blank paper, the program pulls the payor's name and address from the Accounts Receivable form. It also lists your name and address at the top of the invoice if you type your name and address in the System Setup portion of the Utilities menu.

Type **X** next to the unpaid bills, and press F6.

You can print an invoice each month until the bill is paid. Then you can mark it paid and record it in your checking account. You can also print a list of unpaid invoices by pressing F4 from the Accounts Receivable screen or sort them by different criteria by pressing F7.

Making a Five-Year Plan

Managing Your Money includes a Five-Year Planning option, with which you can project a budget for the next five years or use budget records from the past five years with the tax estimator in Chapter 4.

Type **Y** in the Five-Year Planning blank on the Optional Features screen.

When you choose the Five-Year Planning option, additional blanks are added to the Budgets and Actuals screens for each budget category. For example, if you choose five years' worth of data and display the budget and actuals listings for interest, the screen has blanks for year-end totals for the next five years.

To view the Budget Categories screen, press F4 at the mini menu. Highlight the budget category you want to review, and press F2.

Type your best estimates of your year-end totals over the next five years for this budget category. Press F1 to save these totals.

You return to the Budget Categories screen, and the year-end totals are passed along to the Chapter 4 tax estimator, where they can be included in tax estimates.

Changing the Fiscal Year

If your business operates on a fiscal year that differs from the calendar year, you can change the program's annual calendar to reflect the beginning and end of your fiscal year.

From the Optional Features screen, type the month in which your fiscal year ends in the F2 blank and press F2. If your business year goes from August to July, enter July as the last month of the year.

Changing the fiscal year has effects throughout the program. For example, it starts the year-end archiving process—described in the next chapter—in the month that you choose rather than in December. For this reason, I suggest you decide upon your fiscal year before you start using the program. Then you will start out with all your .ARK files ready for a new fiscal year.

If you decide to switch from the calendar year to a fiscal year after you have been using the program for a while, you will need to modify your .ARK files. The program displays four Help screens that explain how to do this when you change the fiscal year with the F2 key.

Home Banking

If you sign up for Chase Manhattan's Spectrum system and you have a modem, you can now pay all your bills from within Managing Your Money. This home-banking option relieves you from printing and signing checks and from licking stamps and envelopes. It also gives you immediate access to your account status (that is, which checks have cleared and your current balance).

Access the home-banking feature from the Optional Features screen by pressing F7 from the mini menu and typing **S** in the Home-Banking Option blank. Press F1 to activate the option.

The home-banking feature lets you record transactions in Managing Your Money as though you were writing checks. Then you can connect to Chase via Chase's toll-free line, and the payment information is sent directly to the bank. (See Chapter 1 to set up your modem.)

First go to the Automatic Transaction screen and note that the F2 function key lets you change any of your normal automatic expense transactions into Spectrum payees. Place the cursor over the transaction you want to convert and press F2. At the View or Edit Automatic Transaction screen, be sure to fill in the address of the payee and then press F3 again to begin the conversion process.

The Convert to Spectrum Payee screen looks like other automatic transactions (see Figure 3-25), but it requires that you enter your bank-account number, the name of the account, and the payee's telephone number. Finally, you must give the payee a "mnemonic" or an abbreviation.

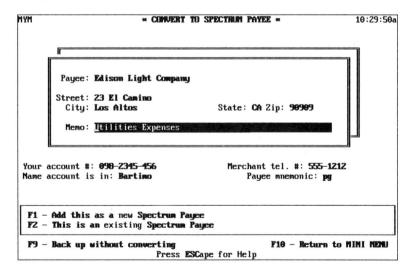

Figure 3-25. *The Convert to Spectrum Payee screen.*

Press F1 to add the transaction as a new payee or F2 to qualify it as an existing payee.

Return to the Automatic Transactions screen. Note that your converted transactions are marked with an asterisk. Mark the home-banking transactions you want to execute, indicate ''Phone'' in the action box, and press F1. The payments are recorded in both Managing Your Money and a file that Spectrum can read. You can use this file with your Spectrum software to pay bills on-line and avoid printing and sending checks.

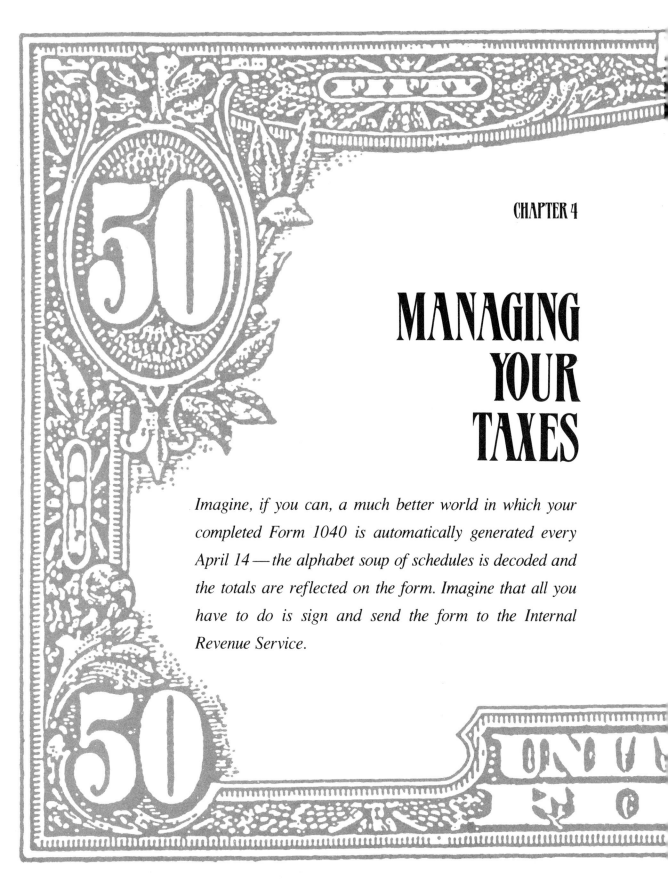

CHAPTER 4

MANAGING YOUR TAXES

Imagine, if you can, a much better world in which your completed Form 1040 is automatically generated every April 14 — the alphabet soup of schedules is decoded and the totals are reflected on the form. Imagine that all you have to do is sign and send the form to the Internal Revenue Service.

This world still doesn't exist, but Chapter 4 of Managing Your Money comes pretty close to making it a reality. The chapter is an electronic version of the IRS tax forms, including the schedules. You can either fill in the blanks of this electronic tax form or use the information you already entered in Chapters 3 and 7. In addition, Chapter 3 generates a variety of budget reports that can be particularly useful for itemizing your personal and business deductions, and Chapter 7 generates reports about your investments and can actually create a completed Schedule D form for reporting investment gains.

Unlike tax preparation packages found in most software stores, the tax estimator does not prepare your taxes for you and print your figures onto Form 1040. Instead, it helps you manage your finances more effectively by letting you estimate, well before December 31, what your income tax is likely to be. If you wait until after December 31 to calculate your taxes, you can do very little to change your tax bill; but if you keep your tax bill in mind during the year, you can take steps to lessen it.

Sometimes it makes sense to reduce your income, perhaps with a salary-reduction plan. You might want to lessen your capital gains, perhaps by holding a stock until January 1 of the following year. You might also lessen your tax bill directly by buying a house instead of renting one.

The tax estimator in Chapter 4 can help you plan your tax bill by projecting your future tax situation based on your current finances and the budget you set up in Chapter 3. You can make hypothetical adjustments and observe their effect on both your income and your taxes. Thus, you can play "what if" games with your capital gains or with your income. You can take advantage of investment opportunities and, even better, you can evaluate those opportunities before you invest.

Managing Your Money keeps up with the changing tax laws by allowing you to modify the tax estimator and keep it current. Chapter 4 already provides two sets of tax schedules, reflecting the new tax brackets for 1988 and 1989, which you can load from the Form 1040 screen by pressing F8 and choosing the year.

ESTIMATING YOUR TAXES

To estimate your taxes, you must fill in estimates for each blank of the tax forms you will use at the end of the year. The income-tax estimator in Chapter 4 provides its own condensed and simplified version of these forms, each of which appears on its own screen.

The program displays a Form 1040 when you first enter Chapter 4. Like a real Form 1040, it is the top of a pyramid of forms, including schedules A, B, C, D, E, and F, as well as forms for alternative minimum tax, Social-Security self-employment tax, investment interest, employee expenses, and moving expenses. In Chapter 4, to move from one schedule to another you simply type its letter. To return to Form 1040 from any of the schedules, you press F9.

If your finances are very simple, Form 1040 may be the only form you ever need to use; but if you're like most people, you will also fill out at least one of the schedules. In any case, Form 1040 is the best place to begin. When you need information from another schedule, go to that schedule, fill it out, and then return to Form 1040 with the values.

Filling Out Form 1040

The first step in using the tax estimator is to enter Chapter 4 and fill out Form 1040.

From the Main menu, press F4.

The Form 1040 screen appears. (See Figure 4-1 on the following page.)

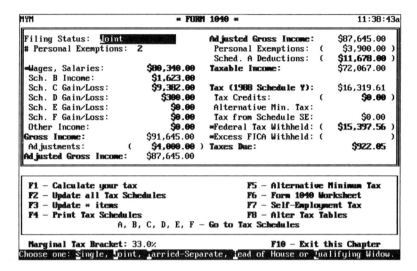

Figure 4-1. *The Form 1040 screen.*

Highlight the Filing Status blank, and type the code for your filing status.

Highlight the Personal Exemptions blank, and type the number of personal exemptions to which you are entitled.

After you type the number of exemptions, the program fills in the appropriate deduction for personal exemptions.

Press F3 to insert in the form values from your budget in Chapter 3.

You can enter data in any or all of the Form 1040 blanks by highlighting the blank and typing the appropriate amount. But the easiest way to fill in the basic information is to let the program use your Chapter 3 budget information. If you kept accurate records, you can press F3 to fill in the values for the blanks marked with an asterisk (*). To fill in the rest of the blanks, you must use the other schedules and forms. The values from all forms are recorded in Form 1040.

The Form 1040 Worksheet

To make an accurate estimate, use the 1040 worksheet to include adjustments you are likely to make to the real Form 1040 at tax time. Include items such as IRA deductions (if you can take them), income from social security, or expenses for child care.

Press F6 from the 1040 screen to reach the Form 1040 Worksheet.

You can fill in the form one blank at a time or use figures from Chapter 3 by pressing F3.

Altering the Tax Tables

The tax estimator is based on ever-changing tax laws and tax tables. The annual updates of the program incorporate the changes, but if you prefer not to upgrade, or if you are using the tax estimator just prior to an upgrade, you can modify the program to reflect changes in the tax tables as well as some types of changes in the tax laws.

If you ever completed your own tax form, you know that after you calculate your adjusted gross income, you check the tax schedule to determine the amount of tax you owe. The schedule contains three tax tables: Schedule Y is for married couples filing jointly, for qualified widows, and for married couples filing separately; Schedule X is for single taxpayers; and Schedule Z is for heads of households. The tax estimator keeps these tax tables in memory to calculate your taxes. However, you can change them from year to year as the tax laws change.

From the Form 1040 screen, press F8 to display the tax tables.

The program displays the tax table that matches the filing status you select on the Form 1040 screen. For example, if you select joint filing status, the Alter Tax Tables screen displays Schedule Y. (See Figure 4-2 on the following page.) You can view a different tax table by changing the selection in the F1 blank and pressing F1.

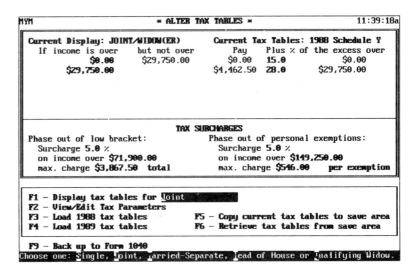

Figure 4-2. *The Alter Tax Tables screen.*

The tax tables have changed each year since the tax reform act passed. You can load the 1989 tax schedules to estimate your 1989 taxes.

At the Alter Tax Tables screen, press F4 to load the 1989 schedules.

The 1989 tax tables should work well for estimated 1989 taxes. But if changes occur in the tax laws before you have a chance to update the program, you can change some aspects of the tax tables yourself.

Press F2 from the Alter Tax Tables screen to see the View or Edit Tax Parameters screen.

The View or Edit Tax Parameters screen has six sections, each with numerous blanks, for changing the rules for personal exemptions, dividend exclusions, FICA tax on wages, deductibles for medical expenses, and more. (See Figure 4-3.) You may need the advice of a tax preparer or a well-indexed tax book to make these changes. (A good reference book is J. K. Lasser's *Your Income Tax,* from Simon & Schuster.)

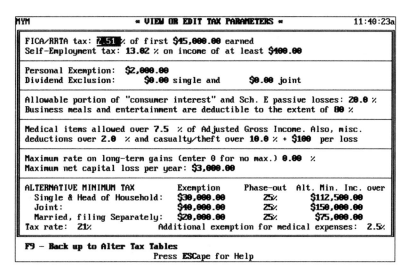

```
MYM              * VIEW OR EDIT TAX PARAMETERS *              11:40:23a

FICA/RRTA tax: 7.51 % of first $45,000.00 earned
Self-Employment tax: 13.02 % on income of at least $400.00

Personal Exemption:   $2,000.00
Dividend Exclusion:      $0.00 single and      $0.00 joint

Allowable portion of "consumer interest" and Sch. E passive losses: 20.0 %
Business meals and entertainment are deductible to the extent of 80 %

Medical items allowed over 7.5 % of Adjusted Gross Income. Also, misc.
deductions over 2.0 % and casualty/theft over 10.0 % + $100  per loss

Maximum rate on long-term gains (enter 0 for no max.) 0.00 %
Maximum net capital loss per year: $3,000.00

ALTERNATIVE MINIMUM TAX        Exemption     Phase-out  Alt. Min. Inc. over
  Single & Head of Household:  $30,000.00       25%     $112,500.00
  Joint:                       $40,000.00       25%     $150,000.00
  Married, filing Separately:  $20,000.00       25%     $75,000.00
Tax rate: 21%               Additional exemption for medical expenses:  2.5%

F9 - Back up to Alter Tax Tables
                  Press ESCape for Help
```

Figure 4-3. *The View or Edit Tax Parameters screen.*

Highlight each value that you need to change, and type the new value. Press F9 to record the changes.

The tax estimator now uses the revised rules in calculating your tax.

Using Schedule A to Itemize Deductions

The government thinks that you shouldn't have to pay taxes on certain expenses. Currently, those expenses include medical bills, home-loan interest, charitable contributions, injury or theft, and other categories found in any good tax book. You can record these deductible expenses on the Schedule A screen.

From the Form 1040 screen or any of the Schedule screens in Chapter 4, press A to display Schedule A.

The Schedule A screen is a mini-version of the actual Schedule A. (See Figure 4-4 on the following page.) You can fill in the blanks in this screen in two ways: Either highlight the blank and type your estimate for expenses in that category, or press F3 to fill in estimates for all your personal expenses using budget information from Chapter 3. As you

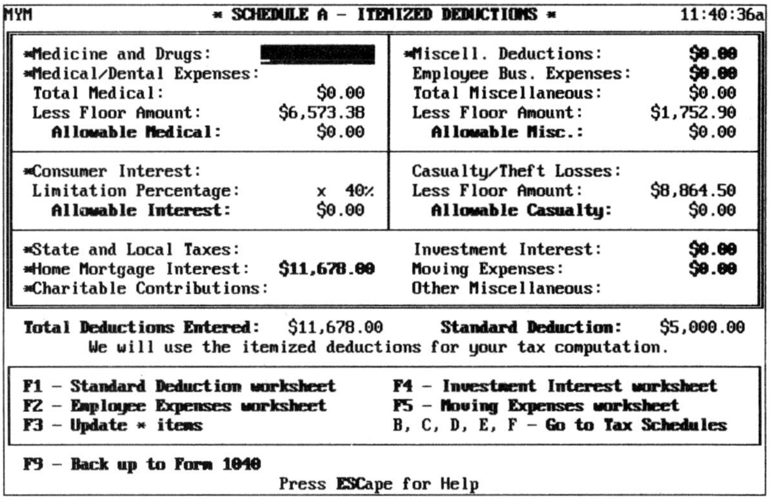

```
MYM                   * SCHEDULE A - ITEMIZED DEDUCTIONS *              11:40:36a
 *Medicine and Drugs:        ▮▮▮▮▮▮      *Miscell. Deductions:          $0.00
 *Medical/Dental Expenses:                Employee Bus. Expenses:       $0.00
  Total Medical:              $0.00       Total Miscellaneous:          $0.00
  Less Floor Amount:      $6,573.38       Less Floor Amount:        $1,752.90
    Allowable Medical:        $0.00         Allowable Misc.:            $0.00

 *Consumer Interest:                      Casualty/Theft Losses:
  Limitation Percentage:      x 40%       Less Floor Amount:        $8,864.50
    Allowable Interest:       $0.00         Allowable Casualty:         $0.00

 *State and Local Taxes:                  Investment Interest:          $0.00
 *Home Mortgage Interest:  $11,678.00     Moving Expenses:              $0.00
 *Charitable Contributions:               Other Miscellaneous:

 Total Deductions Entered:  $11,678.00        Standard Deduction:    $5,000.00
            We will use the itemized deductions for your tax computation.

 F1 - Standard Deduction worksheet       F4 - Investment Interest worksheet
 F2 - Employee Expenses worksheet        F5 - Moving Expenses worksheet
 F3 - Update * items                      B, C, D, E, F - Go to Tax Schedules

 F9 - Back up to Form 1040
                            Press ESCape for Help
```

Figure 4-4. *The Schedule A Screen.*

enter values in the blanks in Schedule A, the program calculates your
total deductible expenses and records your deduction in the Schedule A
Deductions blank on the Form 1040 screen.

Note that you can list only unreimbursed expenses in Schedule A. If
you allocated $1,500 to medical expenses in your budget and were
reimbursed for $1,000 by your insurance company, you may deduct
only $500. Unless you fully detailed your expenses and reimburse-
ments, pressing F3 enters the whole amount.

Using Form 2106   Use Form 2106 to claim deductions for unreimbursed work expenses
from your work as an employee. (Self-employment expenses are
reported on Schedule C.) If you are claiming unreimbursed work expenses, be sure you have proof that your company wouldn't reimburse
you for these expenses. In some occupations, it is assumed that certain
expenses are not paid by the employer. For example, if you are a
salesperson, you may be able to use this form to report expenses for
your car and other transportation as well as business entertainment.

The Form 2106 screen has two parts: Part I is the summary of all your expenses; Part II is a breakdown of car expenses. (See Figure 4-5.)

From the Schedule A screen, press F2 to display Form 2106.

First enter information concerning mileage deductions in the blanks below the information box. This information is used in Parts I and II and so should be entered before you fill in other blanks.

Highlight the depreciation and eligibility blanks that appear between the information and action boxes. Type the appropriate code for each.

Enter in the appropriate blanks the amounts that are deductible before and after your car travels 15,000 miles in one year.

These per-mile amounts change frequently (as you know if you fill out corporate expense forms), so be sure you are using the most current allowable deductions.

Enter your car expenses in Part II.

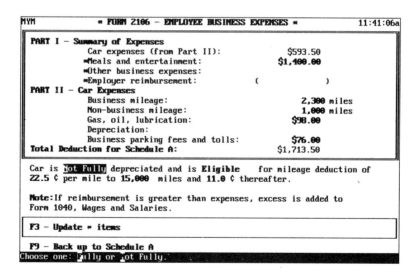

Figure 4-5. *The Form 2106 screen.*

The program totals the expenses in Part II and displays the result in the Car Expenses blank in Part I.

Type your estimates for expenses and employer's payments in Part I.

The employer's payments include any money you receive from your company to contribute to the payment of the expenses reported in this form. These payments are subtracted from the total expenses. If you were reimbursed for more than you expended, the positive result is recorded as wages on the Form 1040 screen.

Press F9 to return to Schedule A.

Investment-Interest Worksheet

Investment interest is the interest you pay on money borrowed for the purpose of investment. A good example is the interest you pay on a margin account with a brokerage firm. A margin account lets you borrow money from the broker and then invest that borrowed money with the hope your return will exceed the interest you're paying to the broker. You must pay interest on the margin-account money, but you may be able to write off this interest on your tax return.

Press F4 from Schedule A to display the Investment Interest Deduction Worksheet.

Enter in the appropriate blanks the amount of investment interest you paid this year and the amount disallowed last year. Or press F3 to call up this year's information from Chapter 3 if you set up an investment-interest category there.

The program calculates how much, if any, investment interest you can write off and plugs it into the information box of Schedule A. It also shows this year's disallowed amount on the worksheet.

Press F9 to return to Schedule A.

**Calculating
Moving Expenses**

Schedule A contains a short screen to help you determine the amount of moving expenses you can deduct if you moved to take a new job and paid some or all of the expenses yourself. Press F5 from Schedule A to view the screen; then enter your figures. (See Figure 4-6.)

> Press F3 to call up these items from Chapter 3 or fill in the blanks individually.

> Press F9 to return to Schedule A.

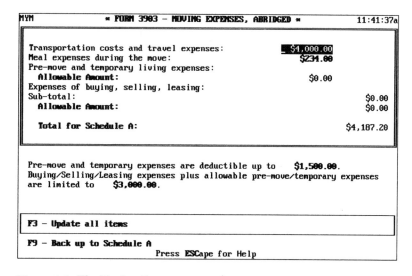

Figure 4-6. *The Moving Expenses screen.*

**Using Schedule B
to Report Interest
and Dividends**

At the end of the year, your broker and banker send you 1099 forms that report dividends and earned interest from your accounts. You, in turn, must report this income to the IRS.

> From the Form 1040 screen or any of the Schedule screens in Chapter 4, press B to display Schedule B.

Because you are estimating your taxes before the end of the year, you probably don't have the 1099 forms to provide the information you need for this schedule. You can estimate this income or use the totals you recorded in Chapter 3, provided you recorded interest and dividends in your budget categories. As with Schedule A, you can enter your estimates in two ways: Highlight one of the blanks and type your estimate or press F3 to call up your budget values. The program calculates your total income from the categories shown and records it in Form 1040 in the Schedule B Income blank.

Using Schedule C to Calculate Business Profit or Loss

If you are a self-employed consultant or if you run your own business with a few employees, you can report the income and claim deductions and losses from your business on Schedule C. Schedule C has three parts: income, deductions, and cost of goods sold (or operations). The program uses two screens to display these three parts.

> From the Form 1040 screen or any of the Schedule screens in Chapter 4, press C to display the Schedule C screen.

Managing Your Money displays the first Schedule C screen, which shows Part II—Deductions. (See Figure 4-7.) You can fill in any expenses you and your tax adviser believe are legally acceptable

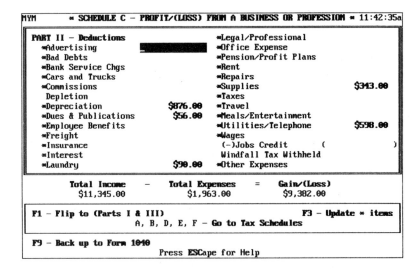

Figure 4-7. *The Schedule C screen, Part II.*

by the IRS as deductions. (Be sure you have receipts for them!) As in the other schedules, you can type in your estimates or use the F3 key to enter values from your Chapter 3 budget.

Note that you can deduct computer expenses on your tax return. You can write off 100 percent of your computer equipment cost as a business deduction if you use the machine only for your own business. If you use the computer for games, home finance, or writing letters, you then have to determine the percentage of time the computer is used for your business and apply the percentage to the original cost as your deduction on Schedule C. If you use the computer only for games or writing letters, it is almost impossible to deduct the cost.

Press F1 to flip to the second Schedule C screen.

The second Schedule C screen displays Part I—Income—and also Part III—Cost of Goods Sold and/or Operations. (See Figure 4-8.) You may need the information from Part III in Part I, so it is best to fill out Part III first. Part III subtracts end-of-year inventory costs from start-of-year inventory costs, accounting for labor and material.

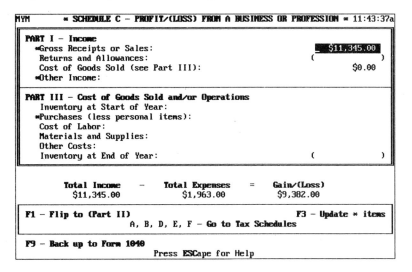

Figure 4-8. *The Schedule C screen, Part I and Part III.*

In the appropriate blanks, type the dollar value of your inventory at the start of the year, purchases, cost of labor and materials, and other costs, as well as the value of your inventory at the end of the year.

The program calculates your cost of goods and records it in the Cost of Goods Sold blank in Part I. There it is subtracted from your business income because excess inventory, labor, and materials are part of your total cost.

Now you can complete Part I. You must provide estimates for your gross receipts or sales. Then enter any loss from returns or allowances in the Returns and Allowances blank. For example, if you have a newspaper route, you might not be able to sell all your newspapers and you would have to pay for them yourself. This expense is subtracted from your income. Next, report any income that does not fall into one of these categories in the Other Income blank.

Type your estimates in the blanks, or press F3 to use your budget values.

Below the information box is the Total Income blank. The program calculates the total income using your business estimates in Part I and Part III. It then records this income minus the expenses from Part II in the Schedule C Gain/Loss blank in Form 1040.

Using Schedule D to Report Capital Gains and Losses

Schedule D reports profits or losses from the sale of investments such as stocks and property. There are two types of capital gains: short-term and long-term. Short-term capital gains come from investments held less than six months, and long-term gains come from investments held longer than six months. Beginning in 1988, tax reform eliminated the difference in the way short-term and long-term capital gains were taxed. Both kinds of capital gains are now taxed at the same rate as ordinary income.

The Schedule D screen in the tax estimator has two parts: Part I lists short-term gains and Part II lists long-term gains. (See Figure 4-9.)

From the Form 1040 screen or any of the Schedule screens in Chapter 4, press D to display the Schedule D screen.

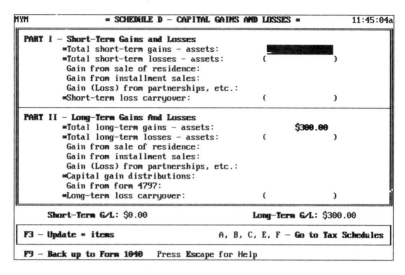

Figure 4-9. *The Schedule D screen.*

If you recorded the sale of investments in the Portfolio Manager in Chapter 7, you can call up the data from that chapter in this schedule, or you can estimate the values and enter them directly.

- In the blanks in Schedule D, type your estimates for each type of gain or loss, or press F3 to use your portfolio values.

Be sure to enter gains in the correct blanks and losses in parentheses. Also, because the tax law allows you to carry over losses from previous years, you should be sure to enter the so-called carryover losses from previous years in both parts, if they apply. After you fill in your estimates for all appropriate fields, the program calculates the total and records it in the Schedule D Gain/Loss blank in Form 1040.

Using Schedule E to Report Supplemental Income

Schedule E lists income from real-estate partnerships, rents, or royalties. Schedule E royalties include certain types of investments, such as oil and gas wells. The Schedule E screen displayed in Chapter 4 is a mini-version of the form, providing blanks for recording only income from real-estate partnerships and rents. (See Figure 4-10 on the following page.)

```
MYM                    * SCHEDULE E - SUPPLEMENTAL INCOME *              11:46:30a
Non-Real Estate Investments with Material Participation
        *Income:                                        $12,000.00
        *Expenses:                                 (    $13,000.00)
Actively-managed Real Estate Investments
        *Pre-enactment Income:
        *Pre-enactment Expenses                    (                )
        *Post-enactment Income:
        *Post-enactment Expenses:                  (                )
         Prior year suspended loss:                (                )
Passive Investments
        *Pre-enactment Income:
        *Pre-enactment Expenses:                   (                )
        *Post-enactment Income:
        *Post-enactment Expenses:                  (                )
         Prior year suspended loss:                (                )

Total Schedule E Gain/(Loss):                          ($1,000.00)


F3 - Update * items                     A, B, C, D, F - Go to Tax Schedules

F9 - Back up to Form 1040
                         Press ESCape for Help
```

Figure 4-10. *The Schedule E screen.*

The Schedule E screen has three sections: The first covers non-real-estate investments with material participation; the second section covers actively managed real-estate investments; and the third covers passive investments. These terms use the language of the new tax laws, some of which is easily understood and some of which is not. The actively managed and passively managed investments sections of Schedule E also have blanks to include income that was carried over from years before the tax reform act was enacted.

A stricter test of participation is material participation. You might be considered a material participant in a business you don't own if, for instance, you are a lawyer and provide legal services for the business. Proving that you are involved in a non-real-estate investment with material participation may be difficult. However, if you are materially participating in a business or venture that is not part of a small business you can list in Schedule C, you may be able to use this section of Schedule E.

Actively managing a real-estate investment refers to the degree to which you are personally involved. For instance, if you are the sole landlord of an apartment building, you are actively participating in the investment. If you are involved to a lesser degree, you should consult a tax accountant or refer to a tax book to determine the qualifications necessary to declare income and losses here.

Passive investments include the once-popular tax shelter called the limited partnership. If you are involved in a limited partnership, you are considered passive if you don't control how the capital is managed. If you became involved in a passive investment before the enactment of the tax reform act, your allowable deductions are decreasing each year and probably will be eliminated completely by 1991. Real-estate partnerships normally issue K-1 forms at year's end to tell you the amount of the expenses you can claim as a write-off. Estimating this write-off yourself is difficult; it's better to refer to the prospectus for the partnership or to your broker.

> From the Form 1040 screen or any of the Schedule screens in Chapter 4, press E to display the Schedule E screen.

If you kept records of any Schedule E figures in your Chapter 3 budget and tax categories, you can use these estimates here.

> Type your estimates for the various types of income and expenses in the Schedule E blanks, or press F3 to use your budget values.

The program totals your income and losses, calculated from all three sections, at the bottom of the Schedule E screen. The total is recorded in the Schedule E Gain/Loss blank of Form 1040.

Using Schedule F to Calculate Farm Income

The Schedule F screen is also a mini-version of the actual schedule. On this form, you record income and expenses for running a farm. (See Figure 4-11 on the following page.)

> From the Form 1040 screen or any of the Schedule screens in Chapter 4, press F to display the Schedule F screen.

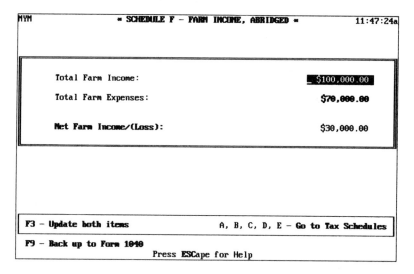

Figure 4-11. *The Schedule F screen.*

If you recorded your farm income and expenses in budget and tax categories in Chapter 3, you can use these figures in Schedule F, or you can estimate the individual values.

> Type your estimates in the Schedule F blanks, or press F3 to call up your budget values.

The program subtracts the expenses from the income and displays the result at the bottom of the form as the net farm income or loss. It also records this net value in the Schedule F Gain/Loss blank in Form 1040.

Estimating Alternative Minimum Tax

Remember when you played Monopoly and landed on the Luxury Tax square? You could either pay a flat fee or determine how much you were worth and pay 20 percent of that amount. The rule in Monopoly is that you have to commit to paying 20 percent before you figure exactly how much you're worth.

The alternative minimum tax is much like the luxury tax in Monopoly, but instead of paying the lower figure, you pay the higher figure. The tax applies only to a few specific tax situations, but it determines the minimum tax the government allows you to pay. Many tax experts predict more of us will have to pay the alternative minimum tax under the new tax laws. Thus, the alternative minimum tax may increase your tax bill, which is Uncle Sam's way of ensuring that those with high incomes pay enough taxes.

You can determine if you must pay the alternative minimum tax on Form 6251.

From the Form 1040 screen, press F5 to display Form 6251.

The Form 6251 screen identifies all types of deductions and preference items that are used to calculate the alternative minimum tax. (See Figure 4-12.)

You can include pertinent information from Form 1040 and Schedules A, B, and E by pressing F3, so be sure you fill out those forms first. After you enter your data, the program calculates the alternative minimum tax and displays it at the bottom of the form. The alternative minimum tax appears only if it exceeds the current tax estimate from Form 1040.

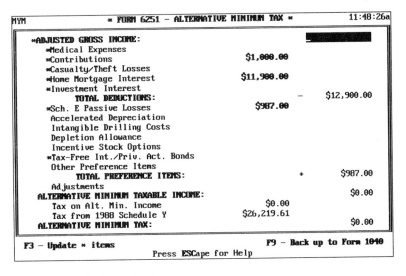

Figure 4-12. *The Form 6251 screen.*

If the program determines that you owe the alternative minimum tax, it then records the amount in the Alternative Minimum Tax blank on Form 1040.

Using Schedule SE to Compute Your Social-Security Tax

Although you report the income from a self-run business on Schedule C or Schedule F, you must use Schedule SE to determine your Social-Security self-employment tax. Even if you and your spouse have full-time jobs, you may be required to fill out this schedule if either of you has a side business. For example, if you tune antique cars for all the members of your car club and receive a fee, you're earning money as a self-employed car mechanic.

From the Form 1040 screen, press F7 to display Schedule SE.

The program displays its version of Schedule SE. (See Figure 4-13.) On this screen, enter all your self-employment earnings as well as information about Social-Security tax that you already paid. If you already completed Schedules C and F, you can fill in some of the Schedule SE blanks automatically.

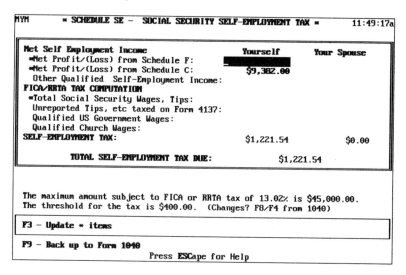

Figure 4-13. *The Schedule SE screen.*

Type any income information not already recorded on Schedules C and F, and then press F3.

Schedule SE displays the tax amounts for you and your spouse as well as the total for both of you. This information is recorded in the Tax from Schedule SE blank on Form 1040.

Calculating Your Taxes

Now that you have filled out all the appropriate forms and schedules, you can calculate your taxes.

From the Form 1040 screen, press F1 to calculate your taxes due.

When you press F1, the program computes your tax from its internal version of the tax tables, adds the tax from Schedule SE, subtracts the amount of tax withheld as well as any excess FICA credit, and displays the total taxes due.

Pressing F1 also calculates the marginal tax bracket. Your marginal tax bracket is computed mainly from your filing status and income and determines the actual worth of your money. If you are in the 33 percent tax bracket, you know that you can keep only $666.67 of a $1,000 windfall. The other $333.33 goes to the government. In other words, the $1,000 is worth only $666.67 to you. Remember your marginal tax bracket because you'll need the figure again in Chapters 6 and 7.

Note that if you change any figures in Form 1040 after you calculate your tax, the program does not update your tax until you press the F1 key again.

ARCHIVING TAX INFORMATION AND BEGINNING A NEW YEAR

Chapter 4 helps you estimate this year's tax bill before the end of the year and at tax time helps you to prepare your tax forms using the year's information from Chapters 3 and 7. If you recorded your transactions in budget and tax categories in Chapter 3, your accounts contain an abundance of tax information. Chapter 7 contains additional information that you can use to create investment reports. Some of this information is already stored in .ARK files on your hard disk. For example, reconciling your transactions in your checkbook automatically stores these records in a .ARK file. These files can take up a lot of space, so at the end of each year, the program automatically starts a procedure for creating a set of archive disks for the entire year's information. Then it removes the data from your hard disk and sets up a new budget—with your help. When you create archive disks, you instruct the program to save the appropriate data in Chapters 3 and 7 in .ARK files so that you can review last year's data whenever you need to.

Note that although this procedure may sound simple, a slipup in any step of the process can delete your entire year's data, and you won't be able to use it at tax time. For this reason, you should back up all your files before you begin the year-end archiving process. In addition, read through all steps in this section before you start the process.

> Make a backup copy of all files.

Be sure you have several blank, formatted floppy disks on hand if you plan to put last year's information on floppy disks.

The first time you use Managing Your Money in the new year, the program automatically begins the archiving process. The Starting A New Year screen appears and indicates it is time to archive last year's information. The screen contains several pages of instructions. (See Figure 4-14.)

> Press F1 to start a new year and archive last year's information. Keep pressing F1 until you have gone through all pages in Starting A New Year.

> On Page 3, press Alt-F1 to begin the actual archiving process, or press F10 if you do not want to archive yet. (See Figure 4-15.)

The program archives any transactions that you did not already archive in Chapters 3 and 7. If you have unreconciled checks, it archives them but does not delete them from the list of unreconciled transactions. If you don't have a hard-disk drive and the .ARK files are not on the disks in the disk drives, the program instructs you to insert first the disk

```
MYM            * STARTING A NEW YEAR...Page 1 *            11:51:25a
┌────────────────────────────────────────────────────────────────┐
│ The last time you used MANAGING YOUR MONEY was 8/25/88, and you  │
│ have entered today's date as 1/2/89.  Since these dates are in   │
│ two different years, you have activated the process for STARTING │
│ A NEW YEAR. If you typed 1/2/89 by mistake, just press F10 now   │
│ and enter the correct date.                                      │
│                                                                  │
│ In Starting a New Year we create a new set of books for the new  │
│ year.  When we do, we reset all of the "actuals" in your budget  │
│ categories to zero and clear last year's archives so that you    │
│ can start with a fresh slate.  It's not much different from      │
│ putting last year's date book away in a drawer and setting up a  │
│ new one.  Don't worry -- we won't erase your budget categories   │
│ or anything like that.                                           │
│                                                                  │
│ If you'd rather not deal with this right now, or want to keep    │
│ the books open for a few more weeks while last year's data       │
│ trickles in, press F2 to postpone.  Otherwise, press F1 to       │
│ continue with STARTING A NEW YEAR.                               │
│                                                                  │
├──────────────────────────────────────────────────────────────── │
│ F1 - Continue with STARTING A NEW YEAR                           │
│ F2 - Postpone it for now                                         │
│                                       F10 - Return to TITLE SCREEN│
└────────────────────────────────────────────────────────────────┘
```

Figure 4-14. *Starting A New Year screen, Page 1.*

```
MYM            * STARTING A NEW YEAR...Page 3 *            11:52:31a
┌────────────────────────────────────────────────────────────────┐
│ OK.  You have a current set of backup disks, should anything go  │
│ wrong (it won't!) and enough blank, formatted disks to store     │
│ your permanent records from last year.  Label these blank disks  │
│ clearly; you wouldn't want to get them mixed up with this new    │
│ year's data.                                                     │
│                                                                  │
│ On the next screens, we're going to:                             │
│                                                                  │
│    (1) Archive any remaining unarchived transactions from last   │
│        year.                                                     │
│                                                                  │
│    (2) Help you make permanent backup copies of last year's data.│
│                                                                  │
│    (3) Give you some choices for organizing your budgets for the │
│        new year.                                                 │
│                                                                  │
│ We're now ready to Start the New Year.  You can still chicken    │
│ out by pressing F10.  Otherwise, press Alt-F1 and we'll begin    │
│ the process. Remember:  Once you've pressed Alt-F1, there's no   │
│ turning back.                                                    │
│                                                                  │
├──────────────────────────────────────────────────────────────── │
│ Alt-F1 - Perform the irrevocable process                         │
├──────────────────────────────────────────────────────────────── │
│ F9 - Back up to the previous screen  F10 - Return to TITLE SCREEN │
└────────────────────────────────────────────────────────────────┘
```

Figure 4-15. *Starting A New Year screen, Page 3.*

containing the BUDGET.ARK file and then the disk containing the PORTFOL.ARK file. These files already exist on your disks even if you haven't archived any data yet. If you never reconciled your checkbook to your bank statement, the archiving process may take up to 15 minutes because the program now has to archive a year's worth of data.

Page 4 of Starting A New Year appears and tells you that the program is about to store last year's information in a separate set of files.

> Press F1 to put those files on a floppy disk, or press F2 to put those files in a subdirectory on your hard disk. (Be sure it is a subdirectory different from the one the program is now in.)

Page 5 appears and asks you to indicate into which floppy drive or hard-disk directory you want to copy last year's files.

> Type **A** in the information box if you are using drive A to store these files.

> Press F1 to copy the .DB files and F2 to copy the .ARK files, or press F3 to copy the entire program and last year's information.

Page 6 of Starting A New Year appears and asks you about next year's budget. (See Figure 4-16.) Setting up a new budget is much easier now than the first time. The program gives you two choices: to use the same budget figures you were using last year in Chapter 3 or to use the actual spending from last year as the basis of your new year's budget.

> Highlight the first blank in the information box and press A or B.

You can also adjust next year's budgets to compensate for inflation— or your more expensive tastes.

> Highlight the second blank and type the percentage by which you want to adjust your budget amounts.

You can then press F1 to continue the archiving process and return to the program, ready to enter information about the new year in Chapters 3 and 7.

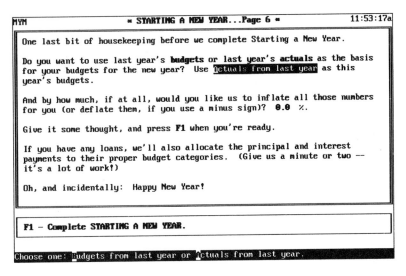

Figure 4-16. *Starting A New Year screen, Page 6.*

Be aware that you don't have to archive everything the first time you enter the program in a new year. The screen indicates it is a new year, but you can postpone the year-end archiving. (See Figure 4-17 on the following page.) This is particularly useful because you can wait until all your previous year's checks have returned from the bank before closing out the year.

If you postpone archiving, you'll have to re-postpone every time you enter the program until you finally do archive. You won't be able to reconcile (archive) your checkbook because doing so would mix the new year's finances with the old. All reconciling menu selections will note that you still must begin a new year. Finally, no actuals are recorded in your budget categories until you do the final archiving. (The transactions you record during postponement are saved and recorded after archiving.)

Press F2 at Page 1 of Starting A New Year to postpone archiving last year's information.

Press F1 to continue postponing and return to the program.

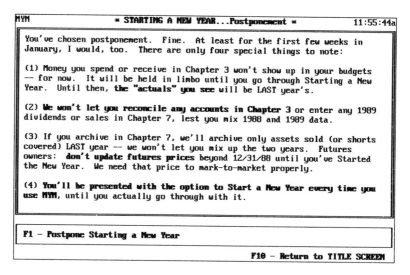

```
MYM                  * STARTING A NEW YEAR...Postponement *              11:55:44a
┌──────────────────────────────────────────────────────────────────────────────┐
│ You've chosen postponement.  Fine.  At least for the first few weeks in         │
│ January, I would, too.  There are only four special things to note:             │
│                                                                                 │
│ (1) Money you spend or receive in Chapter 3 won't show up in your budgets       │
│ -- for now.  It will be held in limbo until you go through Starting a New        │
│ Year.  Until then, the "actuals" you see will be LAST year's.                    │
│                                                                                 │
│ (2) We won't let you reconcile any accounts in Chapter 3 or enter any 1989       │
│ dividends or sales in Chapter 7, lest you mix 1988 and 1989 data.                │
│                                                                                 │
│ (3) If you archive in Chapter 7, we'll archive only assets sold (or shorts       │
│ covered) LAST year -- we won't let you mix up the two years.  Futures            │
│ owners:  don't update futures prices beyond 12/31/88 until you've Started        │
│ the New Year.  We need that price to mark-to-market properly.                    │
│                                                                                 │
│ (4) You'll be presented with the option to Start a New Year every time you       │
│ use MYM, until you actually go through with it.                                  │
└──────────────────────────────────────────────────────────────────────────────┘
┌──────────────────────────────────────────────────────────────────────────────┐
│ F1 - Postpone Starting a New Year                                               │
└──────────────────────────────────────────────────────────────────────────────┘
                                                     F10 - Return to TITLE SCREEN
```

Figure 4-17. *The Postpone Starting A New Year screen.*

ACCESSING INFORMATION FROM PAST YEARS

If you've been using Managing Your Money since 1984 (as I have), you now have five sets of archived disks, one set each for the years 1984, 1985, 1986, 1987, and 1988. If you are audited by the Internal Revenue Service someday, you may want to look back at some of these years and refer to your lists of checks and stock sales.

To ensure access to information from each of the past years, including the current one, you must keep a copy of each version of Managing Your Money along with the archived files for that year. In other words, you must save your 1988 archived files along with version 5.0 of the program. Next year, you'll save 1989 files along with version 6.0 of the program.

Because the program tends to change significantly from one version to the next, you may not be able to read version 4.0 archived information easily with version 5.0, and the problem worsens if you try to read version 1.0 information with version 5.0 of the program. So, at the end of each year when you archive your files, copy those files to a set of floppy disks and label them with the year they represent. Then copy the remaining program files and store them along with the archived files for that year. Label the disks ''1988.''

When you want to refer to 1988 information (perhaps on April 14, when you're preparing your taxes), use the archived information with the copied version of the program. If you have a hard disk, you can copy all these files into a new subdirectory, but don't copy them into the subdirectory you're using for current Managing Your Money activities.

To access another year's information, run that year's version of Managing Your Money. Then, at the opening screen, specify the last day of the year for the year you want to view. To access 1988 information, enter **12/31/88**.

Continue with the program and enter Chapters 3 and 7 to read the archived information you created at the end of that year. In Chapter 3, you can use the Budget Archives feature to read archived information by pressing F9 from the mini menu. In Chapter 7, you can use the Portfolio Archives feature to read archived information by pressing F9 from the mini menu.

CREATING BUDGET REPORTS FOR YOUR TAX FORMS

The Budget Archives feature of Chapter 3 is a flexible tool for designing and printing reports from your budget data. With it, you can print any combination of accounts, budget categories, and tax categories in an almost infinite number of report formats.

You can use this part of the program to read information in the current year or to read last year's information to help you prepare your taxes. For example, suppose you want to create a report as a supplement to Schedule A, your itemized deductions. If you assigned your transactions to budget categories that are marked as Schedule A tax categories, creating such a report is a simple task. You can access your archived information from the Chapter 3 mini menu.

Press F3 from the Main menu to view the Chapter 3 mini menu.

Press F9, Budget Archives, from the mini menu.

If you want to include your unreconciled transactions in your reports, you can temporarily archive them. (If you already temporarily archived your transactions and made no changes since then, you can skip this step.)

Indicate whether you want to temporarily archive your unreconciled transactions by typing **Y** or **N** in the information box.

Type **S** in the action box to save any changes you have made since you entered Chapter 3.

Press F1 and the program reads your archived information, including your temporary archives if they exist.

After it reads the budget data, the program displays a Welcome screen and the number of archived transactions. (If this number is zero, you have not archived any transactions.) The Welcome screen also asks if you want to include the temporary archives in your reports.

Type **Y** in the information box to include the temporary archives or **N** if you do not want to include them. Then press F1.

The program displays the Budget Archive Report Generator screen.

Defining the Budget Report

After you access the archives needed for your report, you can define the content of the report from the Report Generator screen. (See Figure 4-18.) Here you designate the months, accounts, and budget and tax categories to be included in the report.

Type the codes for the first and last months you want to include in the Months Desired blanks.

For example, if you are creating a Schedule A report, you type JA (for January) as the first month and D (for December) as the last month because you want to create a list of budget transactions that took place in the last year.

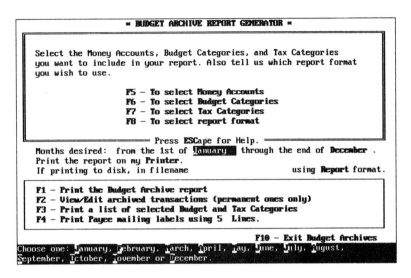

Figure 4-18. *The Budget Archive Report Generator screen.*

Press F5 to display your list of archived accounts.

Type an **X** next to any accounts that you want to include in your report, and press F9.

For example, you should include your day-to-day checking-account information in a Schedule A report.

Press F6 to display your list of budget categories.

Type an **X** next to those categories you want to include in your budget report, and press F9.

The program locates all transactions in the categories you marked when you print the report. (See "The Schedule A Report" on the next page.) For the Schedule A report, mark categories for medical and dental expenses, state and local taxes, loan interest, and charitable contributions.

Press F7 to display a list of tax categories.

The Schedule A Report

A Schedule A report is one of the many reports you can create with the Budget Archive Report Generator. In this sample print-out of a Schedule A report, note that the transactions that were archived from the checkbook and budget in Chapter 3 are listed in the same tax categories as those that appear on a real Schedule A. The report also lists the check dates, amounts, payees, and the total amount of deductions for each category.

```
Tax Category
     Budget Category
          Account Name
               Date     Chk # Payee                        Alloc.
Home Mortgage Interest[A]
     Mortgage Interest
          Bank of Amer
               1/24/88  Phone Home Savings                  -905.87
               2/5/88     571 Home Savings                  -903.41
               3/4/88   Phone Home Savings                  -904.24
               5/13/88  Phone Home Savings                  -901.74
               6/7/88   Phone Home Savings                  -900.90
               7/29/88  Phone Home Savings                  -900.35
               8/8/88     717 Home Savings                  -899.80
               9/8/88     818 Home Savings                  -898.94
               10/8/88  Phone Home Savings                  -898.07
               11/8/88    849 Home Savings                  -897.20
               12/8/88  Phone Home Savings                  -896.32
          Total for Mortgage Interest                    ($9,906.84)

Total for Home Mortgage Interest[A]                      ($9,906.84)

Interest Expense    [A]
     College Loan
          Bank of Amer
               1/30/88    196 ELSI                           -52.00
          Total for College Loan                           ($52.00)

Total for Interest Expense      [A]                        ($52.00)

Medicine & Drugs    [A]
     Medical/Dental
          Bank of Amer
               3/4/88     201 Sandy Dodds D.C.               -80.00
               6/8/88     707 Andrew B. Mann M.D.            -43.00
               6/8/88     708 Marshall Doronberg M.D.        -70.00
               6/8/88     709 Robert Brown M.D.             -305.00
               6/8/88     710 Sandy Dodds D.C.               -80.00
               6/8/88     711 Scott Hoffman DDS              -11.40
               6/8/88     712 Chiropractic Offices Inc.      -19.00
               10/8/88    713 Andrew B. Mann M.D.           -211.00
               10/8/88    714 Robert Brown M.D.             -305.00
               10/8/88    715 Scott Hoffman DDS             -104.40
               10/8/88    716 Chiropractic Offices Inc.      -70.00
          Total for Medical/Dental                       ($1,298.80)

Total for Medicine & Drugs      [A]                      ($1,298.80)

Real Estate Tax     [A]
     Property Tax
          Bank of Amer
               4/2/88     210 Tax Collector,Santa Clara     -841.22
          Total for Property Tax                          ($841.22)

Total for Real Estate Tax       [A]                       ($841.22)
```

Each category is followed by a label in brackets that indicates the tax schedule or form in which the category is reported. (See Figure 4-19.)

Type an **X** next to all categories that pertain to your budget report, and press F9.

If you are creating a Schedule A report, mark all categories that are labeled with the letter A. All checks allocated to Schedule A are then included in the report.

Creating the Budget Report Format

Reports are usually printed with the account name first, followed by the date, check number, payee, income amount, and expense amount. However, you can rearrange this information and choose the order of transactions in your report.

Press F8 to display the Select Report Format screen.

This screen displays several fields. You can specify the element you want to appear in each field. (See Figure 4-20 on the following page.)

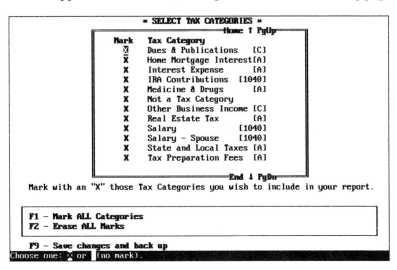

```
                    * SELECT TAX CATEGORIES *
                                    Home ↑ PgUp
          Mark    Tax Category
            X     Dues & Publications   [C]
            X     Home Mortgage Interest[A]
            X     Interest Expense      [A]
            X     IRA Contributions   [1040]
            X     Medicine & Drugs      [A]
            X     Not a Tax Category
            X     Other Business Income [C]
            X     Real Estate Tax       [A]
            X     Salary              [1040]
            X     Salary - Spouse     [1040]
            X     State and Local Taxes [A]
            X     Tax Preparation Fees  [A]

                                    End ↓ PgDn
   Mark with an "X" those Tax Categories you wish to include in your report.


    F1 - Mark ALL Categories
    F2 - Erase ALL Marks

    F9 - Save changes and back up
Choose one: X or  (no mark).
```

Figure 4-19. *The Select Tax Categories screen.*

Highlight the first field in the report, and type the code for the element you want to appear first.

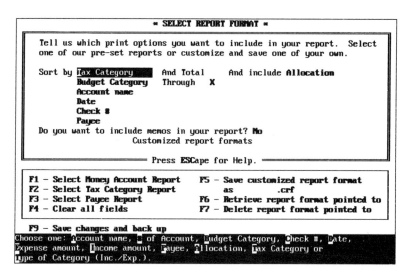

Figure 4-20. *The Select Report Format screen.*

For example, if you want the payee's name to appear first, highlight the first field and type the letter P. You can repeat this process for each field until the information is in the order you want.

You can also use some preset formats for including more or less information.

Press F1 to list the account name first.

Press F2 to list the tax and budget categories first.

Press F3 to include only the payee, date, check number, and income and expense amounts.

Press F4 to clear all fields.

Press F5 to save a report format you created yourself, and press F6 to retrieve it.

The best format for a Schedule A report is the F2 format, which has transactions listed by tax category.

Press F9 to return to the Report Generator screen.

Printing Budget Reports

After you define your report and create the format, you can print your report, save it in a file, or display it on the screen. If you save it in a file, you can modify the report with your word processor or Write On the Money before you print it.

At the Report Generator screen, move the cursor to the third field between the information box and the action box. Indicate whether you want to print the report to the screen, to a printer, or to disk by typing **S**, **P** or **D**. If you choose D, also fill in the blanks to indicate the name of the file and whether you want it stored in ASCII (Report) format or in a format that can be read by Lotus 1-2-3. (See "Lotus 1-2-3 Export Setup" in Chapter 1.)

As a rule, you should display your report on the screen to check the format before printing. Taking the time to do so saves time and paper in the long run.

Press F1 when you are ready to print the report.

The program displays the number of transactions that are included in your report.

Press F1 again to print the report.

Editing Archived Transactions

In addition to generating budget reports, Budget Archives allows you to edit archived transactions. If you made a mistake recording a budget transaction that you want to include in a report at tax time, you can correct the error in the transaction.

From the Report Generator screen, press F2.

The program displays a screen that describes the capabilities and limitations of the editing feature.

Press F1 to display the editing screen.

The editing screen lists the Chapter 3 archived transactions. You can scroll through this list with the arrow keys, the PgUp and PgDn keys, and the Home or End keys.

Press F1 to add a new transaction. Or highlight the transaction you want to edit and press F2.

The program displays the View or Edit Selected Transaction screen, which is much like the screen on which you entered the transaction originally. Here you can change the date, amount, or any other information about the transaction. For example, if the amount is $1,000 and you recorded $10,000 by mistake, highlight the correct amount blank and type in the new amount.

You can also change the budget category to which you first allocated the transaction by pressing F2 at the View or Edit Selected Transaction screen. A screen appears to let you redirect the allocations. You can type in the correct numbers for the correct categories and press F9 to save the changes.

When you press F1 from the View or Edit Archived Transaction screen, the transaction in the .ARK file is permanently changed. However, if the transaction appears in another file, it remains unchanged in that file.

Leaving the Report Generator   When you have finished your work with the Budget Archives feature, you can return to the Chapter 3 mini menu by pressing F10 from the Report Generator screen.

CREATING INVESTMENT REPORTS FOR YOUR TAX FORMS   You can use your information from Chapter 7 to create an investment report exactly as you used your Chapter 3 information to create a budget report. You can use this feature to read any information in the current year or to read last year's information to help you prepare your tax return.

To create an investment report, use the Portfolio Archives feature of
Chapter 7. Chapter 7 information is archived whenever an investment
is sold. Because Schedule D is based entirely on information about sold
investments, the best application for the Portfolio Archives feature of
Chapter 7 is to create a Schedule D report. In fact, one option automatically formats a report for Schedule D.

> To start Portfolio Archives, go to Chapter 7 by pressing F7 from the
> Main menu.
>
> Press F9 to enter Portfolio Archives.

If you want to include your closed-out transactions in your reports, you
can temporarily archive them exactly as you did in Budget Archives,
or you can permanently archive them, which removes them from
Chapter 7 entirely.

> Indicate in the information box whether you want to include unarchived
> information by typing **D** for "don't archive," **T** for "temporary archiving,"
> or **P** for "permanent archiving."
>
> Type **F** in the action box to tell the program to save any changes you
> made since you entered Chapter 3.
>
> Press F1 and the program reads your archived information, including
> your temporary archives if they exist.

After it reads the portfolio information, the program displays a
welcome screen and the number of archived assets. (If this number is
zero, you did not archive any assets.) The welcome screen also asks if
you want to include the temporary archives in your reports.

> Type **Y** in the information box to include temporary archives or **N** if you do
> not want to include them. Then press F1.

The program displays the Portfolio Archive Report Generator screen.

**Defining the
Investment Report** Select the contents of your investment report—the portfolios, assets,
and asset types you want to include—from the Report Generator
screen. (See Figure 4-21 on the following page.)

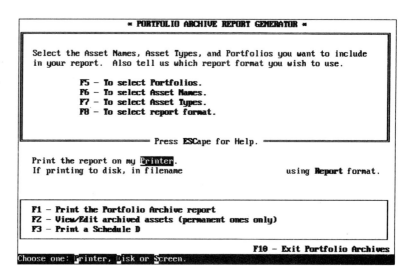

Figure 4-21. *The Portfolio Archive Report Generator screen.*

Press F5 to select the portfolios you want.

The portfolio selection screen lists all your archived Chapter 7 portfolios.

Type an **X** next to each portfolio you want to include, and press F9.

Because Schedule D reports income from all assets sold in a tax year, it is a good idea to mark all your taxable portfolios in case any contains a sold asset.

Press F6 to display your assets.

A list of all your sold assets appears.

Type an **X** next to the assets you want to include, and press F9.

For Schedule D, you should select all reportable assets except those that are reported on other schedules. (Not all assets are reportable.)

Press F7 to select the types of assets you want to include.

The program lists the types of assets.

Type an **X** next to the types of sold assets you want to include in your printed report, and press F9.

Again, for Schedule D, mark only those types of assets with taxable capital gains (or deductible losses). These include common stocks and mutual funds.

Creating the Investment Report Format

You can format an investment report much as you do a budget report. Instead of checks, check numbers, and amounts, this screen has fields for asset type, number of units, and other information about your assets from Chapter 7.

Press F8 to select a report format.

As a default format, the portfolio report lists your portfolio's name first, followed by other information, but you can easily create your own format.

Highlight the field you want to change, and type the code for the element you want to appear there.

You can also use the function keys to choose preset formats for including more or less information.

Press F2 to list your assets by name.

Press F3 to clear all fields and start over.

Press F4 to save a report format you created yourself, and press F5 to retrieve it.

If you are creating a Schedule D report, you can arrange the screen in any format for now. You can set the Schedule D format automatically when you are ready to print the report.

Printing Investment Reports

After you define your report and create the report format, you can print your report, save it in a file, or display it on the screen. If you save it in a file, you can modify the report with your word processor or Write On the Money before you print it.

At the Report Generator screen, move the cursor to the first field between the information box and the action box. Indicate whether you want to print the report to the screen, to a printer, or to disk by typing **S**, **P** or **D**. If you choose D, also fill in the blanks to indicate the name of the file and whether you want it stored in ASCII (Report) format or in a format that can be read by Lotus 1-2-3 (See ''Lotus 1-2-3 Export Setup'' in Chapter 1.)

As a rule, you should display your report on the screen to check the format before printing. Taking the time to do so saves time and paper in the long run.

Press F1 when you are ready to print the report.

The program displays the number of assets included in your report.

Press F1 again to print the report.

Creating a Schedule D

To create a Schedule D, you must reenter the same information you entered on the Schedule D screens of Chapter 4.

Press F3 from the Report Generator screen to prepare a Schedule D for your tax return.

In the two screens that appear, enter information about capital gains, including carryover losses and gains from Form 4767. (For details, see ''Using Schedule D to Report Capital Gains and Losses.'')

Fill in the blanks with capital-gains information. Press F1 to display the second Schedule D preparation screen and fill in those blanks. Press F1 again when you are ready to print the Schedule D.

A message screen indicates the number of assets in your report.

Press F1 to print the report.

The Schedule D Report

You can use the Portfolio Archive Report Generator to produce a Schedule D report, which lists your short-term and long-term capital gains.

```
Part 1.  Short-Term Capital Gains and Losses

                   Date      Date      Gross       Cost +      Gain/
Description        Acquired  Sold      Sale Price  Sale Exp    (Loss)
Apple Computer
        75         1/8/88    5/8/88     5,850.00   6,000.00    -150.00
McDonalds
        93         7/11/87   1/11/88    4,231.50   4,185.00     46.50


Short-term gain from sale or exchange of a principal residence     $0.00
Short-term capital gain from installment sales                     $0.00
Net short-term gain or (loss) from partnerships, S corporations,
   and fiduciaries                                                 $0.00
Short-term capital loss carryover from years after 1969            $0.00
                                                            =============
Net short-term gain or (loss)                                  ($103.50)

Part 2.  Long-Term Capital Gains and Losses

                          Date      Date      Gross       Cost +       Gain/
Description    Units      Acquired  Sold      Sale Price  Sale Exp     (Loss)
IBM           100         10/8/82   10/8/88   10,800.00   12,800.00   -2,000.00
Knight-Ridder 100         1/8/88    10/8/88    4,200.00    3,500.00     700.00
McDonalds      75         7/11/83   10/8/88    3,750.00    3,339.94     410.06
Proctor & Gam 150         7/11/83   10/8/88    9,750.00   10,500.00    -750.00


Long-term gain from sale or exchange of a principal residence      $0.00
Long-term capital gain from installment sales                      $0.00
Net long-term gain or (loss) from partnerships, S corporations,
   and fiduciaries                                                 $0.00
Capital gain distributions                                         $0.00
Gain from Form 4797                                                $0.00
Long-term capital loss carryover from years after 1969          $500.00
                                                            =============
Net long-term gain or (loss)                                 ($1,139.94)
```

If you use the Portfolio Report format instead of the Schedule D format, the same report looks like this.

```
Portfolio
      Units  Asset Name      Pur Date  Pur Price  Term  Gain/(Loss)

E F Hutton
        75   Apple Computer  1/8/88      80.0000  S       -150.00
        75   McDonalds       7/11/83     43.5833  L        410.06
        93   McDonalds       7/11/87     45.0000  S         46.50
       100   IBM             10/8/82    128.0000  L     -2,000.00
       100   Knight-Ridder   1/8/88      35.0000  L        700.00
       150   Proctor & Gambl 7/11/83     70.0000  L       -750.00
Total for E F Hutton                                  ($1,743.44)
```

The format of the Schedule D report should look very much like a real Schedule D. Compare your printout to your Schedule D tax form. If it corresponds exactly, you can staple the printout directly to your Form 1040 in place of the Schedule D form. (The IRS requires that you submit the original form only for Form 1040. You can use replicas for all other forms.) If your Schedule D report differs at all from the real form, however, play it safe and copy the information onto the real form.

Editing Archived Transactions

In addition to generating portfolio reports and a Schedule D, Portfolio Archives includes a feature to correct mistakes, exactly as Budget Archives does.

From the Report Generator screen, press F2.

The program displays a screen that describes the capabilities and limitations of the editing feature.

Press F1 to display the editing screen.

The editing screen lists the Chapter 7 archived assets. You can scroll through this list with the arrow keys, the PgUp and PgDn keys, and the Home or the End key.

Press F1 to add a new asset. Or highlight the transaction you want to edit and press F2.

The program displays the View or Edit Selected Asset screen, which is much like the screen on which you entered the transaction originally. Here you can change most information about the asset.

After you press F1 from the View or Edit Archived Transaction screen, the transaction in the .ARK file is permanently changed. However, if the transaction appears in another file, it remains unchanged there.

Leaving the Report Generator

When you have finished your work with the Portfolio Archives feature, you can press F10 from the Report Generator screen to return to the Chapter 7 mini menu.

MANAGING YOUR INSURANCE

Chapter 5 of Managing Your Money helps you to manage your insurance policies and at the same time adds a little fun to a normally mundane and neglected task. Geared mostly toward life insurance, the chapter helps you to determine your life expectancy, the amount of coverage you need, and the likely cost of the coverage you need. The chapter also helps you organize your policies.

You can keep a list of all your policies, policy numbers, and other information that is usually buried at the back of the drawer when you need it most. Also, the cash value of any life-insurance policies you now hold is recorded in Chapter 8, to be included in your net worth.

CHOOSING A POLICY

The insurance planning parts of Chapter 5 help you choose a life-insurance policy. This choice depends on the answers to three principal questions: How long will I live? What kind of coverage do I need? How much should I pay for that coverage? The insurance planner in Chapter 5 uses the answers to these questions to help you develop the best policy for your needs.

Calculating Life Expectancy

To calculate your life expectancy, you must fill out a questionnaire providing information about your age, sex, marital status, health, lifestyle, frame of mind, occupation, family longevity, and whether or not you smoke, exercise, and wear your seat belt. (See Figure 5-1.)

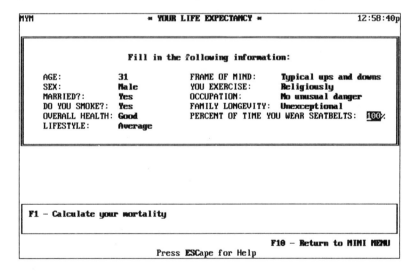

Figure 5-1. *The Life Expectancy screen.*

From the Main menu, press F5 to enter Chapter 5.

The Chapter 5 mini menu appears.

Press F2 to display the life-expectancy questionnaire on the Life
Expectancy screen.

Highlight each blank, and type your response.

The message at the bottom of the screen provides codes for most of the
blanks. For example, the question about your overall health limits your
choices to six possible answers: Excellent, Good, Average, Fair, Poor,
and Terrible.

Press F1 to calculate your life expectancy.

The program calculates your life expectancy and displays a paragraph
about how long you are likely to live. (See Figure 5-2.) It also tells you
your odds of dying this year.

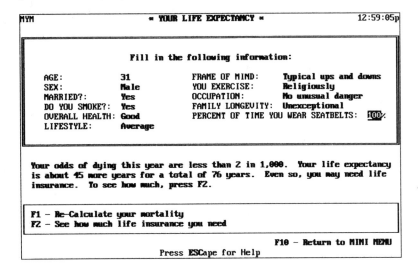

Figure 5-2. *Calculated life expectancy.*

Of course, its prediction is based on statistics that measure how long people generally live if they smoke, wear seat belts, or live wildly. The program assumes that you are an average person and bases its evaluation of your life expectancy on these statistics.

You can change your answers and press F1 again to see how changes in your life-style may affect your longevity. For those who smoke, live wildly, and don't wear seat belts, this screen shows how life expectancy rises as they cut out vices and live more carefully. The screen shows how much longer those who take care of themselves are likely to live. If you do experiment with this screen, note Tobias's comment if you list your age as 14 and answer "yes" to the question about smoking.

Calculating the Amount of Coverage

The next question, "How much coverage do I need?" requires you to answer trickier questions. The Help screens provided for each blank, however, contain truly useful financial advice to help you answer these questions and make decisions about insurance.

Tobias, who wrote a book on the insurance industry called *The Invisible Bankers: Everything the Insurance Industry Never Wanted You to Know*, also provided the useful financial advice in the Help screens. He knows all the ins and outs of insurance, so be sure to read his comments as well as the brief description of each blank.

> Press F2 from the Life Expectancy screen to display the How Much Life Insurance You Need screen. You can also press F3 from the Chapter 5 mini menu.

> Highlight the Number of Years to Provide blanks, and enter your estimates.

There are two blanks for each estimate: one for the number of years until your children finish college and one for the number of years you will live after the children finish college. (Use the figure from the Life Expectancy screen.) If you don't have children or you don't plan to put them through college, enter zero in the first blank. (If your answer for both blanks is zero—in other words, if you don't have dependents who will need money after you die—you probably don't need life insurance.)

> Highlight the Estimated Annual Need blanks, and type your estimates.

Enter the amount of money you think your dependents will need per year after your death. These dependents can be your spouse, children, grandparents, or a disabled relative. The figure you enter is based on factors that only you know. If your spouse is your only "dependent," for example, and he or she makes more money than you do, you might enter zero. But if you have college-bound children, you should enter in the first blank a sum that reflects both the annual cost of raising the children and college financial requirements. The amount in the second blank will be considerably less. If you have no children, you can skip the first blank altogether.

> Highlight the Estimated Social Security blanks and type your estimates.

> Highlight the blank for the rate of interest your heirs will earn, and type your estimates.

To predict more accurately how much insurance you need, the program asks the rate of interest you expect your family to earn on insurance money they receive. The program assumes 3 percent per year, because Tobias thinks this is the most realistic figure when inflation is factored in. If your spouse is a serious investor, perhaps you should raise that figure, because he or she is likely to beat inflation by making shrewd investments.

> Highlight the Final Expenses blank and type your estimate.

Final expenses are basically funeral costs, including burial or cremation. The program assumes $15,000 unless you change the figure.

> Highlight the blank for the assets your heirs may use, and type your estimate.

Record in this blank any assets your heirs are likely to receive. If you have $200,000 in the bank, you may not need any insurance, but if you are $100,000 in debt, you may need quite a bit. You should enter the most liquid of assets, such as stocks and cash, as well as other life-insurance policies, such as the one your employer provides.

> Highlight the blank for any other assets to which your heirs may have access, and type your estimate.

If you think your heirs will become more independent at some point, you may want to subtract some money from this screen's equation. You should include an estimate of their "independence" here. The amount you enter in this blank is subtracted from the total amount of coverage needed.

> Press F1 to calculate your insurance needs.

The number that appears when you press the F1 key is the amount of coverage you need, not the amount of money. To determine how much money you need, go to the next part of Chapter 5.

Calculating the Cost of Insurance

If you filled out the life-expectancy questionnaire and calculated the amount of coverage you need, the program now has enough information to make recommendations and show you how much you will have to pay for the coverage you calculated.

> Press F4 from the Chapter 5 mini menu, or press F2 from the How Much Life Insurance You Need screen.

The program displays the What Life Insurance Should Cost You screen, in which you can confirm or change information about your life expectancy and your coverage needs.

> Press F1 for advice.

The program displays a few words of advice from Tobias about the best method for buying insurance, given your needs. For example, he may advise you to buy insurance in one single lot if your coverage needs are low, because insurance is cheaper by the pound than by the ounce. (In some cases, the single insurance option may not appear, particularly if your health is poor and it is unlikely that you would be eligible for insurance.)

> Press F2 to calculate your insurance costs.

The program displays a list of annual premiums. (See Figure 5-3.) The premiums vary according to your age, so the program shows the premiums for your age until you reach age 69.

The two main types of life insurance are term insurance and whole life insurance. The figures in this screen are based on term insurance.

> Press the Escape key to read Tobias's reasons for including only term life insurance in this portion of the program.

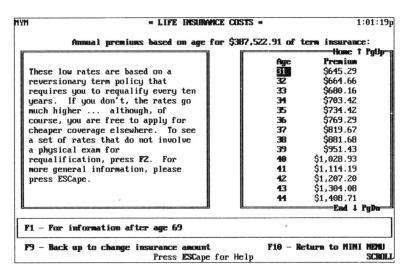

Figure 5-3. *The Life Insurance Costs screen.*

The premiums for term life insurance start low and increase dramatically because they are based on your age and, therefore, on the likelihood of your death. Term insurance is a lot like car insurance, except that the policy pays off only if you are "totaled." You can't cash in a term policy; you can only renew it.

The premiums for whole life insurance start high and tend to stay high because this type of policy is a form of investment. Whole life policies are like savings plans. You can "cash them in" because they have a cash value at all times. Tobias doesn't recommend whole life insurance because he thinks you can get a better return on your money through other savings plans, such as an IRA or a 401(k) salary reduction plan.

Notice that you can scroll through the table of premiums until you reach age 69, where the table stops. To find out why it stops here, press F1 to get information about buying insurance after age 69. Most likely, you can't buy term life insurance after age 69 because the odds are too high that you will die soon. Tobias then explains why you don't need to buy insurance at that time if you have played your financial cards right between the ages of 1 and 68.

Press F10 to return to the Chapter 5 mini menu.

ORGANIZING YOUR POLICIES

You should now know how much, if any, insurance you need, but if you are like most people, you already have some insurance for your health, car, house, and possessions. You can use the policy organizer in Chapter 5 to create a list of your policies and even do a little analysis of each one.

Creating a List of Policies

When you create a list of policies, you must provide information about each policy on the list, including the insurance company, the policy number, the annual premium, and the type of policy. You can usually find this basic policy information on any statement or bill from the insurance company. So gather a few records before you begin.

From the Chapter 5 mini menu, press F1.

The program displays the list of policies. (See Figure 5-4.) If you are creating the list for the first time, you may only have Sid and Sara Sample's policies. If so, delete them by highlighting them one at a time and pressing F3.

Press F1 to add a new policy to the list.

The program displays a form for adding a new policy.

Highlight each blank in the form and enter the appropriate information.

In addition to the other information, you must record the face value and cash value of the policy as well as any outstanding loan amount. The face value is how much will be paid when the policy is paid off. An auto insurance policy that covers you for $300,000 in injuries and $50,000 in damages has a face value of $350,000. The cash-value figure and outstanding loan amount pertain only to whole life insurance. The cash-value figure you enter here eventually shows up alone or in combination with other cash-valued insurance in Chapter 8, where you

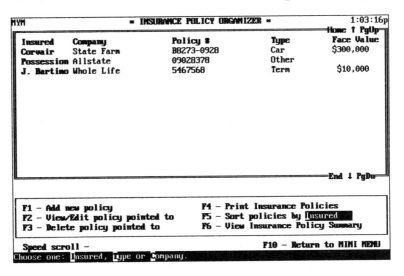

Figure 5-4. *The Insurance Policy Organizer screen.*

calculate your net worth. The outstanding loan amount, however, must be recorded separately in Chapter 3. It is not automatically recorded in Chapter 8 from your list of policies.

Press F1 to record the policy information and add the policy to the list.

After your policy is recorded in the Insurance Policy Organizer, you can make note of changes that occur in your policy by pressing F2. You can also sort your list of policies (by who or what is insured, by type of insurance, or by insurance company) with the F5 key and print it by pressing F4.

Analyzing Your Policies

The main responsibility of the policy organizer is to keep your information in one place for easy access. If you are in a car accident, or if you are robbed (preferably not of your computer and this software), you can refer to this list for all pertinent information. Unlike the budget and portfolio chapters of the program, this list is not a prelude to extensive analysis of your insurance needs. However, the policy organizer has a useful analytic tool: its summary feature.

From the list of policies, press F6 to view the Insurance Policy Summary screen.

The program rearranges some of the information you provided, totaling some of the amounts you entered. (See Figure 5-5). You can see at a glance the total amount of life insurance you currently own, the total annual life-insurance premiums you pay, and the total cash value of your policies. The summary also lists the total annual premiums for your car insurance, home insurance, health insurance, accident insurance, and any other insurance you carry. This summary can help you evaluate your total insurance picture.

Press F9 to return to the Insurance Policy Organizer and then press F10 to return to the mini menu.

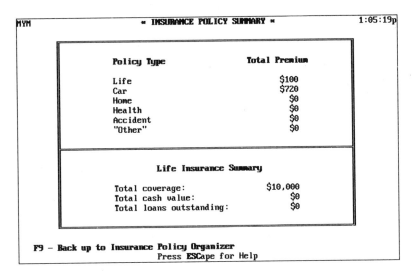

Figure 5-5. *The Insurance Policy Summary screen.*

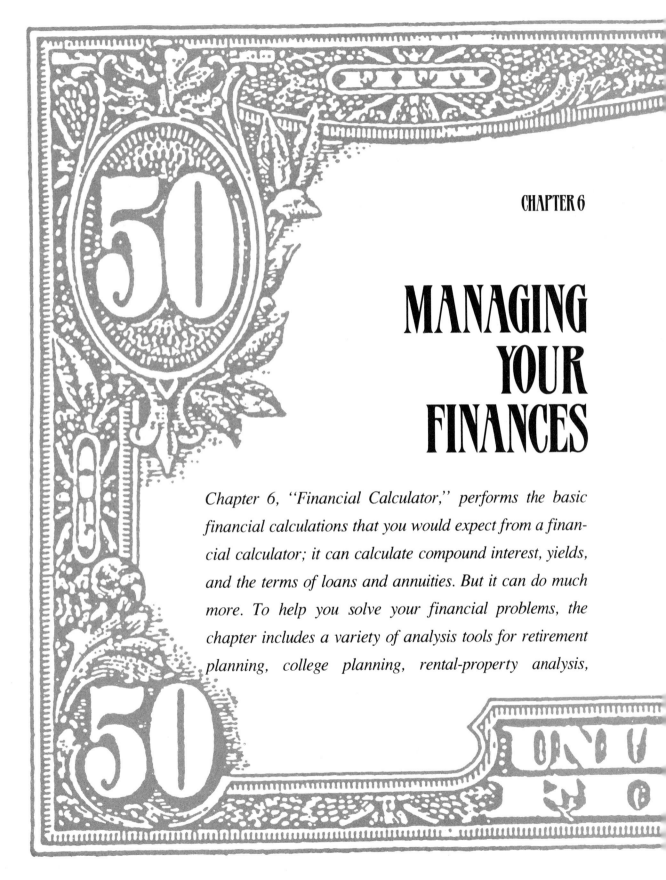

MANAGING YOUR FINANCES

Chapter 6, "Financial Calculator," performs the basic financial calculations that you would expect from a financial calculator; it can calculate compound interest, yields, and the terms of loans and annuities. But it can do much more. To help you solve your financial problems, the chapter includes a variety of analysis tools for retirement planning, college planning, rental-property analysis, refinancing mortgages, making buy/lease/rent decisions, investment analysis, estimating the impact of inflation on your investments, and analyzing loans.

It's not intended that you use Chapter 6 each time you use Managing Your Money, but only as needed. For example, you consider refinancing your house only when interest rates drop significantly below the rate at which you bought it. If you wake up one day and discover the prime rate has dropped to 5 percent, it's time to turn to Chapter 6 and determine if you should refinance your home mortgage.

You may find it necessary to use some of the other tools more frequently, however. You may use the retirement-planning and college-planning sections at least twice a year and the investment-analysis tool even more often.

Most of the tools in this chapter are made up of one screen. You simply enter numbers into the blanks, and the program analyzes them and displays the result. Don't let the simplicity of using these tools deceive you into believing they are not effective. You can get very helpful financial guidance after only a few minutes with one screen.

PERFORMING BASIC FINANCIAL CALCULATIONS
The compound calculator is the first choice on the Chapter 6 mini menu. With it, you can compute compound interest, determine current and future yields, and calculate the terms of a loan or annuity, much as you can in Chapter 3. You can also convert effective annual yield to annual interest rate, or vice versa. These four functions appear on one screen, and each function has its own Help screen that you call up by pressing the Escape key while the cursor is in that function's box. (See Figure 6-1.)

Before you use the compound calculator, first clear the quadrants.

From the Main menu, press F6 to display the Chapter 6 mini menu.

Press F1 to display the compound calculator. Then press F4 to clear the quadrants.

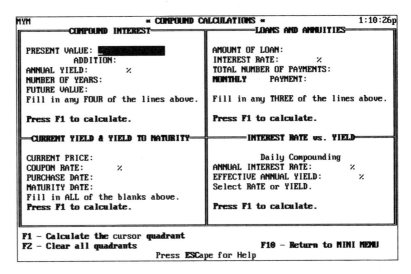

Figure 6-1. *The compound calculator.*

Computing Compound Interest

Compound interest pays you interest on your interest. For example, if you earn 10 percent interest on a $100 investment, you then have $110. If you continue to earn 10 percent interest, the 10 percent is applied to $110. Assuming you receive the interest once a year, your original $100 investment grows yearly as the base number increases. In 20 years, your $100 grows to about $673.

The problem with compound interest is that the U.S. government taxes interest earned each year; therefore, the actual effects of compounding are not quite as dramatic as they may appear. If you are in the 50 percent tax bracket, your $10 in interest is really only $5 after taxes. Ten percent interest on $105 would be only $5.25 after taxes, and the next 10 percent would be computed on only $110.25 instead of $115.50.

Compound interest earned in an individual retirement account (IRA) or a Keogh plan for the self-employed is the exception to the rule and cannot be taxed. For these plans, the compound-interest function in the financial calculator is most useful, so you might want to try this function with a sample IRA problem.

Highlight the Present Value blank and type the amount that is earning interest today.

For example, suppose you have an IRA containing $10,000. Type 10000 in the Present Value blank.

Highlight the first Addition blank and type the code for the frequency with which you plan to add to the starting amount (Daily, Weekly, Monthly, Quarterly, or Yearly). Then highlight the second Addition blank and type the amount you plan to add each time.

Because you can contribute $2,000 annually to an IRA if you do not have a retirement plan at work, type Y in the first blank and type 2000 in the second blank.

Highlight the Annual Yield blank and type the interest rate.

You will have to estimate a bit here. Because your IRA investments can be long-term, and because long-term investments pay higher yields, you might expect a 10 percent yield on your money each year. If you are working with a bank account, enter only the effective annual yield here. (See "Converting Interest Rates to Yields," later in this chapter.)

Highlight the Number of Years blank and type the term.

In the IRA example, type 35 for the number of years to retirement.

Press F1 to calculate the future value.

The future value is the value of the investment plus interest at the end of the term. In this IRA example, the future value is $823,073.11. The program displays this amount in the Future Value blank.

Note that you can calculate the value for any one of the blanks in this function by filling in the remaining blanks and pressing F1. Suppose you decide that $823,073.11 isn't enough money to live on when you're 65. Clear the information and fill in the blanks again. This time, leave the blank for annual yield empty and type 1000000 for future value. The program calculates the interest rate and indicates the amount your investments must earn in order to reach the future value you want.

Determining Yields

If you invest in bonds, you are familiar with the terms "current yield" and "yield to maturity." The second function in the compound calculator calculates how much a bond has yielded to present and how much it will yield at maturity. This function tells you not how much money you earned from your bond investment but the percentage the bond yielded, based on information from your broker or listed in the newspaper.

Highlight the Current Price blank and type the quoted price for the bond.

The bond price is always quoted in cents on the dollar, so if a bond is quoted at 45, type 45 in the Current Price blank. (Bonds are commonly sold in lots of $1,000.)

Highlight the Coupon Rate blank and type the coupon rate or yield.

Most bonds have coupons attached to them which you can tear off periodically and cash in. The coupon rate is also called the yield and is listed in the stock pages. Enter this yield in the Coupon Rate blank.

Highlight the Purchase Date blank and type the date you invested in the bond.

Highlight the Maturity Date blank and type the date on which the bond matures.

Because most bonds don't mature for 15 or 20 years, you may need to enter dates beyond the year 2000. The program doesn't recognize 3/15/00 as March 15, 2000, so you must enter the date as 3/15/100. The "1" stands for the first two digits (20) of any year between 2000 and 2099. For example, 136 indicates the year 2036.

Press F1 to calculate the yields.

The program tells you how much the bond will yield when it matures and how much it has yielded so far. A bond that was quoted at 20 with a 2 percent coupon rate and that was bought in 1985 and matures in the year 2000 has a current yield of 10 percent on March 30, 1986, and a yield to maturity of 16.7 percent.

Calculating Loans and Annuities

The Loans and Annuities box is similar to the loan-calculation tool in Chapter 3, but in addition to calculating loans, this function can calculate the terms of an annuity as well. Annuities are investments sold by insurance companies. When you invest $5,000 in an annuity, you are actually lending money to the insurance company, and the company pays you interest on the loan.

The terms of loans and annuities are calculated in much the same way. You can fill in any four of the five blanks for the function, and the program calculates the remaining variable.

> Highlight each blank in the Loans and Annuities box and type the appropriate values.

For example, to find out if you can afford the monthly payments of a 40-year, $100,000 loan with a 10 percent interest rate, type 100000 in the Amount of Loan blank, 10 in the Interest Rate blank, and 480 in the Total Number of Payments blank (12 months multiplied by 40 years). For the first Payment blank, type M for monthly payments. Leave the second Payment blank empty. The program calculates this value to be $849.15 a month.

> Press F1 to calculate the unknown variable.

Now suppose you want to determine how long it will take for a $5,000 annuity to pay for itself. Type 5000 in the Amount of Loan blank and enter the rate the insurance company promises to pay on the loan— perhaps 10 percent—in the Interest Rate blank.

Calculating the total number of payments is trickier for an annuity, which is often sold on the premise that the buyer will keep it for life (much like an insurance policy). You can enter the number of months you expect to live or the number of months until the penalties for total withdrawal have lessened. If you want to know when the total yield will equal the initial investment, leave this blank empty. Fill in the first Payment blank with the frequency of payments (to you) and the amount of each payment. Then, when you press F1, the program indicates the number of years it will take for this investment to yield a good profit.

Converting Interest Rates to Yields

The final function in the compound calculator converts annual interest rates to effective annual yields. These amounts are always slightly different because annual interest rates do not account for daily compounding—the amount of interest earned on each new daily figure. For example, a bank account with an annual interest rate of 10 percent has an effective annual yield of 10.677 percent.

Highlight one of the two blanks, Rate or Yield, and type the percentage.

Press F1 to calculate the value for the remaining blank.

Because the bank usually tells you only the annual interest rate, you can use this function to find the effective annual yield of your savings account. You can also use it to convert either the results or the input in the compound-interest function if you prefer to work with annual interest rates.

Press F10 to return to the mini menu.

PLANNING FOR RETIREMENT

The retirement-planning tool in Chapter 6 helps you determine how much money you can expect to have at retirement age and how much of that money you can spend per year after you retire. It can also graph some of this information for an overall view of your retirement assets.

Calculating Assets at Retirement

To find out how much money you are likely to have at retirement age, the program adds together your current assets plus your estimated annual contributions to these assets. Then, accounting for inflation, taxation, and the yields of your investments, the retirement-planning tool tells you approximately how much money you can expect to have when you retire.

From the Chapter 6 mini menu, press F2.

The Retirement Planning screen appears. (See Figure 6-2.) Here you enter three types of information for each asset: the current value of the asset, the amount you plan to contribute to the asset per year, and the percentage you expect to make on each asset per year.

Highlight the blanks in the Taxable Savings row and type the values for your interest-bearing investments.

Your taxable savings include investments such as bank savings accounts and money-market funds.

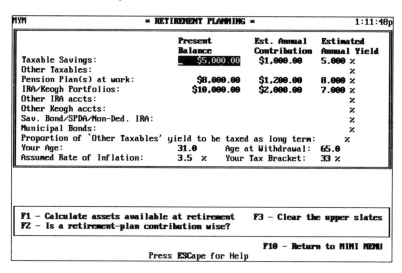

Figure 6-2. *The Retirement Planning screen.*

Highlight the blanks in the Other Taxables row and type the values for your investments that pay dividends.

These investments can include stocks, mutual funds, and any other investments that might rise in value and that pay dividends.

Highlight the blanks in the Pension Plan(s) row and type the values for any pension plans to which you belong through your company.

Most companies with formal pension plans submit a statement of profit sharing and increases (or decreases) in the invested pool of employee funds. Check your most recent statement for the most accurate figures. Note that the values you enter here are automatically entered in Chapter 8 to determine your net worth.

Highlight the blanks in the IRA/Keogh Portfolios row and type the values for these accounts.

If you went ahead and worked with Chapter 7, the present balance of your IRA and Keogh accounts already appears here. You have to add only your annual contributions and your estimate of annual yields.

Highlight the blanks in the Savings Bonds/SPDAs row and type the values for bonds and annuities.

SPDA is an acronym for single premium deferred annuities. The value of these annuities, as well as the value of any bonds you hold, is also calculated and entered here if you label the asset a "savings bond" when you create it in Chapter 7.

Highlight the Municipal Bonds fields and type the values for those tax-free investments.

Highlight each of the two Age blanks and type your current age and your age at withdrawal.

The program uses this information in calculating yields to determine the duration of the investment.

Highlight the Assumed Rate of Inflation blank and type your estimate for inflation.

The program uses this figure to calculate your money's devaluation over time.

Highlight the Your Tax Bracket blank and type your tax bracket percentage.

Remember that the Tax Estimator calculates your marginal tax rate when it calculates your taxes on the Form 1040 screen in Chapter 4. Enter that number here so that the program can determine how much to tax your interest and dividends each year.

Press F1 to calculate the balances at withdrawal.

The program now displays the assets that will be available at your retirement. (See Figure 6-3.) Although the program can't tell you if you will lose all your money before you retire or if you will win the lottery tomorrow, it can tell you what this money will be worth when you retire. The two columns in this screen are somewhat depressing.

```
MYM              * ASSETS AVAILABLE AT YOUR RETIREMENT *              1:13:06a

                                                           Adjusted for
HERE'S HOW YOUR ASSETS WOULD LOOK:          AT 65.0        3.5% Inflation
Taxable Savings:                            $76,998        $23,906
Other Taxables:                                 $0             $0
Pension Plan(s) at work:                   $299,873        $93,103
IRA/Keogh Portfolios:                      $356,299       $110,622
Other IRA accts:                                $0             $0
Other Keogh accts:                              $0             $0
Sav. Bond/SPDA/Non-Ded. IRA:                    $0             $0
Municipal Bonds:                                $0             $0

TOTAL AVAILABLE:                           $733,169       $227,632

By taking advantage of a deductible IRA/Keogh, you put away $22,440 that
would have otherwise gone in taxes, and your savings grew free of tax.  The
$356,299 you accumulated, although taxable as you withdraw it, compares with
$207,463 you would have accumulated (after tax) otherwise.

F1 - Plan for withdrawals over 30  years
F2 - Retirement Analysis graphs

F9 - Back up to Retirement Planning            F10 - Return to MINI MENU
                     Press ESCape for Help
```

Figure 6-3. *The Assets Available at Your Retirement screen.*

The first shows how much your investments would be worth at retirement after accounting for yields, contributions, and taxes, but not inflation. The second column shows how much the first figures are worth after accounting for inflation.

The program also comments on your IRA and Keogh plans. If you have such accounts, it tells you how much they will improve your retirement finances. If you don't have either type, it suggests that you start one.

Graphing Your Retirement Plan

After you have calculated your retirement assets, you can create a set of graphs to see at a glance how your retirement money is invested. (Remember that you can create graphs only if you have a graphics display adapter.)

From the Assets Available at Your Retirement screen, press F2.

The new screen gives you a choice of options for graphing your retirement assets.

Press F1 to graph your retirement assets by type.

A pie chart appears showing how your money is divided among the eight types of assets in the Retirement Planning screen. For example, if 11.8 percent of your retirement money is invested in taxable savings, 11.8 percent of the pie is labeled "Taxable Savings."

Press F2 to graph the impact of your IRA plan or Keogh investment accounts.

This pie chart indicates the portion of your total retirement income that comes from IRA assets. If you have an IRA, the majority of your income most likely comes from this account. Because IRA money is not taxed, it is likely to grow faster than other assets, and this chart shows how a little IRA money will grow to fill a large portion of the pie at retirement.

Press F3 to compare the impact of your annual contributions to the impact of interest earnings and dividends.

This pie chart indicates the percentage of your assets at retirement that will come from your annual contributions and the percentage that will come from appreciation due to interest and dividends on your original (and growing) nest egg. (See Figure 6-4.) Unless you contribute a lot of money toward retirement later in life, the appreciation slice of the pie is larger than the contributions slice.

Figure 6-4. *Graph of contributions and appreciation.*

Spending Your Retirement Income

The amount of money you have when you retire and the continued earnings on that money in your retirement years, together with the number of years you live after you retire, determine how much money you can spend per year during your retirement.

The program assumes you will retire at 65 and live to be 80, so it uses 15 years to calculate your annual spending limit. If you plan to live longer or retire later, change this figure.

On the Assets Available at Your Retirement screen, highlight the F1 blank and type the number of years you expect to live after you retire.

Press F1 to find out how much you can spend each year.

The program calculates how much cash you will be able to spend during each year of your retirement and interprets the effect of inflation—both at the beginning of your retirement and at the end. It also predicts your tax situation during retirement, determines your likely tax bracket after it is adjusted for inflation, and indicates how your tax bracket will affect your annual income.

This information is particularly useful if you are considering an early or late retirement. For example, suppose you are thinking about retiring at 70. Return to the Retirement Planning screen and enter 70 in the Age at Withdrawal blank. Then calculate your assets at retirement, change the number of years in the F1 blank, and press F1 to find out how much money you will have to support yourself per year if you retire at age 70. Note that the Help screen suggests you add $6,000 to $7,000 to your total annual retirement income because you can expect about that much in Social Security benefits.

Generally, this retirement-planning tool is most useful if you are close to retirement age. Obviously, it's hard to predict inflation, taxation, and the general state of the world over 30 years. After all, 10 years ago IRA accounts didn't exist. So, unless you are within 10 years of retirement age, take the results of the retirement planner with a grain of salt.

Press F10 to return to the mini menu.

PLANNING FOR COLLEGE EXPENSES

The college-planning tool helps you determine how much money you will need for each child's college education and how much you must save each year to be ready for the expense. You can create a financial scenario for each child you plan to send to college. After you determine the results, you can print a report.

From the Chapter 6 mini menu, press F3.

Enter in the appropriate blanks the child's name, the number of years until the child enters college, and the number of years he or she will attend college.

A newborn baby has about 18 years until he or she enters college and will probably spend at least four years in undergraduate study.

Highlight the blank for today's annual cost of college and type the yearly cost of the institution you expect your child will attend. Then highlight the blank for annual college-cost inflation and type an estimate here.

Although not as high as it once was, college-cost inflation is still outpacing the inflation rate. A fair estimate of college-cost inflation is about 8 percent.

Highlight the Present Savings blank and type the amount of money you have saved thus far for this child's education. Then highlight the Annual Yield blank and type the yield on those savings.

Press F1 to calculate the amount of money you need to save.

A new screen shows the total cost of this child's college education and three possible methods of saving the money. Before you look at it, brace yourself.

In my own example for a newborn baby, I estimated today's annual college cost at $10,000. I guessed that the inflation rate for college costs would be 4 percent, and I allocated $5,000 of my present savings (yielding 7.25 percent) to the fund. The total cost for this child's four-year education is $86,025.57. And that last $0.57 really hurts.

To save that amount of money in 18 years, I would have to set aside about $1,700 per year—or a little less if I continue to save throughout the four years the child goes to college—according to the program. The last savings alternative is to save considerably less right now (but still more than $1,000 per year) in hopes of being able to save more when I'm older, more successful, and therefore more wealthy.

You can now print a report of these results by pressing F4. Or press F9 to return to the College Planning screen and determine the estimated cost of a college education for your second child.

Press F10 to return to the mini menu.

ANALYZING INVESTMENTS

The investment-analysis tool in this chapter calculates annual cash flow and the internal rate of return (IRR) from your investments. With this information, you can then analyze your investments and determine their true value over time.

Calculating Cash Flows

A cash flow is the amount of income and outgo precipitated by any one investment. It's easy to calculate cash flow for a single investment for one year, but it is difficult to calculate cumulative cash flows over five or more years considering the impact of taxes. The investment-analysis tool can help.

From the Chapter 6 mini menu, press F4 to display the Investment Analysis screen.

This screen lists cash-flow summaries for your investments. If a list of cash flows already appears on the screen, press F5 to clear it. Then you might want to try a simple cash-flow analysis of a money-market account.

Highlight the Year blank in the New Cash Flow Line and type the year you made the initial investment. For example, type **1985**.

Highlight the Actual Cash Out blank and type the dollar amount of your initial investment. Then highlight the Actual Cash In blank and type the amount of all earnings from the investment.

Suppose, for example, you opened your money-market account with an initial investment of $10,000. Type this amount in the Actual Cash Out blank. In 1985, you earned 10 percent interest, so type 1000 in the Actual Cash In blank. If you lost money, enter the Actual Cash In amount in parentheses.

> Highlight the Deductions blank and type the amount of deductions allowed on this investment.

You can claim deductions for certain investments, such as real-estate investments, but you can't claim a deduction for a money-market account. So, for this example, enter 0 (zero) in the Deductions blank.

> Highlight the Ordinary Income blank and type in the amount of income from the investment. Or highlight the Long-Term Gains blank and type in the amount of the gain.

Ordinary income and long-term gains were previously treated differently at tax time, but now they are treated the same. So, you can use either column to record income from your investment. In a money-market account, the Ordinary Income amount is the same as the Actual Cash amount.

In the money-market account, you didn't sell anything in 1983, so enter 0 (zero) in this blank.

> Press F1 to add this cash-flow summary to the list.

You can now repeat this process for all the years you want to analyze. In the money-market example, add cash flows from 1984 to the present, and perhaps add a projection for the coming year. If you made no new investments during these years, leave the Actual Cash Out blanks empty. Be sure to enter Actual Cash In values commensurate with the interest rates for those years.

> Highlight the Tax Bracket blank and type your marginal tax bracket percentage. Then press F2 to analyze these cash flows or F4 to print them.

The program displays the analysis in three columns: The first lists the same figure you entered in the Ordinary Income blank for comparison to the other two columns; the second column lists after-tax cash flow for each year; the third lists your cumulative cash flow.

In the money-market example, the first year's after-tax cash flow, which accounts for the initial $10,000 investment, shows a negative figure. But all figures for the remaining years reflect the profit that resulted from interest earnings minus the taxes for your income-tax bracket.

The cumulative cash flow takes into account income, taxes, and the initial $10,000 investment, spread out over five years. The cumulative cash-flow numbers are all negative because they account for the "loss" you underwent when you initially invested the money.

Calculating Internal Rate of Return

An investment's internal rate of return (IRR) is the interest rate at which future cash flows are discounted to reflect the time devaluation of money so that the present value of those cash flows equals zero. The program's IRR analysis is particularly useful for considering investments that provide large tax deductions, such as real-estate investments. The IRR analysis helps you measure the true income of the investment over time.

If the IRR is only 5 percent, the investment is not to your advantage because you can get that rate from a bank and have total liquidity. Most partnerships predict an IRR when you invest your money. You can use the IRR analysis to track the real IRR against the firm's claim, as years go by.

Add cash-flow summaries for each year of your investment. Or enter predicted cash flows to analyze a potential investment. Then press F2.

The program displays the cash flows and the IRR. If you entered information from a real-estate partnership that provides large tax deductions and small profits in the first few years and the opposite in later years, the IRR should be between 5 and 20 percent, depending on how aggressive and risky your partnership is.

Press F10 to return to the mini menu.

ANALYZING RENTAL PROPERTIES

Few investments benefit more from an analysis of cash flow and IRR than an investment in property that you buy in order to rent for profit. With the cost of property repair, insurance, and missed rent payments, you might wonder whether your investment is actually turning a profit. The rental-analysis tool can give you the answer. It is a specialized version of the basic investment-analysis tool that calculates your cash flows and IRR, but it considers many more factors in analyzing the investment.

> From the Chapter 6 mini menu or the Financial Calculator screen, press F5.

The Rental Property Analysis screen appears. (See Figure 6-5.) Enter information about the property, including purchase date and price, depreciation information, sale date and price if it was sold, mortgage information, and income and expenses associated with the property.

> Highlight each blank that applies to your property and fill in the appropriate amounts or codes.

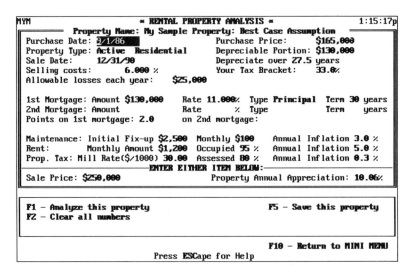

Figure 6-5. *The Rental Property Analysis screen.*

Much of this screen will contain your estimates because you are likely to use the screen well before you sell, and possibly before you buy, property. To estimate the annual appreciation for the property, you might call a local real-estate agent or property assessor for the current rate of appreciation for property in your area.

Pay particularly close attention to the depreciation information you enter because the method of depreciation you choose—either accelerated or straight-line—affects the cash-flow analysis. (The program ignores depreciation completely if you indicate that the property type is personal rather than commercial or residential.)

Press F1 to generate the cash-flow figures and calculate the IRR for the rental property.

The analysis screen that appears shows the actual cash in and out for each year you own the property as well as the depreciation, after-tax cash flow, cumulative cash flow, and IRR. The most telling figures are the after-tax cash flow, which takes into account your tax bracket, and the cumulative cash flow, which takes into account your initial investment and the profit you expect to make on the eventual sale of the property. If you find that the IRR is not higher than the bank rate, you might want to consider whether being a landlord is worth the work for that rate of return.

You can print this analysis by pressing F4.

After you complete an analysis of a rental property, you can save the information by pressing F9 to return to the Rental Property Analysis screen and then pressing F5. From there, you can begin another rental-property analysis.

Press F10 to return to the mini menu.

**REFINANCING
A MORTGAGE**

When interest rates drop, people across America flood the loan departments of banks with applications for mortgage refinancing. Refinancing is, in effect, selling your property to yourself and taking a new loan at a lower rate. The only drawback to refinancing is that you pay closing costs and points again as if you were buying the house for the first time.

So at what point do the savings from a lower interest rate offset the costs of refinancing? You can use the mortgage-analysis tool to calculate the costs and benefits of refinancing your mortgage.

**Defining the
Terms of a
Mortgage**

The first step in analyzing the trade-offs involved in refinancing is to define the terms of your existing mortgage and those of the proposed mortgage, as well as closing costs, inflation, and your tax bracket.

From the Chapter 6 mini menu, press F6.

The Refinancing a Mortgage screen appears. (See Figure 6-6.)

Enter your tax bracket and the after-tax rate of return you expect to receive on your money in the appropriate blanks.

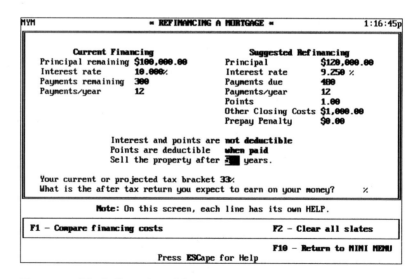

Figure 6-6. *The Refinancing a Mortgage screen.*

Your after-tax rate of return is the return you think you could get on your money if it weren't tied up in a down payment. If you can get 8 percent interest on most of your money, you can assume a personal discount rate of about 8 percent. The program needs to know the possible value of your money before it recommends refinancing.

> Highlight the blanks in the Current Financing section and enter information about your current mortgage.

In this section, enter the balance of your current mortgage, the current interest rate, the term of the loan, and the number of payments to be made per year.

> Highlight the blanks in the Suggested Refinancing section and enter information about the suggested new mortgage.

In this section, enter the amount of the new loan (the amount you owe on your existing loan, not the original amount), the new interest rate, the proposed term of the loan, and the number of payments per year. Next, fill in blanks for points and other closing costs, which are usually between $2,000 and $3,000. (For points, the program assumes the nearly standard 2, but you can change this amount.) If you incur a prepayment penalty for paying off your first loan early, enter the amount of the penalty in the Prepay Penalty blank.

> Enter information about the deductibility of interest and points and your selling plans in the next group of blanks.

You can usually deduct points and interest on your tax return, but you must specify on this screen whether they are deducted in the year of the sale or over the life of the mortgage. For home refinancing, you can usually deduct the points and interest in the year of the sale. However, check first with your banker or accountant.

If you plan to sell the property and you know approximately when, the program can spread the cost of refinancing over the number of years you plan to hold the property.

Comparing Old and New Financing Costs

After you enter your information, you are ready to compare the old and new financing costs.

> Press F1 to analyze the costs of refinancing.

The Comparison of Financing Costs screen appears and indicates how much your property will cost over the life of the loan in today's dollars if you keep your old loan. It then states how much you will pay if you refinance with the loan you described. (See Figure 6-7.)

If you indicated on the Refinancing a Mortgage screen that you plan to sell the property, the difference between the costs of the two loans may vary greatly. For example, if you plan to sell the property in two years anyway, savings from refinancing apply only to those two years. In this case, the costs are high and the benefits are low.

Don't discard the idea of refinancing if the results of the analysis are not positive. You can return to the previous screen and redefine the terms of the suggested loan and adjust the years until you sell the

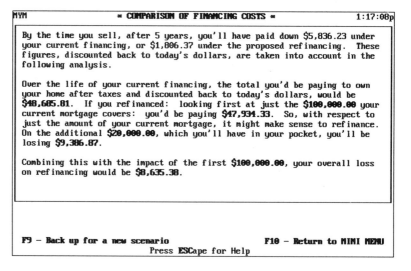

Figure 6-7. *The Comparison of Financing Costs screen.*

property. By changing these variables, you can determine the most profitable way to refinance.

Press F10 to return to the mini menu.

COMPARING BUY/LEASE/ RENT OPTIONS

With the buy/lease/rent analysis tool in Chapter 6, you can compare how much money you will spend over time if you buy, rent, or rent to own (lease) something. You can evaluate these options for the purchase of a home, car, boat, or other major investment.

Analyzing a buy/lease/rent option requires a rather difficult calculation. To be accurate, it must account for the inflation rate, the interest rate, your tax bracket, the resale value of your purchase, and your personal discount rate (the rate that determines the potential worth of your money in hand). The buy/lease/rent analysis tool takes all these into account to calculate your best option.

Defining Buy/Lease/Rent Options

To define these options, you must provide much of the same information you provided when you evaluated your mortgage refinancing.

From the Chapter 6 mini menu, press F7 to display the Buy/Lease/Rent Comparison screen.

This screen has three information sections: one for the purchase plan, one for the rental or lease plan, and one for information applicable to all plans, such as your discount rate and tax bracket. (See Figure 6-8 on the following page.)

Enter the appropriate values or codes for each blank in the Buy section of the screen.

For example, if you are evaluating a buy/rent option for a house, fill in the purchase price of the house, the mortgage amount, the interest rate, and the term. Also fill in the points on the loan and any money you expect to invest in the house initially. Enter the current inflation rate for both maintenance costs and property tax.

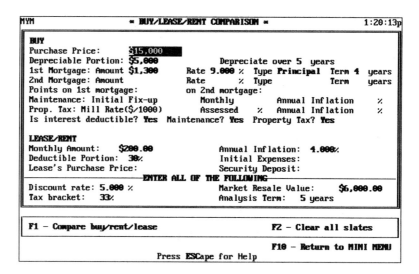

Figure 6-8. *The Buy/Lease/Rent Comparison screen.*

Enter the appropriate amounts for each blank in the Lease/Rent section.

Enter the monthly rent for the house in this section. If you plan to put your monthly rent toward the purchase of the house, enter the price of the house in the Lease's Purchase Price blank. If you don't plan to purchase the house, leave this blank empty. As in the Buy section, you must also enter the inflation rate for rent.

Fill in the blanks in the Enter All of the Following section.

For the house example, enter your tax bracket, the resale value of the house, and your personal discount rate. (See "Refinancing a Mortgage," earlier in this chapter.) In the Analysis Term blank, type the number of years over which you want to make the comparison. If you are renting, chances are you will want to own someday, so make an estimate of this number and use it as the analysis term.

Analyzing the Options

After you enter information in the three sections of the Buy/Lease/Rent screen, you can analyze the options to determine the one that works best for you.

Press F1 to analyze the options.

The program calculates the future net expenses and the net expenses in today's dollars for each of the options and then displays the results in two columns. (See Figure 6-9.) The cost of each option in today's dollars is based on your personal discount rate. (If you entered a discount rate of zero, both columns are the same.) Thus, the second column measures the potential earnings of the money if it weren't tied up in the property.

The cost of buying a house is usually less than renting or leasing because buying lets you earn back your investment in the resale of the house. However, if you plan to live somewhere for a very short time and you might not make up in appreciation what you invest in financing, renting might be the best option. Still, there are no definite rules in this analysis. As with the other tools in this chapter, you can use the buy/lease/rent analysis tool to create different scenarios until you find one that works best for you.

Press F10 to return to the mini menu.

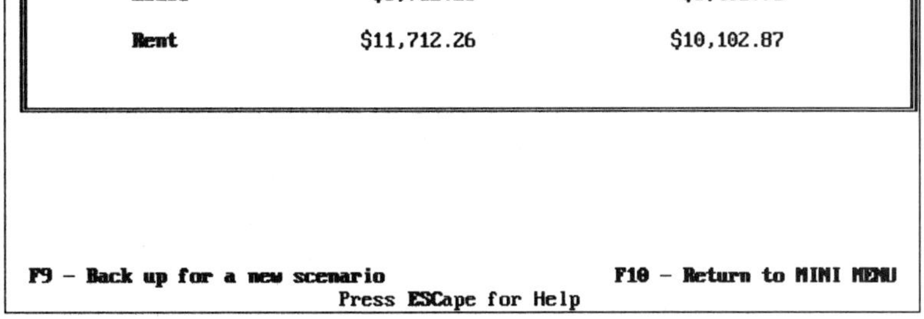

```
MYM                  * BUY/LEASE/RENT COMPARISON TOTALS *             1:20:44p

                                                      Total Net Cost in
                                    Total Net Cost    Today's Dollars

                  Buy                 $7,519.39           $8,870.64

                  Lease               $5,712.26           $5,401.71

                  Rent               $11,712.26          $10,102.87




    F9 - Back up for a new scenario              F10 - Return to MINI MENU
                         Press ESCape for Help
```

Figure 6-9. *The Buy/Lease/Rent Comparison Totals screen.*

ESTIMATING THE EFFECTS OF INFLATION

The inflator/deflator analysis tool helps you determine the effect of inflation on the value of a dollar. It shows you the effect a fixed inflation rate over time has on your money, and also the historical effect of inflation on any sum of money from 1901 to the present.

Calculating the Effect of a Fixed Inflation Rate

To determine how much today's money will be worth tomorrow, you can estimate the rate of inflation and ask the program to calculate how much a given amount will be worth at an indicated time in the future.

From the Chapter 6 mini menu, press F8 to use the inflator/deflator.

The Inflator/Deflator screen appears. (See Figure 6-10.) The first section in this screen is for calculating the effect of a fixed inflation rate. It has two sentences, each with blanks.

Enter the number of years, the rate of inflation or deflation, and the amount you want to evaluate in the three blanks in the first sentence.

The program then determines how much the specified amount will be worth after the entered number of years.

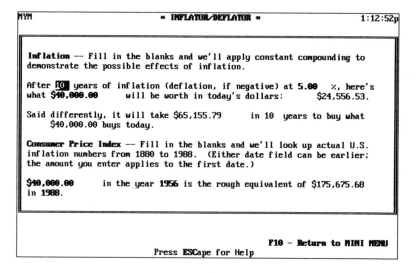

Figure 6-10. *The Inflator/Deflator screen.*

This calculation can help you determine exactly how much your investments really will be worth when you cash them in. Chances are that inflation will slow down the earnings on even the most promising investments.

Evaluating the Historical Effect of Inflation

The second section in the Inflator/Deflator screen contains one sentence with three blanks. Fill in the blanks to determine how much any amount of money in any year since 1901 is worth today or was worth in any past year.

Enter the amount you want to evaluate, the starting year, and the ending year in the blanks in the second section.

The program shows the ending-year value of the amount you entered. For example, to find out how much it cost in 1988 to buy something that cost $1,000 in 1945, type 1000 in the first blank, 1945 in the second blank, and 1988 in the last blank. The program calculates that the cost of the same item at 1988 values is $6,632.65. You can insert ending-year variables in the inflator/deflator up to 1988.

Press F10 to return to the mini menu.

LOAN ANALYSIS The loan-analysis section of Chapter 6 is different from the loan section of Chapter 3 in that it lets you work with loans more directly.

Press F9 from the Chapter 6 mini menu to enter the Loan Analysis screen.

Fill in the field for the loan date and then fill in all but one of the following: type, principal, number of payments, interest rate, and payment amount.

Press F1 to calculate the remaining field.

For most loans, the payments you make cover the original amount you borrowed and the interest that is projected to accrue by the end of the loan's life. The first payments on the loan cover mostly interest (which is tax-deductible), and the last payments cover primarily the original sum, or the principal (which is not tax-deductible). The ratio of payment portion to principal and payment portion to interest changes little by little each year, slowly decreasing the payment to interest and increasing the payment to principal.

Press F4 to print the amortization schedule and see exactly how much of each payment goes to both interest and principal.

If you want to modify the ratio for payments to interest and principal, you can rework the amortization schedule so that the ratio will change after a certain number of payments. You can make a total of four such adjustments.

Press F2 from the Loan Analysis screen to view the Loan Modification screen.

In the Payments, Increase Payment, and Interest Rate fields, fill in the desired changes to your loan.

Press F1 to recalculate and F4 to print the altered amortization schedule.

Press F9 to return to the Loan Analysis screen. Press F10 to return to the mini menu.

MANAGING YOUR PORTFOLIO

Before 1970, people considered shrewd investments to be savings accounts, insurance policies, and a mortgage. Today, these investments are still part of a solid investment portfolio, but many of us are as concerned about making our money work for us as we are about working for our money.

People became more investment-aware after the introduction of the Individual Retirement Account (IRA) in 1970. An IRA allows you to invest $2,000 per year and then deduct the contribution from your annual income. The money is not taxed while it grows in an IRA account, through either investment earnings or accrued interest, and is only taxed as it is withdrawn at retirement age.

Because many IRAs are managed by investment firms, more people are now familiar with different types of investment vehicles, from annuities to zero-coupon bonds. The $2,000 annual tax-free investment quickly becomes a healthy nest egg, and thus much more money is invested by the average person today than 10 years ago. And because more people are investing money, managing an investment portfolio is no longer a task only for the wealthy.

Chapter 7 of Managing Your Money helps you to manage your investments portfolio. If your only investment is an IRA, you can use Chapter 7 to track it more closely, and if you are a high-powered investor, you will find all the tools you need to manage a healthy portfolio.

After you set up one or more portfolios in which you list your investments, you can then use the portfolio manager regularly to update your investment records and to review financial reminders that help you track assets and make buy-and-sell decisions in a timely manner. The portfolio manager also provides several analytical tools to help you examine different aspects of your investments, from commission expenses to the yield or the distribution of risk in your current portfolios.

If you are a serious investor, you may be interested in a special add-on program from MECA called Managing the Market, which provides easy access to the Dow Jones News/Retrieval service for up-to-the-minute stock prices. With it, you can dial and log on to the service and update the prices in your portfolios automatically.

If your current investments consist only of a checking/savings account and an insurance policy, you can still work with Chapter 7 to create a hypothetical stock portfolio. By working with a hypothetical portfolio, you can gain the confidence and experience to consider investing real money when you are ready.

SETTING UP
A PORTFOLIO

Set up portfolios in Chapter 7 in the same way you set up checking and savings accounts in Chapter 3, with each portfolio representing an account. For example, you can list several investments with Shearson Lehman Hutton in your Shearson Lehman Hutton portfolio. If you have an IRA or a Keogh account that is managed by a bank, you can set up a separate portfolio for that account.

Creating
a Portfolio

To list a portfolio, record the name and number of the account, the type of account, and the current cash value of the portfolio.

From the Main menu, press F7 to display the Chapter 7 mini menu. Then press F3 to display the Portfolio Accounts screen.

If you are using the program for the first time, the Portfolio Accounts screen lists Sid and Sara Sample's portfolios. (See Figure 7-1.) You can delete them by highlighting each one individually and pressing F3.

Press F2 to add a new portfolio.

A form for adding a new portfolio appears. (See Figure 7-2 on the following page.)

```
MYM                        * PORTFOLIO ACCOUNTS *                   2:21:31p
                                                            Home ↑ PgUp
   Portfolio       Account #        Type        Cash Balance    Asset Value
   S.F Sample      02C-60000312     Taxable      $34,002.64      $21,025.00
   Fidelity        8A-3563-GG-91837 IRA/Keogh         $0.00       $6,354.22
   Wine Cellar     Downstairs       Taxable          $0.00       $2,228.16




                                                            End ↓ PgDn

   F1 - Work with portfolio pointed to    F5 - Transfer assets between accts
   F2 - Add new portfolio                 F6 - Edit or analyze commissions
   F3 - Delete portfolio pointed to       F7 - Good-Til-Canceleds
   F4 - Print Portfolio Summary           F8 - Rearrange portfolios

   * Ctrl-E - Portfolio notes                     F10 - Return to MINI MENU
                        Press ESCape for Help                      SCROLL
```

Figure 7-1. *The Portfolio Accounts screen.*

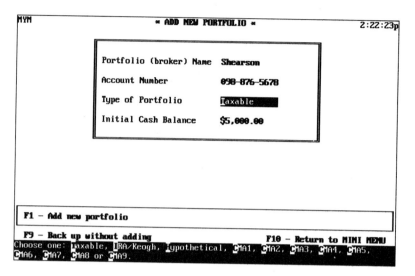

Figure 7-2. *Adding a new portfolio.*

Highlight the blank for the portfolio name and type the name.

Remember that a portfolio is an account, not an individual stock. Don't create a portfolio called ''IBM'' to list your IBM assets.

Highlight the blank for the account number and type the account number.

Highlight the Type of Portfolio blank and enter the code for the type.

Indicating the correct portfolio type is important because the type determines how the program handles the portfolio. The four different portfolio types are: taxable accounts, IRA/Keogh accounts, hypothetical accounts, and cash-management accounts. (See ''What Kind of Portfolio?'' for a definition of each type.)

Highlight the Initial Cash Balance blank and type your current balance.

The initial cash balance is the noninvested portion of your portfolio.

Press F1 to add the new portfolio to the list.

The Portfolio Accounts screen displays your portfolio including the initial information you entered. After you add assets to this portfolio, the program displays the portfolio's asset value, which equals the total worth of your investments—that is, the number of shares multiplied by the price of each share.

Adding an Asset

For each portfolio, list stocks, bonds, and mutual funds relating to the account. These are your unsold assets.

Highlight the portfolio to which you want to add an asset and press F1.

The current list of unsold assets appears. (See Figure 7-3.) If this is a newly created portfolio, no assets will appear on this screen.

Highlight the F1 blank and type the ticker-tape symbol for the asset you want to add. Then press F1.

The program displays the Buy an Asset screen, which contains a form for recording information about the asset. (See Figure 7-4 on page 192.)

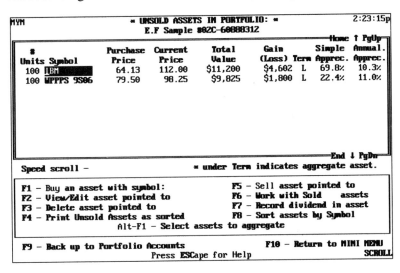

Figure 7-3. *The Unsold Assets screen.*

What Kind of Portfolio?

The portfolio manager works differently with each of the four portfolio types. For example, it does not include IRA or Keogh accounts in tax estimates when it identifies selling strategies. So, after you list a portfolio, you must identify it as one of the following types:

Taxable accounts: A taxable portfolio is one for which you must report dividends to the IRS at tax time. Such a portfolio includes stocks, corporate bonds, and most other investments. The exception is municipal bonds, which are not usually taxable, even under the new tax laws.

IRA/Keogh accounts: A portfolio that lists your IRA/Keogh investments is nontaxable. Any money that you make on an IRA investment cannot be taxed by anyone until you withdraw it at retirement age. Although the new tax laws limit contributions to IRAs, their assets are still not taxable.

Hypothetical accounts: A hypothetical account is a special type of portfolio that you can use to play "What if?" with the portfolio manager. The program regards the investments in a hypothetical portfolio as fictional, which allows you to practice with investments and test the market waters. Note that the program doesn't track a hypothetical account as thoroughly as the other accounts, so be sure to designate only a practice portfolio as a hypothetical account.

Cash-management accounts (CMAs): The CMA portfolios that you list in Chapter 7 are really the second part of the cash-management accounts you set up in Chapter 3. The account is listed in both places because it is basically a checking account handled by your broker. So although you list it in Chapter 7 like any other investment with your broker, the checks you write against it must be recorded in your Chapter 3 checkbook. The balance of your CMA is computed in Chapter 3 and recorded in Chapter 7. (Note that although your money-market account may be handled by a broker, it is not as active as a CMA and can therefore be treated more simply in Chapter 3, where it acts more like a savings account.)

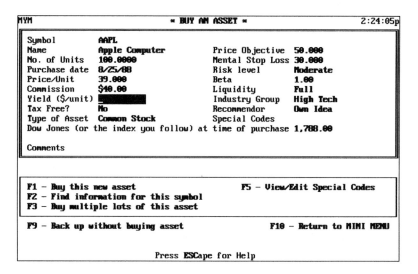

Figure 7-4. *The Buy an Asset screen.*

Here, you provide information such as the amount of commission you paid your broker, the expected yield of the asset, its tax status, type, price objective, risk level, beta value, liquidity, and industry group. You can also indicate who recommended the stock, assign codes for grouping or marking your assets, and include comments about each asset. The quality of the analyses you perform in Chapter 7 depends almost entirely on the quality of the information you enter when you add an asset.

> Enter the name, number of units, purchase date, and price per unit in the appropriate blanks.

Note that the name of the asset is not always apparent from its symbol. In the Price Per Unit blank, enter the amount you paid per unit when you purchased the asset, not its current value.

> Highlight the Commission blank and type the amount your broker was paid for taking part in the transaction.

The broker's commission probably does not appear on your brokerage statement. You can calculate it yourself by subtracting the price of the asset from the amount charged to your account.

Highlight the Yield blank and type the expected yield of this asset.

You can enter the dividend or interest that is listed in the newspaper.

Highlight the Tax Free? blank and type **N** if the asset should be included in a tax report, or type **Y** if it should not.

This answer is important for the Portfolio Archives section of Chapter 7, which you use to create tax reports. (See "Creating Investment Reports for Your Tax Forms" in Chapter 4.) It is also used for the capital-gains analysis in this chapter. Note that most assets are taxable.

Highlight the Type of Asset blank and type the code for the type of asset.

The program displays the categories for types of assets, including common and preferred stock, bonds, mutual funds, options, futures contracts, and metals or collectibles. Filling in this blank allows you to create reports showing the distribution of your assets.

Highlight the Price Objective blank and type the high price you want to achieve for this asset.

When the price of this asset reaches the objective, the program sends a reminder that you reached your price objective. (See "Using Financial Reminders," later in this chapter.)

Highlight the Mental Stop-Loss blank and type the lowest price at which you are willing to retain this asset.

The mental stop-loss price also triggers a financial reminder. The high and low prices set the limits within which you are willing to hold on to an asset.

Highlight the Risk Level blank and type the code for the asset's risk level.

Risk levels range from low to speculative. The level you select, based on your own opinion or that of financial experts, is later used in the overall risk analysis for your portfolio.

Highlight the Beta blank and type the beta value for your asset.

The beta value is a rating that indicates the asset's stability. A beta value of one means that the asset is as stable as the overall market. A higher beta value indicates that the price of the asset increases and decreases with the market, but to a greater extreme. Your broker and most stock guides can help you determine a stock's beta value.

Highlight the Liquidity blank and type the code for the amount of liquidity of the asset.

The liquidity of an asset is a measure of how quickly you can sell it. The three levels of liquidity are: full, semiliquid, and none. A blue-chip stock has full liquidity because you can sell it immediately. A limited real-estate partnership with an 11-year turnaround has no liquidity. A 90-day bank account is semiliquid.

Highlight the Industry Group blank and type the code for the industry to which the asset belongs.

The program gives you a choice of many industries, from the airline industry to textiles. Choose the one that seems most logical for the asset you are adding. Later, you can create a report that shows how much you have invested in each industry, which can be helpful in your overall investment analysis.

For example, if your report shows that 80 percent of your portfolio is invested in the housing industry, and interest rates are climbing to 15 percent, you may want to know about it and take action. (You can use a special code to indicate an industry that is not included in the choices offered by the program.)

Highlight the Recommendor blank and type the code for the source of information for this asset.

At some point, you may ask yourself, ''Who told me to buy this stock, anyway?'' It may be your broker, an idea of your own, a magazine or newsletter, a friend, or none of these. (You can use a special code to indicate a source that is not listed.) The recommendor of an investment may be an important aspect of your portfolio analysis. If 80 percent of your portfolio is recommended by your broker, and you're consistently losing money, it may be time to change brokers.

> Highlight the Special Codes blank and type the code or codes you want to use.

If you are adding an asset for the first time, you won't have special codes yet. To create special codes (or to review them before you assign them to an asset), press F5. The Special Codes screen appears. (See Figure 7-5.)

With this feature, you can make each letter of the alphabet a special code and thus create your own categories for grouping your assets. For example, suppose many of your investment ideas come from *Forbes* magazine. If you assign the code ''a'' to *Forbes* magazine and then

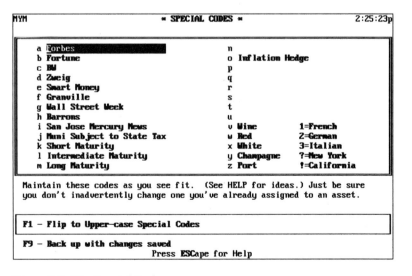

Figure 7-5. *The Special Codes screen.*

enter **a** for each asset that you bought on advice from *Forbes* magazine, you can create a report that shows the percentage of your portfolio acquisitions that were inspired by *Forbes*'s ideas.

You can also use codes to enter other types of information about your asset. Suppose you want to set up a code for Ginnie Mae funds. Type GINNIE MAE in the "g" blank in the Special Codes screen, and then press F9 to return to the Buy an Asset screen. Now you can type S for "Special Coded" in the Type of Asset blank and G in the Special Codes blank for all assets that are Ginnie Mae funds.

> Highlight the Dow Jones index blank and type the Dow Jones index for the day you bought the asset.

From now on, the program will compare the performance of this asset and your portfolio to the Dow Jones average. (See "Analyzing Performance Versus Index," later in this chapter.) This feature helps you determine whether an asset and your portfolio as a whole are performing as well as the rest of the market.

> Highlight the Comments blank and type any notes you want to include. To include longer notes, press Ctrl-E to use the pop-up note feature of Write on the Money.

Here, you might want to include any pertinent facts about the asset or advice you received. For example, you might note that your broker advised against a purchase and you invested regardless.

> Press F1 to add the asset you entered.

If you decide to buy more shares of the same asset, you don't need to type all the information again. On the Buy an Asset screen, type the appropriate symbol and press F2, and the asset information appears. From here, you can alter any information about this asset.

If you are buying the same asset, but at different times or at different prices, you can make multiple entries for the same asset by pressing F3. The Multiple Lots screen lets you enter additional purchase information but repeats the basic information from the Buy an Asset screen.

Press F9 to return to the Unsold Assets screen.

The asset now appears in the list of unsold assets. You can use this list to track the purchase price of the asset, its current price, the total value, your gain to date, and its appreciation.

UPDATING YOUR PORTFOLIOS

A portfolio, like a checkbook, is not static. The prices of stocks can change; you can receive dividends on your assets; you can sell assets or sometimes transfer them from one portfolio to another; or you may have special investment situations such as "short assets" or "good-until-canceled" orders, which are both affected by the changing market.

As the value of your assets changes, you can update your portfolio to track each change. How often you update depends on how active your portfolio is. But whether you work with your portfolio once a day or once a month, it is best to first update the prices of your assets and then review your list of unsold assets to get an overview of your gains or losses to date. From here, you can work in depth with your portfolio to record sales, dividends, and other changing information.

Updating Prices

Current stock prices are listed in the business section of the daily newspaper. Before you begin updating your assets, be sure today's date is correct on the Chapter 7 mini menu. (See Figure 7-6 on the following page.)

Type today's date if it's not correctly entered. Then press F1.

The Update Prices screen appears. (See Figure 7-7 on the following page.) It lists all your assets by symbol, the price you last entered, the yield, and any special codes that apply to the asset. Here, you can enter new prices, yields, and codes.

Highlight the Latest Price blank for each asset and type the new price. Or press one of the Alt-key combinations listed between the information and action boxes.

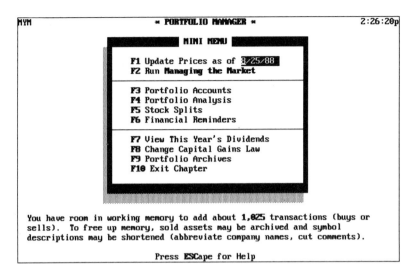

Figure 7-6. *The Chapter 7 mini menu.*

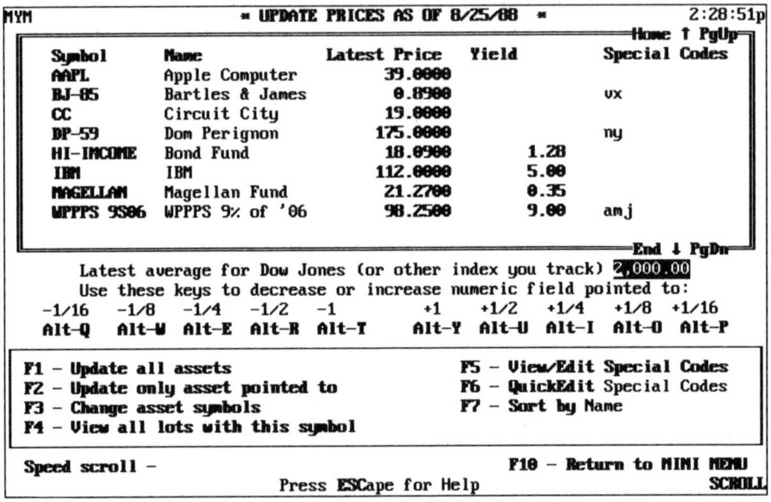

Figure 7-7. *The Update Prices screen.*

Stock, bond, and mutual fund prices are often expressed in fractional amounts. Using the Alt-key combinations saves you the effort of converting fractions typically used in price listings to decimals when calculating dollar amounts. For example, press Alt-P to increase the price by $1/16$. Or press Alt-W to decrease the price by $1/8$. You can use the Alt-key combinations in succession to increase or decrease a price by a fraction not listed. For example, to increase a price by $3/16$, press Alt-P three times.

> Enter the new prices for your assets.

> Highlight the Yield blank for each asset and type the new yield.

The yield is the return per share. You can find it listed on your brokerage statement or calculate it yourself.

> Press F6 and highlight the Special Codes blank. Then type any new codes that apply to each asset.

If you don't remember the meanings of your codes or if you want to change their meanings, press F5 to display the Special Codes screen. Press F9 to return to the Update Prices screen.

> Enter today's Dow Jones average in the blank between the information and action boxes.

You must record today's index in order to compare your asset's performance with the Dow Jones average.

> Press F1 to record the changes you made for all your assets. Or press F2 to update only the highlighted asset.

Note that it is only through the F1 and F2 keys on this screen that you can change asset prices throughout the chapter at one time. You can't change prices of assets individually while working with portfolios. If you did, you might find the same assets listed with different prices in different portfolios.

After you record the new prices, you can review the impact of the change on your assets. For example, if you are updating the price of GM stock, and it rose significantly, you may want to review how many shares you own and how the change in price has affected the total value of the stock.

> From the Update Prices screen, highlight the asset you want to review and press F4.

A new screen lists all lots of the asset you select—that is, all assets with the same symbol, regardless of portfolio. This screen shows the number of units of the asset in each portfolio, the purchase price, the total value based on the new price you entered, and the gain or loss. The screen also indicates whether it is a sold or a ''short'' asset. (See ''Selling Assets'' and ''Tracking 'Short' Assets'' later in this chapter.) You can return to the Update Prices screen by pressing F9, and then you can review another asset.

Changing Asset Symbols

Sometimes the symbol for an asset may change because of a stock merger or a change of company name. You can change this information on the Update Prices screen.

> Highlight the asset whose symbol you want to change. Then press F3.

A form for editing asset symbols appears. (See Figure 7-8.) It shows the current symbol for the asset you selected and a blank for the new symbol.

> Type the new symbol in the blank and press F1.

The new symbol is now recorded in all your portfolios.

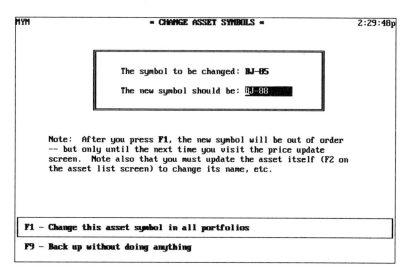

Figure 7-8. *The Change Asset Symbols screen.*

Updating an Asset   You may find it necessary to change the information about an asset. For example, if your estimate of an asset's yield changes from 10 percent to 12 percent, you can record this change for each lot of the asset throughout your portfolios.

Or if you determine that the risk level of Apple stock increased from moderate to high, you may want to change the risk level for your Apple stock in all your portfolios before you perform a risk analysis on your investments.

You can update information about an asset in one portfolio or in all your portfolios at the same time.

> From the Chapter 7 mini menu, press F3 to display your list of portfolios. Highlight the portfolio that contains the asset you want to update and press F1.

The list of unsold assets in the portfolio appears.

Highlight the asset you want to update and press F2. The program displays the form for updating an asset.

Highlight the blank you want to change and type the new information.

For example, to modify the risk level for Apple stock, highlight the Risk Level blank and type H.

Press F2 to record the change for all assets with the same symbol. Or press F1 to record it only for this asset.

Note that the F2 key does not change the units, date of purchase, original price, or commission throughout your portfolios because these figures may be different for each asset.

Transferring Assets Between Accounts

At some point, you may find it necessary to transfer assets from one account to another. For example, you may decide to change brokers and transfer one or all of your assets to the new broker.

From the Portfolio Accounts screen, press F5.

The Transfer Assets screen appears. (See Figure 7-9.) It lists your portfolios with a blank next to each.

Highlight the blank next to the portfolio from which you want to transfer the asset and type **F**. Then highlight the blank next to the portfolio to which you want to transfer it and type **T**.

Be sure you enter only one F and only one T on the screen.

Press F1 to display the assets in the FROM portfolio.

A complete list of the assets in the portfolio appears, with a blank next to each asset.

Type an **X** in the blank next to each asset you want to transfer.

Note that you can mark more than one asset.

Press F1 to transfer the assets.

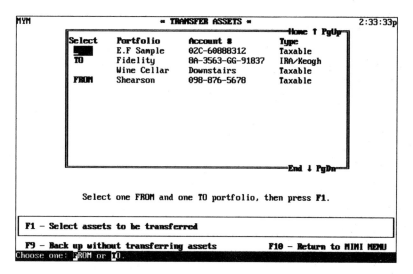

Figure 7-9. *The Transfer Assets screen.*

If you transferred all the assets out of a portfolio, you can delete the empty portfolio by pressing F3 at the Portfolio Accounts screen. You can press F8 to view the Rearrange Portfolios screen and rearrange the order of the portfolios in the list.

> Type **1** next to the portfolio you want listed first, **2** next to the second, and so on. Then press F1 to return to the Portfolio Accounts screen, where your assets are listed in the new order.

Recording Dividends

If you own stock, you most likely receive dividend checks in the mail. You can accept a dividend as cash or reinvest it in the same asset. When you buy a stock, mutual fund, or other asset, your broker asks you which you want to do. You need to indicate your answer in the program so that the dividend is recorded properly.

If you reinvest the earnings, the program displays the new stock as a separate holding in the list of unsold assets. The date you bought it is the date your dividend was issued. For example, if you receive a $100 dividend from General Motors (GM) and you automatically reinvest it, the stock appears on the unsold assets list as GM stock. The purchase price is the price on the day you bought it, calculated from the total dividend and the number of shares you bought. If you accept the dividend as cash, the program reminds you to enter the amount of cash as income in the budget and checkbook in Chapter 3. In either case, you record the dividend on the Unsold Assets screen.

Press F3 from the mini menu to view the Portfolio Assets screen.

Move the cursor to the desired portfolio and press F1.

Move the cursor to the asset paying a dividend and press F7. If you own more than one lot of the asset, it makes no difference which you highlight.

The program displays the Record Dividends and Interest screen. At the top, you can review the information about the asset—how many units you own, how much each unit was worth when you bought it, how long you've owned it, and how much it is worth now. Below this information are blanks for recording the dividend.

Highlight the Date blank and type the date you received the dividend. Then highlight the Amount blank and type the amount of the dividend.

Highlight the Status blank and type **I** if you received the cash directly; type **B** if the broker is holding the dividend for you; or type **A** if it is automatically reinvested.

If your dividend is automatically reinvested in more shares, you must tell the program the number of shares. This information is listed on your brokerage statement.

Highlight the New Shares Bought blank and type the number of shares.

Next you can enter information about capital gains, which can be found on your brokerage statement.

Highlight the Capital Gain blank and type the portion of this dividend to be recorded as a capital gain.

Information entered in the Capital Gain blank is also recorded in the Schedule D screen in Chapter 4.

Press F1 to record the dividend.

Reviewing Dividends

You can view a list of the year's recorded dividends by pressing F7 from the Chapter 7 mini menu. The Year's Dividends and Interest screen shows the asset symbol, date of dividend, total amount, the portion that is capital gain, the amount recorded on Schedule B, and the way the dividend was handled (received as cash, held by broker, or reinvested). You can then print the list by pressing F4 or sort it by highlighting the F7 blank, choosing one of the categories displayed, and pressing F7.

Selling Assets

Any asset in which you invest can either increase in value so much that you decide to sell some or all of it in order to cash in on your wise investment (known as ''profit taking''), or it can plunge so low that you sell it before it hits zero and you lose your entire investment (known as ''losing your shirt''). In either case, you must be sure to record the sale of your asset.

Highlight the asset you want to sell and press F5.

The screen that appears displays the initial purchase price and date of the stock, its latest price, and your loss or profit to date. Below, it lists three blanks for recording information about the sale of the asset. (See Figure 7-10 on the following page.)

Enter the sale date, price, and commission in the appropriate blanks.

This information should be included on the sell slip your broker sends when you make a transaction. Note that you can sell all units in the asset or only a portion of them. You can also sell all lots of this asset listed in this portfolio.

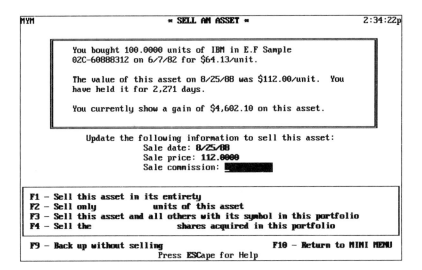

Figure 7-10. *The Sell an Asset screen.*

Press F1 to sell all of this asset. Or type the number of units you want to sell in the F2 blank and press F2 to sell only a portion of the asset. Press F3 to sell all of this asset as well as all assets with the same symbol in this account. Or fill in the F4 blanks and press F4 to sell a specific number of the oldest or newest shares of the stock.

When you press one of these four function keys, the program transfers the sold asset to the Sold Assets screen. You are not rid of the asset completely; the dividends you received before you sold it and the profit or loss from selling it both continue to influence your tax estimates for the remainder of the year. Even after you sell an asset, you can continue to work with it in the Sold Assets screen.

To display the sold assets, highlight the F6 blank on the Portfolio Assets screen, type **SO**, and then press F6.

You can move among the unsold, sold, and ''short'' assets by pressing F6. You can print a list of your sold assets by pressing F4. If you make a mistake when entering information about the sale, you can update the sold asset by pressing F2 to work with the Update a Sold Asset screen. Here you can make changes to the prices, commissions, or dates, and then press F1 to return to the Sold Assets screen.

Note that the F3 key deletes a sold asset. You will most likely use this key only when working with a hypothetical portfolio.

Tracking "Short" Assets

Selling short is a rather advanced investing technique in which you never really buy a stock or an asset—you borrow it from your broker and then sell it to someone else.

The reason you sell short is because you believe the price of the stock will go down. If it does, then the person to whom you sold the stock is forced to sell it back to you for less. You make a profit on the deal and return the borrowed stock to your broker.

If the price of the stock goes up, you must pay the person who bought your borrowed stock. And although you can lose only your original investment when you buy a stock, you can lose much more if you short a winning stock to someone. When the price of the stock rises, you must pay the difference.

> From the Unsold Assets screen, highlight the F6 blank and type **SH**. Then press F6 to display the Short Assets screen.

The Short Assets screen appears. (See Figure 7-11 on the following page.) Here you can add a short asset the same way you add an unsold asset.

> Press F1 to add a short asset.

The form for adding a short asset appears.

> Fill in the Short Assets form and press F1 to add the short asset.

The asset now appears in the list of short assets. You can track it the same way you track an asset in the Unsold Assets screen until you are ready to buy it back. Buying back a short asset is called "covering."

> To cover a short asset, highlight the asset you want to buy back and press F5.

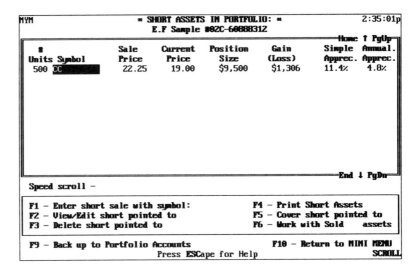

Figure 7-11. *The Short Assets screen.*

The program displays three blanks for the purchase date, price, and commission.

> Enter the purchase date, price, and commission in the appropriate blanks.

As in the case of selling assets, you can cover all the short asset or only part of it. If you have additional lots of this asset in the portfolio, you can cover them at the same time.

> Press F1 to cover the entire asset. Or type the number of units you want to cover in the F2 blank and press F2. Or press F3 to cover all lots of this asset in this portfolio.

The covered asset now appears in the Sold Portfolio Assets screen.

Tracking "Good-Until-Canceled" Orders

A "good-until-canceled" (GTC) order tells your broker to buy or sell a stock when it reaches a certain price. For example, suppose you see Apple stock dropping daily (as it did in 1985). You decide that if it ever gets as low as $13 a share, you definitely want to buy 100 shares.

Rather than check Apple stock each day, you call up your broker and place an order for 100 shares of Apple stock if and when it reaches $13. Your order is valid until you call to cancel it.

Now suppose that Apple hits $13 a share one day while you are in Hawaii. Your broker buys 100 shares on the basis of your GTC order. You then return from vacation and call your broker to place a new good-until-canceled order. This order says to sell Apple when it reaches $25. Again, your broker assumes you want to sell unless you call and cancel the order. If Apple reaches $25, your stock is sold automatically.

From the Portfolio Accounts screen, press F7.

The current list of good-until-canceled orders appears. (See Figure 7-12.) For each order, the program displays the number of units and the symbol. It shows whether the order is a buy or sell order and the price at which you want to buy or sell. It also has a new GTC Line for adding new orders.

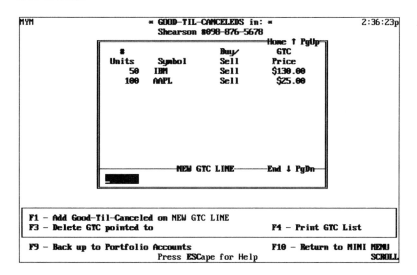

Figure 7-12. *The Good-Til-Canceled screen.*

In the New GTC Line, enter the number of units you want to buy or sell and the asset symbol in the first two blanks. In the Buy/Sell blank, type **B** for buy or **S** for sell. Then type the stock price and press F1.

The new order appears in the list. Unfortunately, this screen is only a list. It is not connected to the stock prices that you update, so no warning bells can alert you when one of your orders is actually executed. You have to rely on a report from your broker. You can, however, print your list of good-until-canceled orders by pressing F4. When an order has been executed, you can delete it from the list by highlighting it and pressing F3.

Recording Stock Splits

It is unusual to find a $200 stock on most stock exchanges. Stock prices don't climb that high because it becomes awkward to invest in such a stock; you could only buy five shares of a $200 stock with $1,000. When a stock's price rises to a point at which it is considered too expensive, the stock may be split. A split doesn't make your stock more valuable; you own twice as many shares of the stock (if it is split in half), but each share is worth only half of what it was worth before.

For example, if a company's stock is priced at $150 per share and you own 100 shares, it is worth $15,000. But if it splits 2 for 1, you own 200 shares of it at $75 a share—still worth $15,000. However, a split is an indication that the stock is doing well and is likely to continue rising.

You can record a stock split in Chapter 7's Stock Splits screen.

From the Chapter 7 mini menu, press F5.

A list of all asset symbols in all your portfolios appears on the screen. (See Figure 7-13.)

Highlight the asset for which you want to record a split and press F1.

The program displays a screen for specifying the way the stock is split. (See Figure 7-14.) The split must be recorded as a ratio. For example, if you receive two shares for every one you own, it is a 2-for-1 split. If you get four shares for every one, it is a 4-for-1 split.

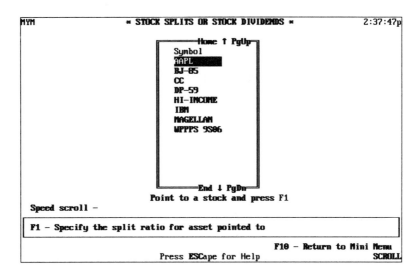

Figure 7-13. *The Stock Splits or Stock Dividends screen.*

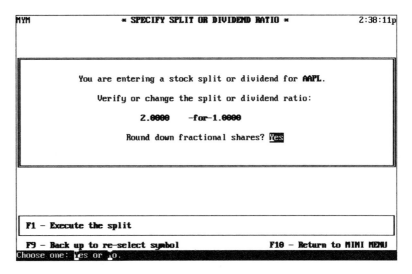

Figure 7-14. *Specifying a stock split.*

Type the ratio in the first two blanks.

The screen also asks if you want to round fractional shares to the lowest whole share. Usually you do, because shares are normally rounded down in stock splits.

Press F1 to record the split and return to the mini menu.

The split is then recorded for every lot of the stock recorded in your portfolios. If you record a 2-for-1 split, the price of the stock is halved, and the number of shares you own is doubled. If you want to check this change quickly, press F1 from the mini menu to display your list of stocks with the latest price.

USING FINANCIAL REMINDERS

In addition to keeping your records up-to-date, the portfolio manager in Chapter 7 can help you keep your investment decisions up-to-date. You can use financial reminders to help you track your assets. They alert you when an asset has reached either your price objective or the mental stop-loss price that you set when you first added the asset to your portfolio.

The financial reminders in Chapter 7 are much like the daily reminders in the Chapter 2 reminder pad; but unlike the daily reminders, financial reminders are generated automatically by the program.

For example, suppose you own stock in Apple Computer, and when you first added your Apple stock to the list of assets in your portfolio, you entered a mental stop-loss price of $30. When and if the Apple stock drops that low, you want at least to consider the idea of selling it.

Imagine that one day as you regularly update your stock prices, you update the price of Apple stock to 29¾. When you review your financial reminders, you will find one that lists all the Apple stock in all your portfolios and indicates, ''Below your Stop Loss of $30.00.''

Now suppose you entered a price objective of $50 for your Apple stock when you added it as a new asset. You update the prices regularly, and one day Apple stock reaches $51. When you review your financial reminders, a reminder lists your Apple stock with the message, "Reached your Objective of $50.00."

Viewing Financial Reminders

The best time to view your financial reminders is after you update asset prices, because one or more of the price changes might have triggered a reminder.

From the Chapter 7 mini menu, press F6 to display your financial reminders.

The Financial Reminders screen appears (See Figure 7-15.) Each reminder lists an asset symbol, the number of units you own, the asset's current price, and a message. You can review any asset in the Financial Reminders screen for more detailed information.

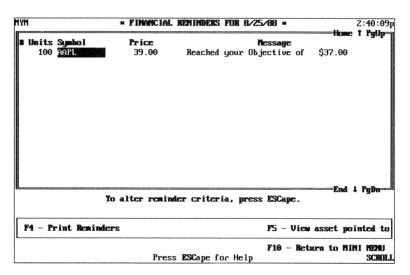

Figure 7-15. *The Financial Reminders screen.*

Highlight the asset you want to review and press F5.

The program displays the information you entered when you added or updated this asset. You cannot change the information in this screen, only review it.

Press F9 to return to the Financial Reminders screen.

Press F4 to print your list of financial reminders.

Changing the Reminder Criteria

You can modify financial reminder criteria to suit your portfolio in the Help screen for the Financial Reminders screen.

Press Escape to display the Help screen.

The Help screen displays three paragraphs with five blanks. (See Figure 7-16.) You form your financial reminders criteria by filling in these blanks.

```
║║║║║║     THIS IS A HELP SCREEN.  TO GET RID OF IT, JUST PRESS ESCAPE.  ║  2:40:36p

    If you've listed securities in this chapter, we'll automatically remind
    you when a position is within █5█ days of going long-term.  We won't
    bother reminding you if the gain or loss is less than $250.00  .  Also, we
    will Omit    assets in your hypothetical portfolios and Omit    assets in
    your IRA/Keogh portfolios.  (Type over any of these parameters to change
    them; enter "0" days if there is no capital gains holding period or you
    don't care to be reminded of it.)

    If you've specified price objectives for any of your stocks, we'll remind
    you when they've been met.  (Will you sell?  Or raise your objective, only
    to see the stock fall back to where you bought it?)  If you've entered
    mental stop losses, we'll remind you when they've been reached.  (Will you
    sell?  Or lower the stop loss, only to see .  .  .  )

    If you've used the proper options symbols (see page 132 of the Version 3
    manual, page 7-45 of the V4 manual or the page listed for "Options,
    Expiration" listed in the index of the V5 manual), we can deduce its
    expiration month.  We assume options expire the 3rd Friday of each month
    (as all currently do), and begin reminding you 20  days in advance
    thereof.
```

Figure 7-16. *The Financial Reminders Help screen.*

Don't change the value in the first blank.

Highlight the second blank and type the minimum gain or loss for which you want to be warned.

Highlight the third blank and type **I** if you want to include your hypothetical portfolios in your reminders or **O** if you want to omit them.

Highlight the fourth blank and type **I** to include your IRA/Keogh portfolios or **O** to omit them.

Because assets in IRA/Keogh portfolios are tax-free, the six-month mark doesn't have much bearing on how you manage them, but you can include them to track price objective and stop loss.

Highlight the fifth blank (near the bottom of the screen) and type how many days you want to be warned in advance of the expiration date of an option.

Press Escape to leave the Help screen.

Automatic Financial Reminders

When you leave Chapter 7 after using it for the first time that day, you are asked if you want to view the Financial Reminders screen.

Type **Y** if you want to see the screen or **N** if you don't.

I recommend that you answer ''No'' to this question. If you answer ''Yes,'' the Financial Reminders screen appears before you update the asset prices. It is more useful to view it after you update, because then the reminders should be based on today's prices, not those you entered the last time you worked with Chapter 7.

ADJUSTING FOR CHANGE IN THE CAPITAL-GAINS LAWS

The tax laws indicate that short-term and long-term capital gains are to be handled as regular income from 1988 onward. If the law changes, consult a good tax accountant and then modify the way Chapter 7 handles capital gains.

Press F8 from the Chapter 7 mini menu.

The single screen that appears lets you adjust for changes in the tax laws beginning at a time when short-term and long-term capital gains are handled differently than at present.

Change the values displayed to match the new laws. Then press F10 to save these changes and return to the mini menu.

ANALYZING YOUR PORTFOLIOS

Chapter 7 allows you to do much more than record information about your investments. The portfolio manager includes tools for analysis that can help you make better decisions about your investments. With these tools, you can analyze the overall risk profile of your investments, compare appreciation of various assets, and analyze your yield.

You can perform these analyses on all assets in all your portfolios or only on assets that you select according to criteria such as when you purchased them, their risk level, or their liquidity. The first step in analyzing your portfolios is to select the assets you want to analyze.

Setting Up the Analysis

To set up an analysis, you must tell the program which portfolios to analyze and which assets to analyze within those portfolios.

From the Chapter 7 mini menu, press F4 to analyze your portfolios.

The program lists your portfolios and asks you to select those that you want to include in the analysis. (See Figure 7-17.)

Type an **X** in the blank next to each portfolio you want to include in the analysis. Then press F1.

The Analyze Selected Portfolios screen appears, which lists criteria for selecting assets, including the acquisition date, risk level, yield, tax status, beta level, sold or unsold status, annual appreciation, liquidity, type of asset, industry group, and source that recommended them. (See Figure 7-18.)

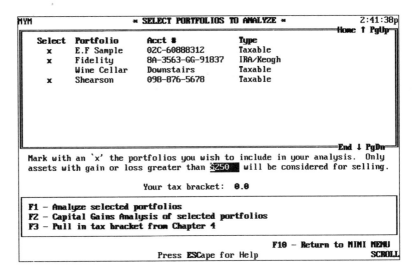

Figure 7-17. *The Select Portfolios to Analyze screen.*

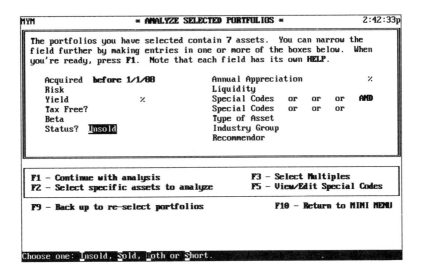

Figure 7-18. *The Analyze Selected Portfolios screen.*

You can also use one or more of the special codes that you set up as criteria for including an asset. The program then uses the information you provided when you first added an asset to determine whether or not the asset meets the criteria that you specify.

Enter the criteria you want to use in the appropriate blanks.

For example, if you want to analyze only high-risk assets, highlight the Risk blank and type **H** for "high." Only high-risk assets will be used for the subsequent analyses.

For the asset type, industry group, and recommendor criteria, you can include more than one category by typing **MUL** for "multiple." Then press F3 to display a list of choices. For example, if you want to include several types of assets, type **MUL** in the Type of Asset blank and then press F3 to display the types of assets. Then type an **X** next to each type you want to include in the analysis and press F1 to return to the Analyze Selected Portfolios screen.

If you want to specify the assets by symbol, press F2; the program lists the symbols for all your assets. You can type an **X** next to the ones you want to include and then press F1 to return to the information-retrieval screen. This approach is one of the most useful ways of analyzing an asset. Although it may be helpful to select assets by beta, yield, and liquidity, I find it best to look at one asset and review its progress. For example, if you want to analyze how IBM is doing, select all your portfolios, display the asset symbols, and type an X next to IBM. Then when you select an analysis option, all lots of IBM stock that you own are included in the analysis.

Using the special codes can be tricky. The two lines for special codes allow you to select assets that meet two different criteria. For example, if you type A in a blank on the first Special Code line and B in a blank on the second, the asset must be marked with both code A and code B to be included in the analysis. If you type several codes in the first line only, any asset that is marked with any one of these codes is then included in the analysis. If you need to review your list of special codes, press F5.

Note that if you want to include all assets in the selected portfolios, you should leave all blanks empty.

> Press F1 from the Analyze Selected Portfolios screen to display a preliminary report.

The program selects the assets that meet your criteria and displays a preliminary report on the Analysis of Selected Assets screen. (See Figure 7-19.) Included in this report are the number of assets that meet all your criteria and their total value. These assets represent a percentage of your selected portfolio (or portfolios), and the preliminary report indicates that percentage. It gives the total gain or loss for the selected assets as well as their weighted average beta value. It also shows the distribution by risk of the selected assets. You can now analyze the assets you have selected in more detail.

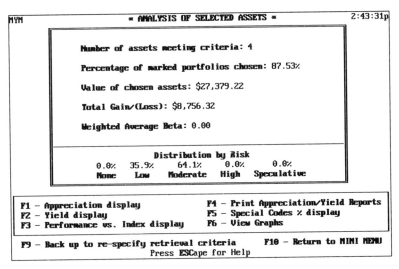

Figure 7-19. *The Analysis of Selected Assets screen.*

**Graphing
Characteristics
of Assets**

The simplest analysis you can perform is to graph characteristics such as risk, tax status, liquidity, industry group, recommendor, and type of asset. The program graphs this information in a series of six pie charts.

From the Analysis of Selected Assets screen, press F6 to display the graph options.

The six graph options are represented by six function keys, F1 through F6. (See Figure 7-20.)

Press the function key that corresponds to the type of graph you want to produce.

For example, suppose you want to graph the risk associated with your selected assets. Press F1, and a pie chart appears. (See Figure 7-21.) It shows the distribution of your selected assets across risk categories. One slice might be labeled ''Low 35.9%'' and another ''Moderate 64.1%.''

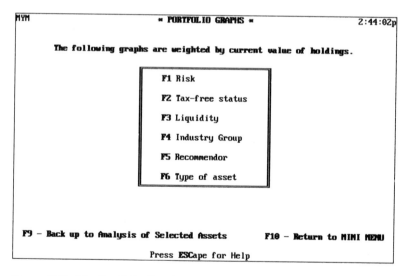

Figure 7-20. *The Portfolio Graphs screen.*

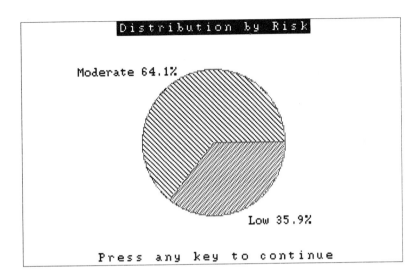

Figure 7-21. *Graph of selected assets by risk categories.*

The pie slices for these graphs are based on how much the assets are currently worth. So if you own highly speculative mining stock and its worth accounts for 80 percent of the value of the selected assets, the pie chart has a large pie slice labeled "Speculative 80%."

To display another graph, press any key to return to the Portfolio Graphs screen. Then press the function key for the next graph you want to create.

Press F9 to return to the Analysis of Selected Assets screen.

Calculating Appreciation

Appreciation is the amount an asset has increased or decreased in price from the time you bought it to the present. You can display the total value, gain or loss, and annual appreciation for each of the assets you select, as well as the totals for all of those assets combined.

From the Analysis of Selected Assets screen, press F1 to display the appreciation analysis.

The Appreciation Display screen is much like the list of unsold assets, but it differs in two ways: It displays the appreciation information only for those assets you selected, and it also computes and displays the totals for all selected assets. If you want to review information about one of the assets, you can highlight the asset and press F4.

Analyzing Yield

Yield is the annual dollar amount you receive in interest or dividends. After you select assets you want to analyze, you can display the yield per share, the total yield for an asset, and the yield as a percentage of the total price per share. You can also display an asset's total return.

From the Analysis of Selected Assets screen, press F2 to display the yield analysis.

The Yield Display screen lists the assets you selected, the portfolio to which they belong, and the date you purchased them, with four columns of information about yields. The "Yield" column shows how much dividend or interest is paid per share of stock. (You enter this figure when you add or update an asset.)

In the "Total" column, the per-share figure in the "Yield" column is multiplied by the number of shares you own to display how much you earned from an asset's yield. So if you own 50 shares of Procter & Gamble and that stock pays a $2.60 dividend, the total yield is $130.

The "%" column shows the per-share yield as a percentage of the total per-share stock price. So if General Motors pays a $1 dividend and its stock price is $100 per share, the "%" column shows 1.0%, because $1 is 1 percent of $100.

The total return is a complex figure. It combines the amount you earned on the asset's annualized appreciation plus the amount you earned on yield, and then it shows this combined value as a percentage of the original investment. The total amount of money yielded by the selected assets and the yield as a percentage of the total asset prices are shown at the bottom of the information box.

Now you can analyze the yield further by displaying a summary analysis.

Press F4 to display the Yield Summary Analysis screen.

The summary analysis shows how the total yield from the assets you selected is distributed across tax categories, risk categories, and types of assets. It also indicates how much this yield is worth to you, based on your income-tax bracket. (The tax bracket is determined in Chapter 4, and you can change it there if it is not correct.)

Press F9 to return to the Yield Display screen.

Displaying an Aggregate Analysis

After you perform an aggregate analysis, you cannot return to the yield or appreciation analyses or print them, and you also cannot graph your selected assets. If you want to work with the same set of assets after you display an aggregate analysis, you must start again by setting up a new analysis and reselecting the assets.

The aggregate analysis combines separate purchases of the same asset. So if you have GM stock in three different lots listed in two separate portfolios, the aggregate analysis displays your total holdings of GM.

From the Yield Display screen, press F2 to display the aggregate analysis.

The aggregate analysis shows the total value of each asset, that is, the number of shares of that asset multiplied by the price. It also shows the total yield from each aggregate asset and the total gain or loss, including yield.

The last column in the display shows the value of each aggregate asset as a percentage of the total value of the portfolio from which it came. (Note that this is not the percentage of the selected assets, so the numbers don't add up to 100 percent.) The combined totals and averages for all assets appear at the bottom of the screen.

Printing Appreciation, Yield, and Aggregate Analyses

You can print the appreciation and yield analyses before you display an aggregate analysis, and you can print the aggregate analysis after it is displayed.

To print the appreciation or yield analysis, press F4 from the Analysis of Selected Assets screen.

To print the aggregate analysis, press F2 from the Yield Display screen, and then press F4 from the Aggregation Display screen.

Press F9 to return to the Select Portfolios to Analyze screen.

Analyzing Performance Versus Index

You can now take advantage of the Dow Jones information you entered in the chapter.

From the Select Portfolios to Analyze screen, press F1.

Press F1 again to select assets based on selection criteria.

Press F3 to view the Performance Versus Index Display screen.

Listed on this screen are all the assets you updated with the Dow Jones index, along with their appreciations and purchase prices. The program compares the prices and appreciations for the asset against the index.

For example, suppose you bought a stock at $18.25 when the market was at 1800, and the price didn't change but the market went up to 2000. Compared to the index, the stock's simple appreciation is now a negative 11 percent because the rest of the market left it behind. You can also compare the asset and the index for purchase price and annual appreciation and view the totals at the bottom of the screen.

Press F10 to return to the mini menu.

Analyzing Capital Gains

Capital gains are the amounts you earn or lose whenever you sell an asset. They can make a big difference in your tax bill at the end of the year. The capital-gains analysis in Chapter 7 can help you to understand how they are likely to affect your tax bill so that you can make better decisions about when to sell an asset.

Before you analyze your capital-gains position, however, remember that you won't know how your tax bill is shaping up until the third or fourth quarter of the year, when the capital gains and losses on all your year's investments become apparent. Although it may look like a lean income year in April, you may sign a lucrative movie deal with MGM in November.

In autumn, when you do start to consider capital gains, press F4 from the Chapter 7 mini menu to start the analysis portion of the portfolio manager. Setting up a capital-gains analysis is a little different from setting up the other analyses in this chapter.

> On the Select Portfolios to Analyze screen, type an **X** next to the portfolios you want to include in the analysis.

> Press F2 to display the Capital Gains Analysis screen.

The Capital Gains Analysis screen lists the gains you have realized so far as well as unrealized gains. (See Figure 7-22.) Here you can record losses carried forward and other gains and losses before you analyze your capital-gains position.

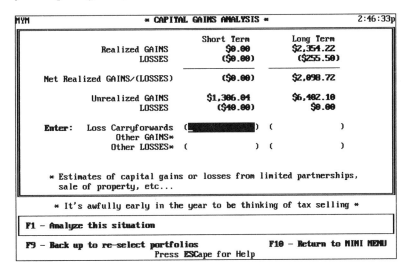

Figure 7-22. *The Capital Gains Analysis screen.*

Realized gains represent money that you actually received as a result of selling your assets this year. Losses represent the money you lost when you sold an asset for less than the amount for which you bought it. This information is entered automatically from the Sold Assets screen. When you subtract losses from gains, the balance is the net realized gains.

Unrealized gains and losses represent the money that you would gain (or lose) if you sold the assets you now hold. This set of figures helps you decide what to sell, considering your gains and losses to date. If the realized capital gains for this year are very high or very low, you can use the profits or losses from the as-yet-unrealized gains to offset them. The unrealized gains for the assets you selected are entered automatically from information in the Unsold Assets screen.

It may be necessary to carry forward a loss from the previous year. If you have more than $3,000 in capital losses in a year, you must carry forward the amount in excess of $3,000 to the next year. Because Managing Your Money works with only a year's worth of data at a time, you must enter any amount to be carried forward by hand.

You should also include other miscellaneous gains and losses in this analysis. For example, if you lost money on the sale of your cabin cruiser, you would enter the loss in one of the Other Gains or Other Losses blanks.

Press F1 to analyze your capital-gains position.

The program displays a simple paragraph analysis of your capital-gains position. It explains how your taxes will be affected by the gains and losses you've recorded so far. For example, if you have $1,000 in losses this year and you are in the 33 percent tax bracket, the program indicates that you achieve a tax savings.

Press F1 again for advice on your capital-gains position.

Sometimes the best strategy is to maximize your losses, and sometimes the best strategy is to do nothing. Tobias offers advice for all the different scenarios you can describe in the Capital Gains Analysis screen. Experiment with different scenarios and test Tobias's advice.

> Press F1 again to see a list of assets you could sell to change your capital-gains position.

The Selling and Covering Candidates screen shows a list of assets you might want to consider selling in order to change your capital-gains position.

> Select the assets you want to consider selling by typing an **X** next to those assets and then press F1.

The program indicates how selling these assets can change the way you are taxed on your overall capital gains.

> Press F1 to return to the original screen. Or press F2 to select a new combination of selling candidates.

Note that capital-gains scenarios alone probably aren't reason enough to sell an asset. Consider that you specified a minimum loss or gain when you began the analysis. Also, before you sell for tax reasons, be sure that other market factors, such as market price and the economy in general, are also right for the sale of the asset in question.

> Press F10 to return to the mini menu.

Analyzing Commissions

Brokers (or financial consultants, as some firms now call them) are salespeople. Each time they sell an investment, they take a commission off the top. If your broker's commission is 10 percent, your investment has to earn 10 percent back before it starts to become profitable for you. So the image of a high-powered investor with a phone in each ear shouting "Sell!" and "Buy!" into both phones is not very realistic because anyone who trades that much that fast can probably never pay the broker's commission and still make a profit.

One solution to the problem of high commissions is the discount brokerage firm. Discount brokers don't really employ brokers; they employ people who take your buy and sell orders. You pay a much lower commission when you use a discount broker because you're not paying for a full-service broker's advice.

Some people use only a full-service broker or only a discount broker. Some use both. Either way, you can get an instantaneous calculation of the commissions you've paid so far this year on any portfolio with the commission analysis in Chapter 7. The commission analysis is a simple but important analysis that you can perform from the Portfolio Accounts screen.

> From the Chapter 7 mini menu, press F3 to display the Portfolio Accounts screen.

To set up a commission analysis, simply select the portfolio you want to analyze.

> Highlight the portfolio you want to analyze and press F6.

The Commission Analysis screen appears and indicates how many trades you made in the selected portfolio and how much money you paid for commissions and sales fees. (See Figure 7-23.) Then it estimates how much less a discount broker would charge you for the same number of trades.

Of course, the quality of this analysis depends entirely on how accurately and religiously you enter brokerage fees when you add an asset to the Unsold Assets screen or when you sell an asset. The program adds those fees and then reduces the total by a percentage to arrive at a possible discount brokerage fee.

To add or edit commissions information in the selected portfolio, press F1. The Quick Edit Commissions screen appears.

> Press F10 to return to the mini menu.

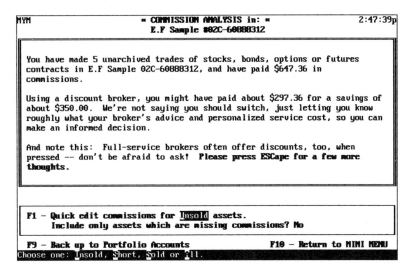

Figure 7-23. *The Commission Analysis screen.*

MANAGING THE MARKET

For most users of Managing Your Money, the portfolio management strategies described in this chapter are adequate. But if you are a very sophisticated investor who needs up-to-the-minute information about stock prices, you may want to consider buying another program from MECA called Managing the Market.

Managing the Market is an add-on program for Managing Your Money. If you have a modem, you can use it to call up the Dow Jones News/Retrieval service, retrieve stock price information, and automatically update the prices in your Chapter 7 portfolios. You also need more than 256 KB of memory to run Managing the Market from Managing Your Money.

Managing the Market saves the time you might spend looking up prices in the newspaper, typing updated stock prices for each asset, and learning the esoteric commands necessary to navigate the Dow Jones service. It also saves you the expense of on-line charges that you pay while you learn the Dow Jones service.

Quotes from the Dow Jones service are only about 20 minutes old, whereas those you find on the newspaper financial page may be 12 hours old. It's up to you to decide if the cost of the Dow Jones service and Managing the Market justify this 11-hour-and-40-minute time savings.

Running
Managing
the Market

You can access Managing the Market from Chapter 7. By pressing F2 at the Chapter 7 mini menu, you can jump right into Managing the Market, call up Dow Jones, update stock prices, and return to Chapter 7 to analyze the new information.

This function works best if you have a hard disk. If you have a two-floppy system, you can still run Managing the Market from Chapter 7, but you need to switch disks, which can be inconvenient.

To get Managing the Market running, you need to copy all the Managing the Market files into your Managing Your Money subdirectory.

Press Ctrl-D from the Chapter 7 mini menu.

Insert your Managing the Market disk in drive A and type
COPY A:*.* C:\MYM from the DOS prompt.

Type **EXIT** at the DOS prompt to return to Managing Your Money.

Press F2 to run Managing the Market.

Press F2 from the Managing the Market screen.

You are sent first to the Managing the Market System Setup screen. Fill in the blanks in this screen to set up the automatic dialing and logon procedures for Managing the Market.

Highlight the News/Retrieval Password blank and type your password.

When you open an account with Dow Jones, you are assigned a password. Enter this password here.

Highlight the Name of the Modem blank and type the code for the modem your computer is using.

Chances are that you will use the code for the Hayes Smartmodem, because most modems these days adhere to the Hayes standard. If you don't have a Hayes, type **O** for other.

> Highlight the Baud Rate blank and type the baud rate.

Most modems communicate at 1200 bits of information per second, known as the baud rate. Type **300** if you communicate at 300 baud.

> Highlight the Communications Port blank and type the code for the port you are using.

Your modem is most likely connected to the first communication port, but if a printer or mouse is connected to your first port, type **2** in this blank.

> Highlight the Type of Monitor blank and type the code for color or black and white.

This choice sets the screen colors for Managing the Market.

> Highlight the first Phone Number blank and type the telephone number and the name of the network you want to use. Then highlight the second Phone Number blank and type your second choice.

Two common networks are Tymnet and Telenet, but MCI, Sprint, and AT&T also offer long-distance computer networks. Most likely, you will want to enter the least expensive network as your first choice and a more expensive network as your second. When you tell Managing the Market to call Dow Jones, it tries the first number three times and then moves on to the second. After three attempts, it goes back to the first, and repeats the process until it connects.

> Press F10 to return to the Chapter 7 mini menu.

Your settings are saved. You can now call Dow Jones simply by choosing an option from the Chapter 7 mini menu.

Press F2 from the Chapter 7 mini menu.

Select the portfolios you want to update by pressing F1 and typing an **X** in the blank next to each portfolio you want to update.

The program updates all the assets in each portfolio you select. If you have the same stock in two different portfolios and you select only one portfolio for updating, the program automatically updates both portfolios.

You can select all portfolios from this screen by pressing F2, or you can clear all existing selections by pressing F3.

Press F1 to call the Dow Jones service.

When you press F1, Managing the Market calls the Dow Jones service, retrieves the prices, and inserts them in all the selected portfolios.

Creating "Hot Lists"

With Managing the Market, you can create a "hot list," which is a list of stocks you want to track on a regular basis. A hot list may include some stocks that you have in your portfolio, but a hot list's purpose is not to update your portfolios. Instead, it provides a quick way to find the most current prices for any stocks that interest you.

You can create up to three hot lists, each with up to 75 assets. So you can track as many as 225 assets with only a few keystrokes, and you can update the prices in this list automatically by calling the Dow Jones service.

Press F2 from the Chapter 7 mini menu. Then press F2 to go to the Managing the Market menu.

Press F3 from the Managing the Market menu to create your hot list.

If you are using Managing the Market for the first time, the program displays the Create or Edit Hot List screen, which is a grid of blanks in which you enter asset symbols and define the type of asset.

Highlight the first blank on the screen and type the name of the hot list.

Press F10 to name the hot list.

The next time you press F3 from the Managing the Market menu, the name of this hot list appears on the Hot List screen.

Highlight the first Symbol blank and type the exact symbol used on the stock exchange. Then highlight the Type blank and type the code for the type of investment instrument.

The program gives you a choice of five instrument types: stocks, options, bonds, treasuries, and mutual funds. You can enter symbols and types for up to 75 assets.

Press F10 to return to the Managing the Market menu. Then press F3 to display the hot lists.

When you press F3, the program displays a list of your hot lists. If you have created only one, you can create another by pressing F1. Or you can edit your existing list by pressing F2.

Type an **X** next to each hot list you want to price and press F3 to update the prices.

Press F10 at the Managing the Market menu to return to the Chapter 7 mini menu.

The price information is updated throughout the chapter.

CHAPTER 8

MANAGING YOUR NET WORTH

*Now that you've entered a year's worth of checks, ana-
lyzed your stock portfolio, created a list of insurance
policies, and planned your retirement, you can combine
all this information and determine your net worth. Net
worth equals the value of all your assets minus the value
of all your debts. To determine your net worth, you create
balance sheet that lists your possessions, investments,*

cash, and debts. Managing Your Money uses information from other chapters to create a preliminary list of your assets and liabilities. For example, if you maintain an up-to-date record of the cash in your checking and savings accounts in Chapter 3, Managing Your Money automatically collects the balances from all your Chapter 3 accounts and enters them in your list of assets. It also compiles the asset and liability information from Chapters 3, 5, 6, and 7 to add to the balance sheet. You can then enter manually other assets, such as furniture, stereo equipment, or stamp collections.

You can print your balance sheet and present it to a loan officer if you're requesting a loan, or to an insurance company in case of a fire or burglary. You can also graph your lists of assets and liabilities to show exactly where your wealth lies.

CREATING A BALANCE SHEET

Think of the balance sheet in Chapter 8 as a pyramid. The top is your net worth, computed from your assets and liabilities. If you want to view your total assets and total liabilities, you move down to the next level on the pyramid. If you want to see the individual assets or individual liabilities used to compute those totals, you move down still another level.

When you start adding assets and liabilities manually, you can add many more levels to the pyramid. For example, under assets, you may add an item called "Inventory of Possessions." This inventory represents the total value of items listed at the next lower level—such as your house and automobile. Your house, in turn, may represent the total value of items you list at a still lower level. For example, you may list the value of your living room separately from the value of your bedroom or kitchen. Finally, the value of each room may represent the combined value of all the items in the room, listed individually at a level lowest of all.

So your balance sheet is really a series of lists of assets and liabilities, each of which is totaled as a single value in another list, until you get to the single total of assets and liabilities, which is your net worth.

An item in a list may be an extract item, an individual item, or an aggregate item. An extract item is one that the program adds automatically, using information from the other chapters. An aggregate item is one with a value that is calculated from several items at the next level down. For example, you may list your living room as an aggregate item, since its value is calculated from the value of items such as your couch, coffee table, and other furnishings. An individual item is one whose value is not calculated by totaling any other items. In other words, it has no levels below it.

To create your balance sheet you must first tell the program to extract the information from Chapters 3, 5, 6, and 7 to create the backbone of your balance sheet, and then you must add any other assets or liabilities one at a time. If you are using the program for the first time, remember to clear the existing balance sheet of the sample data.

> From the Main menu, press F8 to enter Chapter 8.

The program displays the Net Worth screen. (See Figure 8-1.) It is the top level of the pyramid and the bottom line of your balance sheet.

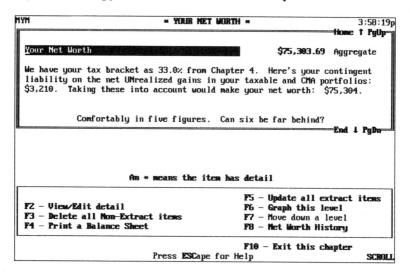

Figure 8-1. *The Net Worth screen.*

> To erase the existing data from the balance sheet, press F3, and then press F1 to confirm.

The F3 key is labeled "Delete all Non-Extract items," which means it will delete all items except the extract items that the program enters automatically from the other chapters. You can't delete extract items, but you can change them.

Extracting Assets and Liabilities

The balance sheet shows several asset and liability categories for which the program can extract the current values from your data in Chapters 3, 5, 6, and 7. The table in Figure 8-2 lists all these built-in assets and liabilities and indicates the chapters from which each value came. You can extract values for these assets and liabilities individually or all at one time.

> To extract all your assets and liabilities at once, press F5 from the Initial Net Worth screen.

The program now computes any necessary totals from the other chapters and enters the values for each asset or liability.

Assets	*Liabilities*
Checking accounts and cash (3)	Balance on mortgages (3)
Savings and money-market accounts (3)	Balance on auto loans (3)
Accounts receivable (3)	Balance on credit cards (3)
Loans I own (3)	Balance on education loans (3)
Insurance cash value (5)	Balance on personal loans (3)
Pension/profit-sharing plans (6)	Balance on other loans (3)
Portfolio cash (7)	Accounts payable (3)
Marketable securities (7)	Margin debt (7)
Unrealized gains on shorts (7)	Unrealized losses on shorts (7)
Bonds (7)	
Savings bonds/SPDAs (7)	
IRA/Keogh portfolios (7)	
Metals and collectibles (7)	
Real estate (7)	
Tax shelter (7)	

Figure 8-2. *Assets and liabilities with chapter locations.*

> From the initial Net Worth screen, press F7 to move down a level to the asset and liability totals.

The asset and liability totals appear on the Net Worth screen. (See Figure 8-3.)

> Highlight the Assets line and press F7 again to display the extracted values.

The list of assets appears on the Net Worth screen. (See Figure 8-4 on the following page.) After you add new information in the other chapters, you can update the extract items individually.

> Highlight the extract item you want to update and press F5.

The program extracts the most up-to-date information from the appropriate chapter, enters it in the Value blank, and recalculates your balance sheet.

If you did not enter necessary information in earlier chapters, the program leaves the Value blank empty. You can type the exact amount or

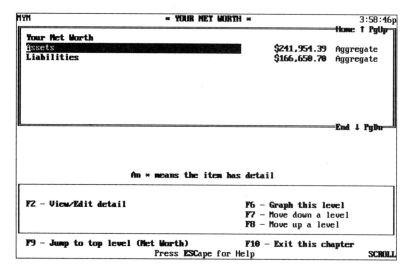

Figure 8-3. *Asset and Liability totals.*

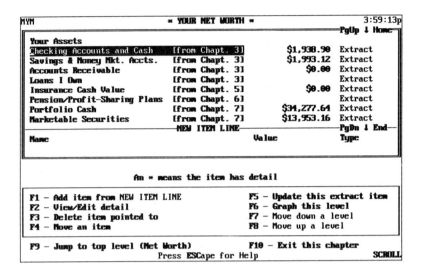

Figure 8-4. *The list of assets.*

your estimate directly in the Value blank. Note that if the program extracts a value from another chapter, you can change it here, but the value in the other chapter will not change.

Deleting Items

After you pass the first two Net Worth screens, you can delete certain items from your balance sheet. Note that you can't delete extract items because the program draws them from other chapters. You also can't delete an aggregate item until you delete its subordinates. You must first press F7 to move down a level and delete the subordinate items and then return to the aggregate item by pressing F8.

Position the cursor over the item and press F3 to delete it.

Adding Assets and Liabilities Manually

Although the values that the program extracts from other chapters form the backbone of your balance sheet, you most likely have many assets and liabilities that are not recorded in any of the chapters. You can add these additional assets and liabilities manually.

After you pass the first two Net Worth screens, you can add asset or liability items using the New Item Line.

Highlight the Name blank in the New Item Line and type the name of the
item you want to add.

For example, suppose you want to create a balance-sheet item called
"Automobiles." Type Automobiles in the Name blank. Then you
must decide whether this item is an aggregate item or an individual
item. If it's an aggregate item, you don't enter a value for it; the value
is computed automatically from a subordinate list. If it's an individual
item, you simply enter the value; no further computation is necessary.

If the new item is an aggregate item, leave the Value blank empty and
type **A** in the Type blank. If it is an individual item, type the value in the
Value blank and type **I** in the Type blank.

Suppose you own two automobiles. In this case, the "Automobiles"
item in your list of assets should be an aggregate item.

Press F1 to add the new item to the list.

The new item appears in the list. If it's an aggregate item, you must
continue to the next level and add the items that determine the value of
this new item. For example, in the case of your automobiles, you must
add an item for each automobile you own.

Highlight the aggregate item and press F7 to view the next level.

You can add a new item here exactly as you did at the previous level. If
you own a Chevy and a Toyota, add a new item for each of them.

Press F8 to return to the previous level, or press F9 to return to the initial
Net Worth screen.

The program automatically tallies the impact of the new assets. In the
automobile example, the value of the two automobiles is calculated and
displayed in the blank for the "Automobiles" item. The program also
adds this value to your assets and displays the new value in the Assets
blank, and the initial Net Worth screen displays your new net worth.

When you list your valuable possessions in this way, you create the kind of list your insurance company will want if you make a claim. In the event of a fire or theft, this list of possessions may help prove that you once owned the things you say you did. You may also want to include in the list serial numbers of high-ticket items such as computers, compact-disc players, and videocassette recorders.

CREATING GRAPHS AND PRINTOUTS

Now that all your assets and liabilities are in one place, you can graph their value or print a list of them. Graphs can give you an overall view of your financial position and help you determine where your money is. Printouts can help you get financial advice or monetary assistance.

Graphing Assets and Liabilities

If your computer has graphics capability, you can produce a pie chart for any aggregate item in your balance sheet except your net worth. This pie chart graphs all the items that make up the aggregate item to display how your wealth—or your debt—is distributed.

> Highlight the item you want to graph and press F7 to display the list of subordinate items.

For example, suppose you want to graph your assets.

> From the initial Net Worth screen, press F7 to view your list of assets and liabilities. Then highlight the Assets blank and press F7 again to display the list of assets.

> Press F6 to graph the list of items.

The program creates a pie chart representing the items on the list. (See Figure 8-5.) For example, if you graph the list of assets, the pie chart shows each asset as a slice of the pie chart. If most of your assets lie in your household goods, that slice is the biggest.

You can create pie charts for other aggregate items as well. For example, you can graph the assets listed under "House" to determine

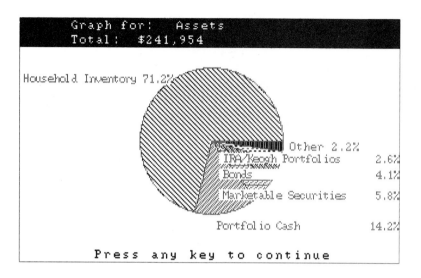

Figure 8-5. *A sample graph of assets.*

your most expensive room. You may be surprised to see where most of your assets and liabilities—the biggest slices of the pies—really are.

Printing Your Balance Sheet

If you ever applied for a bank loan, you know that you must sit with a loan officer and answer questions about all your debts, investments, and savings. The loan officer takes down your answers and then checks your credit.

The printed balance sheet that you produce with Chapter 8 of Managing Your Money is essentially the same balance sheet that the loan officer creates. (See ''The Balance Sheet'' on the following page.) Creating your own balance sheet can save you time with the loan officer but is also useful in other ways. It's a handy way to encapsulate all your investments for your own personal files. And if you ever hire a financial planner to help you decide which stocks to buy, you can bring a printout instead of paying your adviser $75 to $100 per hour to interview you about your investments. This way, you can spend that money being advised about where to invest next.

THE BALANCE SHEET

The personal balance sheet that you prepare in Chapter 8 shows your net worth—your total assets minus your total liabilities. It also lists all your assets and liabilities. The following is an example of a balance sheet that lists major asset categories and details significant personal possessions.

```
Net Worth                                     $75,303.69
    Assets                                   $241,954.39
        Checking Accounts and Cash   [from Chapt. 3]    $1,938.90
        Savings & Money Mkt. Accts.  [from Chapt. 3]    $1,993.12
        Portfolio Cash               [from Chapt. 7]   $34,277.64
        Marketable Securities        [from Chapt. 7]   $13,953.16
        Unrealized Gains on Shorts   [from Chapt. 7]    $1,306.04
        Bonds                        [from Chapt. 7]    $9,825.00
        IRA/Keogh Portfolios         [from Chapt. 7]    $6,354.22
        Household Inventory                            $172,306.31
            Living Room set and Stereo (boom box)         $600.00
            Kitchen                                       $186.86
                Super Griddle                              $80.00
                1943 Kelvinator "Frosty" Refrig. #218097-43 $93.91
                    Three cans, Hunt's tomato paste          $1.89
                    Four Woolworth ice trays                 $2.89
                    18 Harry and David miracle grapefruit   $18.00
                    Sam's medication (the big pink ones)    $24.50
                    Sally's medication (the little yellow ones) $16.78
                    Sid's pastrami sandwich                  $1.85
                    Sarsaparilla - 2 cases                  $28.00
                    The cat, til we find a final place for her $0.00
                Rival popcorn popper                       $12.95
            Study                                      $8,764.50
                IBM AT with quadram board   #12-09384   $1,500.00
                Hazeltine 1500 dumb terminal #45-9283-001  $25.00
                File cabinets (seven, suspension)         $750.00
                Horseshoe teak desk                     $1,500.00
                Reference books                           $250.00
                Office TV                                 $189.50
                Hayes 1200 Smart Modem #9834589457        $250.00
                Convertible sofa, 4 office chairs         $700.00
                Xerox copier  #1203494C                 $1,100.00
                Office carpet (wool)                    $1,200.00
                Kroy Type lettering machine  #834748290   $600.00
                Sony recorders/transcriber; Pearlcorder   $600.00
                Telephone equipment                       $100.00
            Basement                                       $54.95
                Hammer                                     $15.00
                Sickle                                     $39.95
            Bedrooms                                   $17,700.00
                Kids' beds                                $500.00
                Small TV                                  $125.00
                Clothing                                $2,000.00
                Antique bureau                         $15,075.00
                    Socks                                  $50.00
                    Underwear                              $25.00
                    Sara's uninsured diamond tiara     $15,000.00
        Vehicles                                      $20,000.00
        The House                                    $125,000.00
    Liabilities                                      $166,650.70
        Balance on Mortgages         [from Chapt. 3]  $134,944.89
        Balance on Auto Loans        [from Chapt. 3]    $1,973.74
        Balance on Credit Cards      [from Chapt. 3]      $457.50
        Balance on Education Loans   [from Chapt. 3]    $4,274.57
        Other                                         $25,000.00
            Contingent liabilities                    $20,000.00
            Estimated tax due for 1987 audit, when done $5,000.00
```

From the initial Net Worth screen, press F4 to print your balance sheet.

The Print a Balance Sheet screen appears. Position the cursor in the Type of Report blank.

You can print your balance sheet in several different formats. You can include all levels of an outline format by typing **A** in the Type of Report blank. You can limit the levels of detail in the outline by typing **1**, **2**, **3**, or **4**. These numbers indicate the level of balance-sheet detail your printout will contain. You can produce a simple balance sheet with only a listing of basic assets and liabilities by typing **1**. You can type **B** for a bank-style format, which arranges your assets and liabilities in two adjacent grids in an extra-wide format. (With this format, you will need to use the compressed-print mode or use a wide-carriage printer.) Or you can type **C** for a corporate format, which is similar to the bank-style format but has the grids placed one under the other instead of side by side.

Press F1 to print the balance sheet in the format you selected.

Tracking Your Net-Worth History

If you use Chapter 8 frequently, you can keep a history of your net worth as it increases or decreases.

Press F8 from the initial Net Worth screen.

You can add today's net-worth total to the Net Worth History screen by pressing F1. The program lists today's date, assets, liabilities, and total net worth. This entry on its own is of little use, but as you add net-worth entries on days in the future, you'll create an entire list of net-worth balances over time. (See Figure 8-6 on the following page.)

After you enter two or three net-worth totals, you can press F6 to graph your net-worth history, which helps you determine the likely direction of your future net worth. You can also print your net-worth history by pressing F4 or delete your net-worth history by pressing F3.

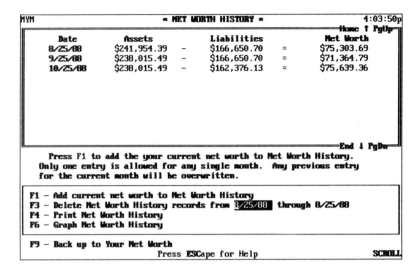

Figure 8-6. *The Net Worth History screen.*

**Adding Detail
with Write
on the Money**

You can use Write on the Money's pop-up feature to attach a note to any net-worth item. (See "Write on the Money" in Chapter 1.)

Position the cursor over any item on any net-worth screen and press F2.

Write on the Money pops up to let you write notes about the item. You might attach a note to the "Automobile" item to record the mileage, insurance information, and other details about your cars. Note that if you enter numeric information in a pop-up note, it will not be transferred and reflected on your Net Worth screens.

Press F2 to leave Write on the Money.

After you leave Write on the Money and view the Net Worth screen again, the net-worth item will show an asterisk, which indicates that a note is attached to the item.

You can view the note attached to an item by highlighting the item and pressing F2.

MANAGING YOUR CARD FILE

If you work in an office, you probably have a card file or a Rolodex on your desk. At home, you may be less organized. Telephone numbers may be recorded anywhere, from the backs of envelopes to a misplaced address book.

Chapter 9 of Managing Your Money, the electronic card file, can help you become as organized at home as you are at the office—perhaps even more organized. The card file can not only organize phone numbers and addresses, it can track birth and anniversary dates by sending information to Chapter 2, where the reminder pad will alert you to upcoming dates.

You can use the program to dial a telephone number with a Hayes-compatible auto-dialing modem. You can print mailing labels, phone and address lists, and separate information lists of friends, relatives, and business associates. You can also create form letters using Write on the Money.

SETTING UP YOUR CARD FILE

To begin the organization, you must first set up the card file.

From the Main menu, press F9 to enter Chapter 9.

The Card File screen appears, which includes the first and last name from each card, as well as the home phone number and a brief note identifying the person. (See Figure 9-1.)

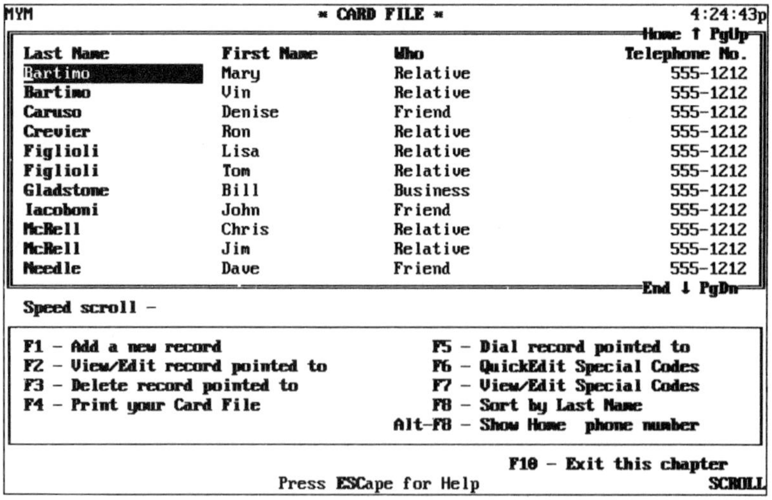

```
MYM                          » CARD FILE »                          4:24:43p
                                                               Home ↑ PgUp
   Last Name          First Name      Who                Telephone No.
   Bartino            Mary            Relative               555-1212
   Bartino            Vin             Relative               555-1212
   Caruso             Denise          Friend                 555-1212
   Crevier            Ron             Relative               555-1212
   Figlioli           Lisa            Relative               555-1212
   Figlioli           Tom             Relative               555-1212
   Gladstone          Bill            Business               555-1212
   Iacoboni           John            Friend                 555-1212
   McRell             Chris           Relative               555-1212
   McRell             Jim             Relative               555-1212
   Needle             Dave            Friend                 555-1212
                                                              End ↓ PgDn
   Speed scroll -

   F1 - Add a new record              F5 - Dial record pointed to
   F2 - View/Edit record pointed to   F6 - QuickEdit Special Codes
   F3 - Delete record pointed to      F7 - View/Edit Special Codes
   F4 - Print your Card File          F8 - Sort by Last Name
                                   Alt-F8 - Show Home phone number

                                           F10 - Exit this chapter
                      Press ESCape for Help                   SCROLL
```

Figure 9-1. *The Card File screen.*

If you are using Chapter 9 for the first time, the Card File screen contains Sid Sample's entries, which you can delete by highlighting each entry and pressing F3.

> Press F1 to add a new record.

The Add a New Record screen appears and displays the first card, with several blanks for three different addresses and phone numbers. You can include addresses and numbers for home, work, and another location. (See Figure 9-2.)

> Fill in the Title, First Name, M (middle initial), Last Name, and Who blanks at the top of the screen.

> Enter information in the blanks in the Home, Work, and Other boxes. (You don't have to fill in all the blanks.)

Below the address fields are blanks for personal information. The program includes a few categories of important information you may want to record.

> Fill in those blanks with information you think is useful.

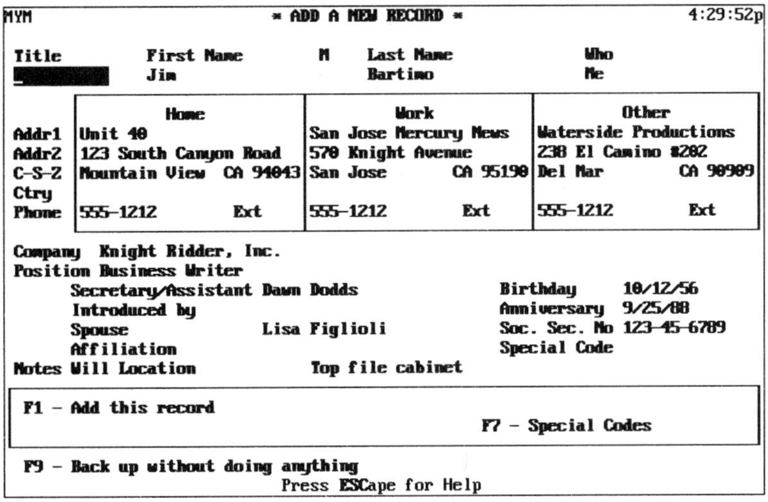

```
MYM                       * ADD A NEW RECORD *                         4:29:52p

 Title          First Name    M    Last Name          Who
 ▇▇▇▇▇▇         Jim                Bartimo            Me
                Home                    Work                  Other
 Addr1  Unit 40                San Jose Mercury News  Waterside Productions
 Addr2  123 South Canyon Road  570 Knight Avenue      238 El Camino #202
 C-S-Z  Mountain View  CA 94043 San Jose     CA 95190 Del Mar        CA 90909
 Ctry
 Phone  555-1212       Ext     555-1212       Ext     555-1212       Ext

 Company   Knight Ridder, Inc.
 Position  Business Writer
      Secretary/Assistant Dawn Dodds           Birthday      10/12/56
      Introduced by                            Anniversary   9/25/88
      Spouse              Lisa Figlioli        Soc. Sec. No 123-45-6789
      Affiliation                              Special Code
 Notes Will Location          Top file cabinet

 F1 - Add this record
                                              F7 - Special Codes

 F9 - Back up without doing anything
                         Press ESCape for Help
```

Figure 9-2. *The Add New Record screen.*

If you want to enter information that doesn't fit into the program's categories, you can enter this information in the Notes field at the bottom of the screen.

> Highlight the Notes blank and type the information you want to keep with the card.

You can use Write on the Money's pop-up feature to add pages of information to your card.

> Press Ctrl-E to enter Write on the Money and record your information.

> Press F2 to exit Write on the Money and reenter the Add a New Record screen.

Notice the Special Code blank near the bottom of the screen. You use this blank for sorting when you print lists from your card file. (See ''Using the Special Code Feature'' later in this chapter.) For now, leave the Special Code blank empty.

> Press F1 to record the card in the card-file list and return to the Card File screen.

Add a card for each of your friends, family members, and associates. If you need to add or change information on a card in this file, you can edit by positioning the cursor over the entry at the Card File screen and pressing F2.

Searching for Cards

After you set up your card file, you can use it to look up phone numbers, addresses, and other information. You may have several screens of entries in your card file; to reach an individual entry, you can use the arrow keys, the PgUp and PgDn keys, and the Home and End keys to scroll through the list. But to save time, you can use the Speed-Scroll feature.

> Position the cursor on any Last Name blank in the information box. Type the first one or two letters of the last name for which you want to search. The cursor jumps to the first matching entry on the list.

> Press F2 to view the card.

Sorting Cards

The Card File screen lists names alphabetically by last name. You can change the order to list alphabetically by first name, alphabetically by the Who field, or numerically by telephone number.

> Position the cursor in the F8 field in the action box and type **L** for last-name sorting, **F** for first-name sorting, **W** for Who-field sorting, and **P** for phone-number sorting.

> Press F8 and the card-file list is reordered in the information box.

DIALING FROM THE CARD FILE

To dial automatically with a Hayes-compatible modem, first plug your telephone into the modem. Then indicate the dialing procedure if you are calling long distance. (See ''Modem Setup'' in Chapter 1.) The simplest and fastest way to dial is to press F5 at the Card File screen, but you can also dial from individual cards.

> Highlight the name of the person you want to call in the Card File screen. If you want to dial from the card, press F2 to display the card and highlight the desired number.

> Press F5 to dial.

Be sure the telephone receiver is in its cradle. The modem will open a phone line and produce the tones necessary to simulate touch-tone dialing. After the number is dialed, a message at the bottom of the screen tells you to pick up the receiver and then press any key. The modem then releases the line to your telephone and you can start talking. Note that the phone line will disconnect if you press a key before picking up the receiver.

MARKING ENTRIES FOR PRINTING

Before you print your card file, you must first decide which cards to include and what format to use. After selecting the cards you want to print, you can then print lists that show only the name and number; name, number, and address; or all the card-file information. You can also print mailing labels or merge the names and addresses with a Write on the Money document.

From the Card File screen, press F4 to display the Print Your Card File screen.

This screen displays the Last Name, First, and Who fields of all your card-file entries. It also shows three columns: ''Home,'' ''Work,'' and ''Other.'' If a name on the list has one short line in one of these columns, a phone number is listed in the corresponding card-file field. If it has two short lines, an address is present; if it has three lines, both are present. (See Figure 9-3.)

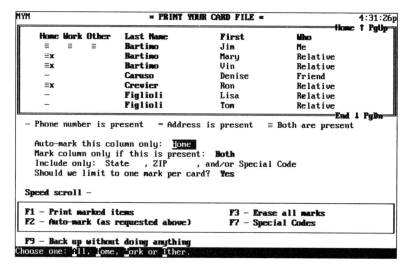

Figure 9-3. *The Print Your Card File screen.*

Marking Individual Entries
You can mark each entry for printing one card at a time. You might use this method to create a guest list for a party. You can look through your list, consider whom to invite, and then mark the chosen entries.

Type an **X** in the appropriate column next to each name you want to include on your list.

To erase all marks and start over, press F3.

Auto-marking Entries

You can quickly select cards based on information in the Home, Work, and Other boxes by filling in the blanks between the information box and the action box and then instructing the program to auto-mark.

> To limit marking to a single column, highlight the first blank and type **H** for the "Home" column, **W** for "Work," or **O** for "Other." If you don't want to limit the marking, type **A** for all columns.

You can further limit the focus of your list by eliminating cards that lack addresses or phone numbers.

> Highlight the second blank and type **P** to include only cards that have phone numbers; type **A** to include only cards that have addresses; or type **B** to include both. If you don't care whether the phone numbers and addresses are present, type **D**.

> Move the cursor to the State field and type a two-letter state code if you want to mark only cards with addresses in that state.

> Move the cursor to the Zip field and type all or part of a zip code to mark only cards with that zip code.

> Move the cursor to the Special Code field and type a special code to mark only cards with that special code.

After you fill in the appropriate information, press F2 to auto-mark those cards.

Using the Special-Code Feature

You can focus your card-file list on a particular category of people by using the special-code feature.

For example, suppose you want to print separate sets of mailing labels for Christmas gifts and Christmas cards. You plan to send your friends baskets of fruit and your business associates Christmas cards. You then create a category for friends and a category for business associates.

> Type a one-character code for the appropriate category in the Special Code blank on each card.

For example, you might type F in the Special Code blank to indicate friends or B to indicate business associates. You might type R as a code for relatives.

You can also add codes to cards by pressing F6 from the Card File menu and entering your special codes in the "Codes" column next to each name. If an entry belongs to more than one category, you can enter more than one code. In fact, you can enter as many as six codes when you first set up your card file, or you can enter them later as it becomes appropriate.

After you code every entry in your card file, you can use the Special Code field on the Print Your Card File screen to mark only names containing a certain code. For example, to mark a list for printing labels only for business associates, type B in the Special Code field and press F2.

PRINTING THE CARD FILE

After you mark all the entries you want to print, you can choose a format to print your card-file entries or merge your card-file names with a Write on the Money document. (See Figure 9-4.)

Press F1 from the Print Your Card File screen to view the Card File Reports screen.

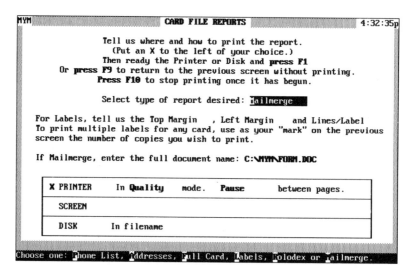

Figure 9-4. *The Card File Reports screen.*

Printing Lists and Labels

From the Card File Reports screen, you can print lists of names, phone numbers, and addresses separately or together in different combinations. You can also apply the printing to mailing labels by defining margins and line limits.

To print a list of names and phone numbers only, type **P** in the Select Type of Report field.

To print a list of names, phone numbers, and addresses, type **A** in the report type field.

To print all the information on each card, type **F** in the Select Type of Report field.

To print mailing labels, position the cursor in the Select Type of Report field and type **L** for labels. Then fill in the next three fields to indicate the mailing label margins and the number of lines that can be used per label.

Press F1 to print.

Using the Mail-Merge Feature

With the mail-merge feature, you can actually produce a mass mailing for any purpose, using Write on the Money and your card file. The first step is to create a Write letter, but instead of typing a person's address on the letter, you can type a "substitution code," and the program enters addresses from your card file when you print.

Press Ctrl-W to enter Write on the Money.

Press F1 to create a new document.

Create a letter, but in place of a name and address, use Write's substitution codes, which correspond to different card-file fields such as Title or Name. The following is a list of substitution codes and the card-file fields to which they correspond:

[ti]	= Title		[ci]	= City
[fn]	= First Name		[st]	= State
[ln]	= Last Name		[zi]	= Zip Code
[po]	= Position		[ph]	= Phone Number
[a1]	= 1st Address		[wh]	= Who
[a2]	= 2nd Address		[da]	= Today's Date

You can insert these codes in place of names, addresses, and phone numbers, and then Managing Your Money pulls the information from the individual cards. (See Figure 9-5.)

Save the Write document by pressing F2, entering a name in the F5 blank, and then pressing F5.

Press F10 to leave Write on the Money.

Press F1 from the Print Your Card File screen to return to the Card File Reports screen.

Fill in the Select Type of Report field. Then, move down to the Full Document Name field and enter the name of the Write document that contains your form letter and substitution codes.

Press F1 to print copies of your form letter with names and addresses from your card file. (See Figure 9-6.)

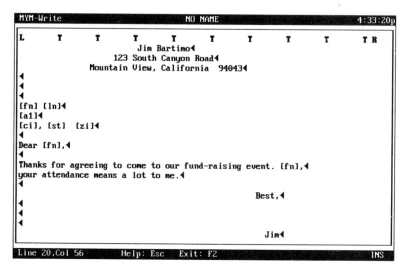

Figure 9-5. *Mail-merge letter using substitution codes.*

```
                               Jim Bartimo
                          123 South Canyon Road
                       Mountain View, California  94043


           Dave Needle
           415 Pt. Reyes Dr. #714
           Sunnyvale, CA  94090

           Dear Dave,

           Thanks for agreeing to come to our fund-raising event. Dave,
           your attendance means a lot to me.

                                                     Best,


                                                     Jim
```

Figure 9-6. *Printed letter using mail merge.*

EXPORTING TO THE REMINDER PAD

Before you leave Chapter 9, you are asked if you want to ''export'' birthdays and anniversaries listed in your card files to your reminder pad in Chapter 2. If you export them, you'll be reminded of those dates when you enter Managing Your Money.

Press F10 from the Card File screen to exit Chapter 9. The Leaving Chapter 9 screen appears.

Type **E** in the first field on the Leaving Chapter 9 screen to export the dates to Chapter 2. (See Figure 9-7 on the following page.) Then type the number of days before each date that you want an entry to appear in Chapter 2. Between 15 and 30 warning days gives you enough time to shop for a gift or card, but you can enter as many as 365 and be reminded every day of the year.

Press F1 to save the changes you made.

Before you can use these dates in Chapter 2, you must ''import'' them into Chapter 2 by pressing F8 at the Chapter 2 Reminders screen. Export the dates in Chapter 9 first, and then see Chapter 2 for further instructions.

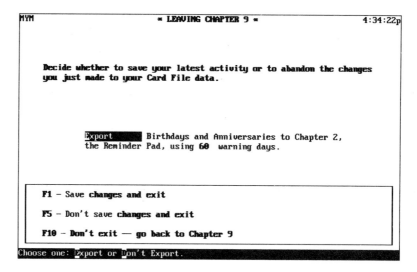

Figure 9-7. *The Leaving Chapter 9 screen.*

YOU'RE ON YOUR OWN— ALMOST

Now that you have completed your tour of Managing Your Money, you probably have many ideas about how the program can work for you— how you want to organize your financial and personal information, how frequently you want to use the checkbook and budget, and how the reminder pad fits into your life. You might already have special tasks you want to accomplish with the program. If you have worked through the chapters, you also have a lot of personal data already stored.

You're on your own now, so go ahead and put the program to work for you. But if you still don't have a complete picture of how the program fits into your life, you might want to look at Part II, ''People Who Manage Their Money.'' In these case studies, you get a chance to see how people in different financial situations use the program to help them achieve their financial goals.

PART II:
PEOPLE WHO MANAGE THEIR MONEY

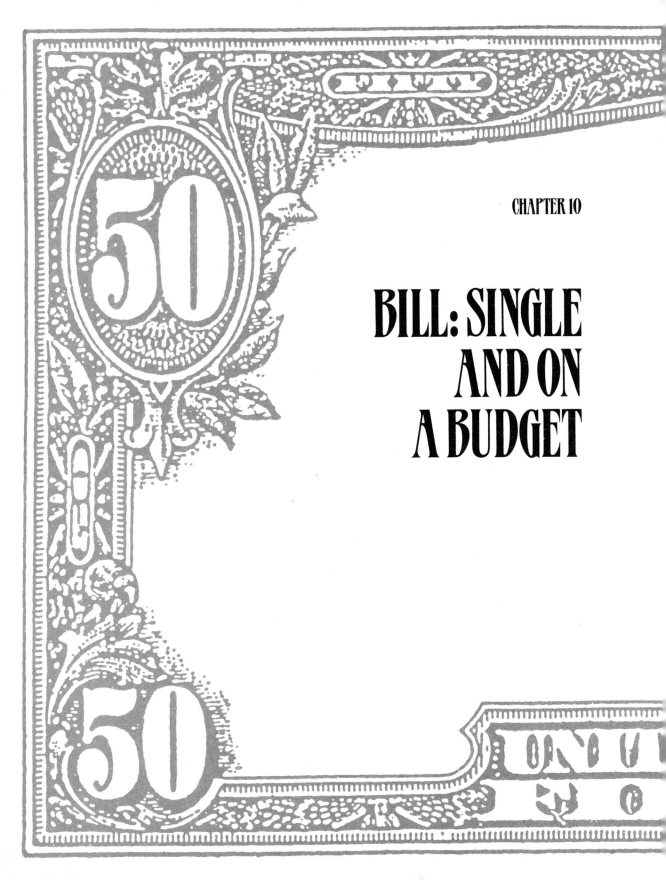

BILL: SINGLE AND ON A BUDGET

Bill is single and lives alone. He makes $21,000 per year—a salary many young people make a year or two after graduating from college. Bill lives in a one-bedroom apartment, eats out often, and likes to go out with friends on weekends. Bill hasn't thought a lot about budgets and saving in the past and has been content meeting his basic expenses from month to month. Recently, however, he began to think about the future. He dreams of buying his own condominium some day but will not be able to do so for a long time. Bill realizes that he has to start saving some of his monthly income if he wants to accomplish some of his long-term goals.

Bill's more immediate goal is to eliminate his daily bus ride to work. Although he knows that keeping an automobile in the city can be expensive, he wants to buy a new economy car with a bank loan. To do so, he must save enough money for a down payment, and he has set the end of the year as his goal.

Because his finances are so basic, Bill can get the most use from the budget and checkbook section (Chapter 3) of Managing Your Money. The budget and checkbook features can help him save time when he pays bills and can help him keep track of where he spends most of his money. He can also monitor his savings with the cash-forecasting tool in Chapter 3 to determine if it's possible for him to save enough for the down payment by the end of the year.

AN ELECTRONIC BUDGET

A PAYCHECK BELONGS IN A 1040 TAX CATEGORY.

Chapter 3 of Managing Your Money will act as the electronic version of Bill's checkbook and budget. To create his electronic checkbook, he turns to Chapter 3 and selects Money Accounts from the mini menu. There he creates an account called "First Saving," an abbreviation of the name of his bank, and labels it as a checking account. (See Figure 10-1.)

To set up a realistic budget, Bill will attribute each check he writes and receives in the coming months to a budget category. After one or two months, he can check his spending against his budget to determine if he is overspending or if he should revise his budget.

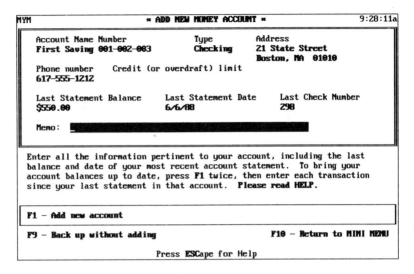

Figure 10-1. *Bill adds a new money account.*

Bill takes the first step toward creating his budget by selecting the Budget Categories option at the Chapter 3 mini menu. He asks himself where he earns and spends his money. The answer to the first question is simple—he earns his money at work, where he receives a bimonthly paycheck.

BILL'S PAYCHECK

Bill's first move is to create a budget category called ''Paycheck.'' Knowing that he must report earned income on a Form 1040, he assigns this budget category to the Form 1040 Items tax category and then further identifies it as Salary on the Choose Tax Category screen.

Continuing, Bill moves to the Budgets and Actuals screen. Here all 12 months of the year are listed in two columns, one for the monthly budget and one for actual receipts from his paycheck. For each month in the ''Budget'' column, Bill enters his total gross pay for a whole month. (The gross amount does not reflect FICA and income-tax deductions.) He doesn't make an entry in the "Actual" column because the program fills in this column automatically as he enters transactions in his checkbook.

When Bill returns to the list of budget categories, he locates the "Paycheck" category listed there. Also listed is the category type (Income), the annual total (Bill's projected salary for the rest of the year), and the tax category to which he allocates his paycheck (Salary).

TAXES ON BILL'S PAYCHECK

Bill knows that his paycheck reflects expenses as well as income. Federal income tax and Social-Security taxes are automatically deducted from his paycheck. To account for these expenses, Bill must create budget categories for each. He creates one called "SS Tax" and labels it an expense. He assigns it to the Form 1040 Items tax category, but with the subcategory FICA—the standard abbreviation for Social-Security tax. Bill continues to the Budgets and Actuals screen, where he enters the amount deducted for FICA from two paychecks. He then repeats this process for federal tax, but instead of selecting FICA as the tax subcategory for Form 1040, he selects Federal Withholding.

BILL'S EXPENSES

To determine his expenses, Bill makes a list of all the places he spends money. The entries on this list, along with his tax withheld, make up his expense budget categories.

Bill's first expense category—Rent—takes the largest portion of his income. He pays $450 per month. Because rent payment is not tax-deductible, he selects Not a Tax Category when he adds the Rent category to his expense list. Then he moves on to the Budgets and Actuals screen and types $450 for each month of the year in the "Budget" column. Unless he has a rent increase later in the year, Bill should have no trouble sticking to this part of his budget all year.

Other expenses in Bill's budget are not so easy to predict. His telephone bill, for instance, varies widely from month to month. He often calls his parents, who live only a few miles away. And sometimes he calls several of his college friends who live in other cities.

THE MONTHLY BUDGET FOR RENT IS USUALLY PREDICTABLE BUT OTHER EXPENSES ARE LESS SO.

Bill creates an expense budget category called "Telephone." (This category is also not a tax category.) Then he makes some rough estimates for the "Budget" column on the Budgets and Actuals screen. His most expensive phone bill was approximately $100, and his least expensive bill was around $25.

At first, Bill types $25 in the "Budget" column for every month of the year. Then he looks at the months in which his phone bill is likely to be higher. He knows he usually calls friends around the holidays, and so he estimates a $50 phone bill for November and a $75 phone bill for December. (See Figure 10-2.) In the summer months, Bill is too busy vacationing and taking weekends at the beach to make a lot of phone calls. So he leaves the estimate of those bills at $25.

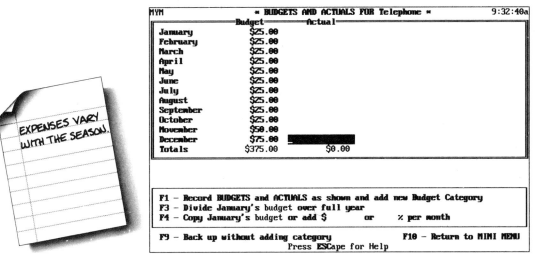

Figure 10-2. *Bill's monthly phone budget.*

EXPENSES VARY WITH THE SEASON.

The telephone budget might not be exact, but at least Bill has made a start at creating a budget that he can follow. He might even be able to discipline himself to reduce it. After a few months of spending, Bill can return to these budget estimates and make any necessary adjustments.

Bill completes his budget by creating a budget category for each expense he incurs. This includes categories for utilities, restaurants, groceries, clothing, toiletries, household expenses, furniture, doctor bills, and dentist bills.

He keeps his expense categories general so that he won't need to remember where he spends every dollar. He doesn't create a category just for ties, for instance, because that expense can be included in the general category "Clothing." If he forgets any expenses now, he can always add some more as he starts to pay his bills.

FORECASTING BILL'S BUDGET

After Bill builds his budgets based on what he assumes are accurate projections, he still doesn't know how much he can save at the end of each month. To find out, he selects Cash Forecasting from the Chapter 3 mini menu.

The Cash Forecasting screen displays Bill's projections for his total income and expenses for each month. It also subtracts Bill's monthly expense projections from his monthly income projections to show his monthly profit or loss. Finally, it shows his total cash position at the end of each month, which includes figures from each previous month.

The Cash Forecasting screen helps Bill in two ways. First, it helps him assess whether his budget is workable. If the cash at the end of the month is exceptionally high, he may have misjudged his budget by not allocating enough for expenses. If the cash at the end of each month is negative, Bill must return to his budget and look for categories in which he can cut his spending.

Second, it helps him determine whether his budget can meet his financial goals. To ensure that he will have $1,200 at the end of the year for a down payment on a car, Bill verifies that his budget allows him to save $200 per month. He adjusts his various budget categories until the Cash Forecasting screen shows a monthly $200 surplus of money projected over the next six months.

**BILL'S
CHECKBOOK**

With his preliminary budget complete, Bill returns to his electronic checking account. Because it is a newly created account, no checks or receipts are listed on the Unreconciled Transactions screen.

To record this month's first paycheck, Bill adds a transaction record for the *net* amount of his bimonthly check. He then moves to the Allocate to Budget Categories screen, finds the "Paycheck" category, and enters the *gross* amount of his check. Then Bill moves the cursor to the SS Tax and Federal Tax categories and enters the amounts of those expense categories as part of his paycheck budget transaction. After allocating his paycheck to budget categories, he records the check and returns to the Receive Money screen.

Bill entered the net amount of his paycheck in the Receive Money screen, but in his budget the gross amount of the check is recorded so that it matches his budgeted gross income. Budget estimations and actual tax amounts for the SS Tax and Federal Tax categories will also match provided that Bill records the amounts from each check in the correct categories.

With his income recorded, Bill returns to his list of unreconciled transactions. He is now ready to record checks on the Spend Money screen. On the electronic check, he enters information about his first check. He fills in the check number, date, payee's name, and the amount of the check, exactly as he would on a real check. On these checks, however, he also fills in the address of each company whose bill he pays. (See Figure 10-3 on the following page.)

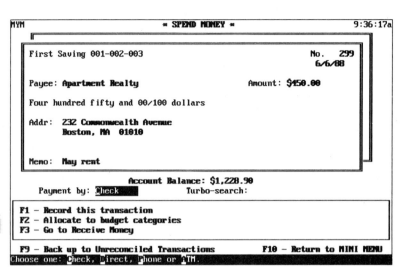

```
MYM                          * SPEND MONEY *                      9:36:17a

   First Saving 001-002-003                           No.    299
                                                            6/6/88

   Payee: Apartment Realty                  Amount: $450.00

   Four hundred fifty and 00/100 dollars

   Addr:  232 Commonwealth Avenue
          Boston, MA  01010


   Memo:  May rent

                          Account Balance: $1,228.90
        Payment by: Check               Turbo-search:

   F1 - Record this transaction
   F2 - Allocate to budget categories
   F3 - Go to Receive Money

   F9 - Back up to Unreconciled Transactions       F10 - Return to MINI MENU
Choose one: Check, Direct, Phone or ATM.
```

Figure 10-3. *Bill's monthly rent check.*

After filling in each check, Bill allocates the amount to a budget category. When he pays the gas bill, he allocates the check to the Utilities category of the budget. When he pays the rent, he allocates the check to the Rent category.

ALLOCATING EACH TRANSACTION TO A BUDGET CATEGORY ENSURES THAT YOU CAN MONITOR YOUR BUDGET.

THE CHECK PRINTER

The first few times Bill uses the program, he uses the electronic checkbook to record checks that he already wrote by hand. Later, he decides to try the program's check-printing option and buys form-feed checks from a local computer store.

After he records the checks for his monthly bills in his electronic checkbook and allocates them to budget categories, Bill prints them from his list of unreconciled transactions. He indicates the checks he wants to print using the Print Checks screen. Then he loads his printer with the form-feed checks and, after a few trial attempts to line up the printer with the check forms, prints all the marked checks.

INCLUDING ADDRESSES ON THE CHECKS MAKES IT EASY TO USE WINDOW ENVELOPES AND SAVES THE TIME IT WOULD TAKE TO ADDRESS THE ENVELOPES.

Because Bill also includes the addresses of his payees on his electronic checks, he can print his checks with those addresses. In this way, he can save himself the trouble of addressing envelopes by using window envelopes. He then signs the checks, stamps the envelopes, and drops them in the mail.

THE AUTOMATIC CHECK

After a few months, Bill realizes that many of his bills are from the same companies every month, and often they are for the same amount. Rather than fill in each check separately every month, Bill decides to set up automatic transactions.

At the Automatic Transactions screen, Bill finds that he can create an automatic payment much as he created a check. He adds an automatic spend transaction and fills in the necessary information (including the address) to pay his rent. Then he allocates the automatic transaction to the Rent budget category and saves the automatic transaction.

The list of automatic transactions now consists of a listing for a fixed payment to Bill's landlord and the amount of the check. Bill then creates automatic transactions for all the bills he pays on a regular basis and allocates them to the correct budget categories. For payments such as gas bills, he enters an approximate amount. He can change the amount of the check for such transactions each month but keep the payee and budget allocations the same. Bill even creates one automatic receive transaction for his bimonthly check and allocates it exactly like a regular transaction.

THE FULLY AUTOMATED CHECKBOOK

These days, Bill spends very little time paying his bills. He simply starts the program and goes to the Automatic Transactions screen. He marks the bills he wants to pay this month and types in any new amounts for the checks. (See Figure 10-4 on the following page.) He presses one key to execute all automatic transactions and allocate them to budget categories.

```
MYM                     * AUTOMATIC TRANSACTIONS in: *              9:41:24a
                            First Saving 001-002-003
                                                           ┌─Home ↑ PgUp┐
┌Payee/Payor          Mark Last Use Type    $ In      $ Out    Chk# Budget│
│Apartment Realty       x          U                 $450.00        Rent  │
│Cartier Enterprises               U     $594.18                    Split │
│Commonwealth Gas Company x        U                 $55.00         Utili │
│Edison Light Company   x          U                 $60.00         Utili │
│Federated Savings & Loan x        U                 $140.00        Line  │
│Loan Servicing Corp    x          U                 $75.00         Stude │
│Meyer's Furniture                 U                 $35.00         House │
│Seaboard Telephone                U                 $25.00         Telep │
                        Account balance: $1,854.78═══════════End ↓ PgDn┘
   Speed scroll -
   Mark those transactions you wish to execute by █Check█  . For recording
   checks, begin with #382   or alternate number in "Chk#" column. Execute
   transactions on 8/26/88  or on an alternate date in "Last Use" column.

  ┌─────────────────────────────────────────────────────────────────────┐
  │ F1 - Execute marked transactions     F4 - Print Automatic Transactions│
  │ F2 - View/Edit transaction           F5 - Add a Spend Transaction     │
  │Alt-F2 - View/Edit allocations        F6 - Add a Receive Transaction   │
  │ F3 - Delete transaction                                               │
  │                                                                       │
  │ F9 - Back up without doing anything        F10 - Return to MINI MENU  │
  └Choose one: █Check, ↑TM, █Direct or █hone .───────────────────────────┘
```

Figure 10-4. *Bill's Automatic Transactions screen with bills marked to be paid.*

Then Bill adds individually any checks that are not automatic transactions. After printing the checks, he signs them and slips them into window envelopes for mailing.

BALANCING BILL'S CHECKBOOK

Bill saves so much time paying his bills that he decides to start doing something he always knew he should do but never did. He decides to balance his checkbook against his bank statement.

From his list of unreconciled transactions, he chooses the option for reconciling his checkbook. A new screen lists Bill's recorded checks and deposits. Here he types an X next to each check or deposit that appears on his bank statement. Then he enters the balance from the bank statement. The reconciling option compares this balance to the balance in his electronic account. If they do not match, Bill can investigate the checks and deposits recorded in the program (or look for ones that he forgot to record), or he can call his bank to report an error.

When Bill balances his checkbook, all the reconciled transactions disappear from the screen. The new balance is exactly the amount of money Bill currently has in the bank.

RENT IS AN EXAMPLE OF A FIXED TRANSACTION - IT IS NOT LIKELY TO CHANGE OFTEN.

GAS BILLS ARE EXAMPLES OF VARIABLE TRANSACTIONS-- THE AMOUNTS CHANGE EACH MONTH, BUT THE PAYEE AND BUDGET CATEGORIES DO NOT.

INCOME CAN BE AN AUTOMATIC TRANSACTION, TOO.

BALANCING BILL'S BUDGET

After a few months of paying his bills automatically, writing checks with his printer, and balancing his checkbook with the program, Bill still finds that he's not saving as much money as he would like. He has made the bill-paying process easier and has even prevented a few bounced checks by keeping a balanced checkbook, but he has still done little to save for a car.

Bill decides to examine his original budget. He selects "Budget Categories" from the mini menu, but this time, instead of creating budget categories, he examines how his projected budgets compare with his actual spending of the past few months.

From the Budget Categories screen, Bill can review any budget category that he set up and then compare the "Budget" column with the "Actual" column, which now lists his monthly totals for his actual spending. Suspecting that he has overspent his restaurant allowance, Bill examines the "Restaurants" budget category, to which he has been allocating portions of his MasterCard bill. (See Figure 10-5.)

THE PROGRAM SHOWS WHERE YOU ARE OVERSPENDING OR UNDERSPENDING YOUR BUDGET-- CATEGORY BY CATEGORY.

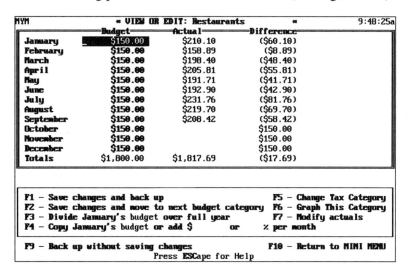

MYM	* VIEW OR EDIT: Restaurants		* 9:48:25a
	Budget	Actual	Difference
January	$150.00	$210.10	($60.10)
February	$150.00	$158.89	($8.89)
March	$150.00	$198.40	($48.40)
April	$150.00	$205.81	($55.81)
May	$150.00	$191.71	($41.71)
June	$150.00	$192.90	($42.90)
July	$150.00	$231.76	($81.76)
August	$150.00	$219.70	($69.70)
September	$150.00	$208.42	($58.42)
October	$150.00		$150.00
November	$150.00		$150.00
December	$150.00		$150.00
Totals	$1,800.00	$1,817.69	($17.69)

F1 — Save changes and back up   F5 — Change Tax Category
F2 — Save changes and move to next budget category   F6 — Graph This Category
F3 — Divide January's budget over full year   F7 — Modify actuals
F4 — Copy January's budget or add $ or   % per month

F9 — Back up without saving changes   F10 — Return to MINI MENU
                    Press ESCape for Help

Figure 10-5. *Bill's restaurant budget screen.*

The program not only shows his budget projections and actual spending, but also subtracts the budget projection from the actual amount spent and displays the difference between the two. In other words, it tells Bill how much he has overspent or underspent for the category. In the "Restaurants" category, he has overspent his budget by about $50 per month.

As he reviews his other budget categories, Bill discovers that he has kept close to the budget he set up. So he knows that in order to save the required $200 per month for his car, he must cut down on eating out. Vowing to reach his financial goal, Bill starts to eat at home more often, dining out on weekends only.

REACHING THE GOAL

By the beginning of the next year, Bill has finally saved the $1,200 for a down payment on a new car. In the meantime, he has also received a raise at his job, which will help him better afford the car payments. His rent has increased, but only slightly. Now, to account for the changes in his finances, Bill returns to his budget and makes changes to reflect his new income, his pending new expenses, and his next goal— saving enough for a down payment on a condominium.

CHAPTER 11

STEVE AND ANN: A TWO-INCOME COUPLE MOVES UP

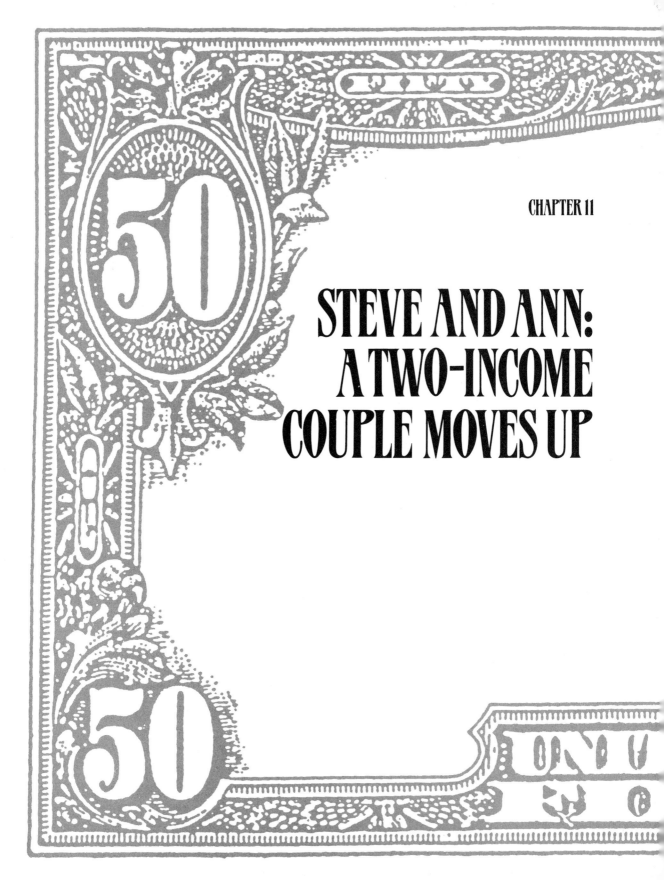

Steve and Ann, both 30 years old, are a typical up-and-coming couple. Married three years ago, they have worked since they graduated from college, and their combined income is now $60,000 a year. Together, they have saved $10,000.

Their immediate goal is to buy their first home. Steve and Ann would like to keep their monthly mortgage payments below $700. They know that both the amount of the loan and the interest rate affect their monthly payments, so they plan to shop around for the best buy on a home as well as the best buy on a loan.

When they find both, Steve and Ann will need to provide information about their assets and liabilities to a loan officer, who will decide whether they qualify for the loan. If they do, their budget will change, and so will their taxes, because they will be able to write off the interest portion of their monthly house payments.

Managing Your Money can help Steve and Ann in all the stages of buying their new home, from determining how much they can afford to pay for a house to setting up automatic loan payments after they close the deal. They can use the financial calculator in Chapter 6 to calculate monthly mortgage payments for different loan amounts and interest rates. And, for their interview with the loan officer, they can create a personal balance sheet with Chapter 8.

After they secure the loan, they will need to update their budget and checkbook in Chapter 3, setting up automatic loan payments and recording both the interest and principal payments in budget categories. Then they can use Chapter 4 to estimate the impact that owning their own home will have on their taxes.

HOUSE HUNTING WITH THE FINANCIAL CALCULATOR

Steve and Ann set out to purchase a house. After looking at condominium townhouses, they finally find a three-level unit they like. The asking price is $100,000. With their $10,000 as a down payment, they need a $90,000 loan. They wonder if $700 a month will cover the loan payments.

To find out, Steve starts the Managing Your Money program, turns to Chapter 6, the financial calculator, and enters the compound calculation. It can perform four basic types of calculations. The one he wants is called "Loans and Annuities." Using this part of the calculator, Steve can juggle some mortgage figures to determine if he and Ann can afford a $90,000 home loan.

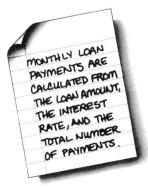

Steve enters the amount of the loan and then types his bank's current interest rate—9.9 percent—in the Interest Rate blank. He knows he wants a standard 30-year loan, so he types 360 in the Total Number of Payments blank. He leaves the Monthly Payment blank empty for the program to calculate. The result is $783.17 per month.

"That's not bad," Steve thinks, but he still would like to keep his monthly payment below $700. So he tries another approach. This time, he enters his ideal payment of $700 in the Monthly Payment blank. Using the same interest rate and the same number of payments as before, he leaves the Amount of Loan blank empty, and then he recalculates. (See Figure 11-1.)

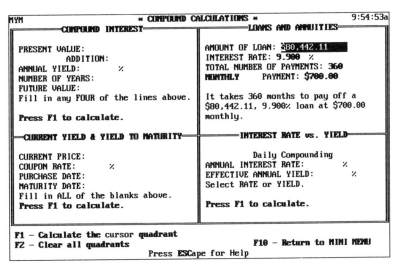

Figure 11-1. *Working with the compound calculator.*

The loan amount that appears is $80,442.11, the amount Steve and Ann can afford to borrow at his bank's interest rate and still keep their monthly payment at $700. This means they must either find a less expensive townhouse or convince the sellers of the one they want to drop the price.

LOAN SHOPPING WITH THE FINANCIAL CALCULATOR

Try as they might, Steve and Ann can't get the sellers of the townhouse to come down from their price of $100,000, and they must still borrow $90,000 in order to buy it. But Ann saw a sign in the window of Downtown Bank, near where she works. It advertised mortgage rates at 8.9 percent interest over 40 years.

Again, Steve turns to the financial calculator in Chapter 6 and enters some new figures. In the Amount of Loan blank, he enters $90,000 again, but he changes the interest rate to 8.9 percent and the total number of payments to 480. He leaves the Monthly Payment blank empty. This calculation shows that he can pay $687.30 per month and still afford to buy the $100,000 townhouse with the $10,000 as a down payment.

A PERSONAL BALANCE SHEET

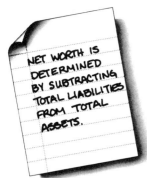

NET WORTH IS DETERMINED BY SUBTRACTING TOTAL LIABILITIES FROM TOTAL ASSETS.

Now that Steve and Ann know they can afford their dream house, they visit the seller and agree to buy the townhouse for $100,000, depending on approval of the $90,000 loan from Downtown Bank.

Downtown Bank will want to know about Steve and Ann's finances before it accepts their application for a loan. So, before they see the loan officer, Steve turns to Chapter 8 of Managing Your Money to create a personal balance sheet. Because Steve keeps track of all their finances with the program, he can quickly create a printed list of their bank accounts, investments, and personal property.

When Steve first turns to Chapter 8, the program displays one figure that reflects his and Ann's total net worth—the total of their assets minus the total of their liabilities. But this figure by itself won't convince the loan officer that Steve and Ann are really worth that much. So, Steve displays the lists of assets and liabilities that are used to compute these totals. The assets list includes bank accounts, insurance policies, pension plans, and other investments, along with their cash values. (See Figure 11-2.) In the liabilities list, Steve finds a list of all their debts, including their car loan, and the outstanding balances. Their assets and liabilities are listed automatically from information in Chapters 3, 5, and 7. But Steve can also enter the cash value of his stereo, computer, and other high-ticket items in the assets list.

After he enters their assets, Steve prints their personal balance sheet. He plans to use this balance sheet to show the loan officer how much money they have and how much they owe. Because the loan officer will want to verify Steve's figures with the appropriate institutions, Steve also prepares a list of the names, addresses, telephone numbers, and account numbers.

When Steve and Ann finally visit the loan officer at Downtown Bank, the interview proceeds quickly. The loan officer is impressed that Steve and Ann have a printed list of all their assets and liabilities

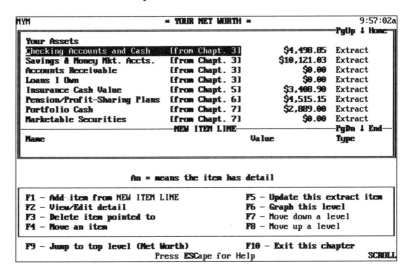

Figure 11-2. *Steve and Ann's assets.*

because most couples come in with only a hazy recollection of all their accounts. Steve and Ann's professional-looking personal balance sheet makes the loan officer's job of checking their financial resources much easier. As a result, the 8.9 percent loan application is approved quickly. Steve and Ann soon close the deal on their townhouse.

A NEW LOAN IN THE BUDGET

As moving day approaches, Steve realizes he must include his monthly mortgage payments in his checkbook and budget. When he and Ann were renting, Steve simply wrote the rent check from their checking account and recorded it in the Rent category in their budget. He set up an automatic transaction to print the rent check each month. But keeping track of a monthly mortgage payment is a little more complex, and so Managing Your Money has a special section—the "Loan Records" section in Chapter 3—for making automatic loan payments and recording them.

Mortgage payments are more complex because each monthly payment is really two payments—one to pay interest and one to pay the principal. In the early life of a loan, most of the monthly mortgage payment is applied to the interest, and later payments contribute more toward the principal. The interest-to-principal ratio changes a small amount each month.

It is important for Steve and Ann to track the interest-to-principal ratio because one of the advantages of owning their new home is that they can deduct all the interest on their federal income-tax return. They cannot, however, deduct their principal payments.

To account for the interest/principal split in his budget, Steve first creates two new budget categories: "Mortgage/Interest" and "Mortgage/Principal." He assigns the "Mortgage/Interest" category to a Schedule A tax category and further identifies it as Interest Expense. The "Mortgage/Principal" category is classified as Not a Tax Category. Now Steve can allocate a portion of his monthly mortgage payment to each category and track the portion that is tax-deductible.

AUTOMATING LOAN PAYMENTS

Now that Steve has added the loan to his budget, he returns to the Chapter 3 mini menu and selects "Loan Records." Steve enters information about the new mortgage on the New Mortgage Calculator, specifying the amount, interest rate, terms, monthly payment, and other information. (See Figure 11-3.) He then adds this mortgage to his and Ann's list of loans.

The next task is to set up an automatic monthly loan payment. Then Steve can use his electronic checkbook to write the mortgage check automatically each month, record it, and allocate it to his mortgage budget categories. He creates this automatic payment from the Loan Records screen.

Even though the amounts of principal and interest vary with each payment, Steve knows he will be paying Downtown Bank the same amount every month. The electronic check that appears when he creates the automatic payment already includes the lender's name and the amount of the monthly payment, which the program enters from the information in the Loan Records screen.

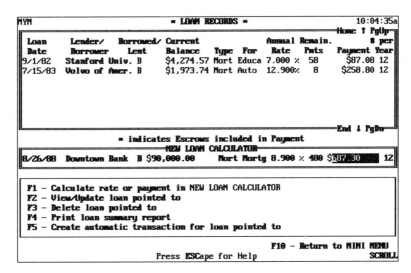

Figure 11-3. *Entering the new loan.*

Of course, Steve wants to allocate this monthly payment automatically to the two mortgage budget categories. The loan records section of Chapter 3 is especially designed to handle interest/principal splits. The program can determine exactly how much to allocate to each of the two budget categories for every monthly payment because it contains internal amortization tables.

To use the program's internal amortization schedule, Steve must indicate which budget category receives allocations for interest and which category receives allocations for principal. When he chooses the Allocate to Budget Categories option, the program lists all Steve and Ann's budget categories. Steve highlights the ''Mortgage/Interest'' category and types I for interest in the blank next to it. Then he highlights the ''Mortgage/Principal'' category and types P for principal next to it. (See Figure 11-4.)

The next time Steve works with his checking account, he can select the Automatic Transactions option and see his monthly mortgage payment listed as an automatic transaction. To record the mortgage payment,

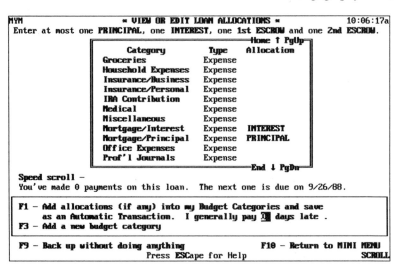

Figure 11-4. *Allocating mortgage payments to budget categories.*

Steve marks it with an X and executes the transaction. The monthly payment is recorded in Steve and Ann's checkbook, and the interest/ principal split is recorded in their budget. When Steve prints his checks, one will be made out to Downtown Bank for $687.30.

ESTIMATING THE IMPACT ON TAXES

Steve and Ann know that although their monthly mortgage payment is now higher than the rent they paid previously, they will save money in the long run by paying considerably less tax to the federal government. And they would like to know exactly how much less they will pay in taxes.

Although it's not possible to know in January exactly what next April's tax bill will be, it is possible to estimate what the tax bill is likely to be, based on actual and projected expenses and income. Steve now turns to the tax estimator in Chapter 4.

The opening screen of Chapter 4 is an electronic version of Form 1040. Because Steve allocates his and Ann's income and expenses to budget and tax categories in Chapter 3, he can fill out Form 1040 with current information at the touch of a key.

One of the blanks in Form 1040 is for Schedule A deductions. Steve wants to use his Chapter 3 figures to calculate his taxes, so he presses A to display an electronic version of Schedule A. This form shows all the itemized deductions that Steve allocated to a Schedule A tax category in Chapter 3. They include medical expenses, charitable contributions, and other deductible expenses such as his mortgage interest payments.

Of course, the item of most interest to Steve and Ann is the category for home mortgage interest. To be sure this category reflects the amount he budgeted for mortgage interest, he tells the program to use the budget values from Chapter 3 to fill out the form.

When Steve returns to Form 1040, he can see roughly what this year's tax bill will be. The $7,000 that he and Ann will pay in mortgage interest has lessened their taxable income from $54,500 to $50,184. Their total federal tax is likely to be $10,184 instead of $11,393. Because Steve and Ann now have an annual total of $15,000 taken from their paychecks for federal withholding, they can expect a tax refund of almost $5,000 this year.

Thus, by using the tax estimator, Steve and Ann realize that they can reduce the amount withheld from their taxes and apply the money to their mortgage payments. Then they can return to Chapter 3 and change the budget estimates to account for their higher income.

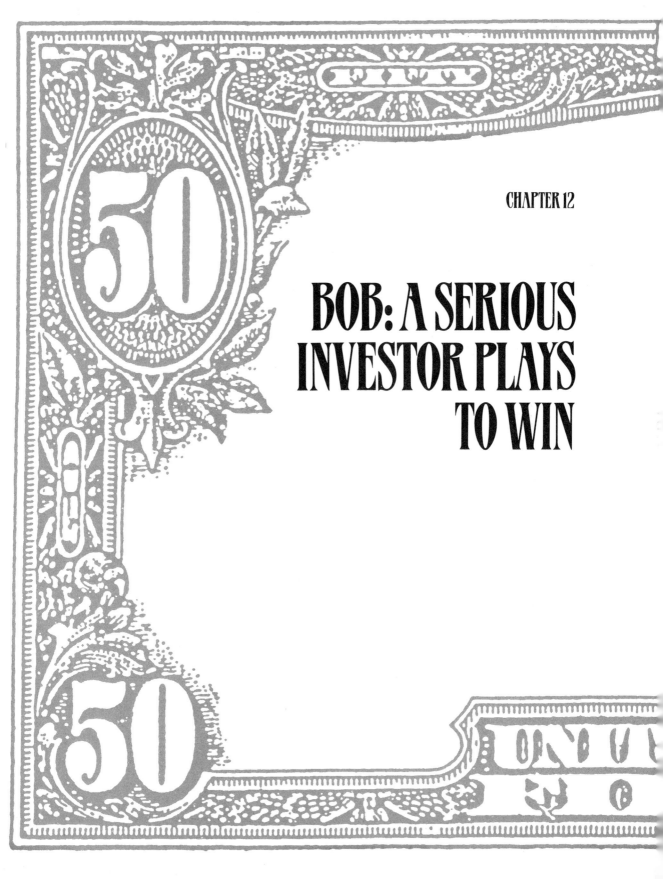

CHAPTER 12

BOB: A SERIOUS INVESTOR PLAYS TO WIN

Bob isn't a high-powered Wall Street broker, but he is a serious investor. A middle-aged professional who makes $60,000 a year, Bob has much of his money tied up in his company's stock-purchasing plan, its 401(k) retirement program, and his personal individual retirement account (IRA). He also has invested money in his own home, a real-estate partnership, several blue-chip stocks, and two mutual funds.

Bob is a conservative investor. He wants to keep his money safe because most of it is earmarked to help with college costs for his two children. Besides, he knows he still has quite a few years of earning power in him, and he doesn't need to take big risks for big profits. Bob is happy if his investments earn a bit more than the current money-market rates.

Every now and then, however, Bob strays from his conservative path to something a bit more risky. In mid-1985, Bob believed that Apple Computer stock was undervalued. At about $20 per share, he thought the stock was sure to rise to at least half of the $60-per-share high it had reached only a few years earlier. So Bob bought 100 shares of Apple for about $2,000.

By mid-1986, Bob's instincts proved to be correct. After an initial dip below $15, Apple stock rose to $37 per share and continued to rise a few fractions of a percentage point each day. The talk of an Apple takeover that had persisted when Bob bought the stock was long gone as Wall Street reacted favorably to Apple's healthy quarterly reports.

Bob wondered if the time were right to sell and used Chapter 7 of Managing Your Money to help him decide. Using the portfolio manager, he tracked the price of all his assets and checked his original price objective for the Apple stock. He analyzed the stock to determine his capital gain. After he made a decision, Bob recorded the stock sale in Chapter 7, which transferred the information to Chapter 4 in order to estimate next year's tax. He then recorded the income in Chapter 3. And when tax time arrived, he used the Portfolio Archives feature of Chapter 7 to produce a copy of Schedule D, which he attached to his Form 1040 to report capital gains.

HOW THE STOCK WAS RECORDED

When Bob first bought his 100 shares of Apple stock in 1985, he started his copy of Managing Your Money and turned to Chapter 7, the portfolio manager. He then viewed his list of portfolios on the Portfolio Accounts screen and opened the account called "Fidelity." (Fidelity Investments is the discount brokerage firm through which Bob bought his 100 shares of Apple stock.) Bob then recorded his purchase as a new asset in the "Fidelity" portfolio. Apple uses the symbol "AAPL" on the NASDAQ stock exchange, so Bob used that symbol for his new asset. He filled out the Buy an Asset screen, listing the company's name, the number of units, the purchase price, and the purchase date— May 30, 1985. He indicated that the Apple stock is a high-technology common stock, fully liquid, and somewhat speculative. In the Recommendor blank of the form, he noted that buying Apple was his own idea. He set a price objective of $35 a share. He decided that his mental stop-loss figure—the price at which he would have to sell or fear losing the entire investment—was $10 per share. (See Figure 12-1.) Bob also recorded the Dow Jones Industrials average at the time he purchased the Apple stock.

THE DAILY NEWSPAPER LISTS THE CURRENT PRICES OF STOCKS. AN ON-LINE SERVICE CAN PROVIDE UP-TO-THE MINUTE QUOTES.

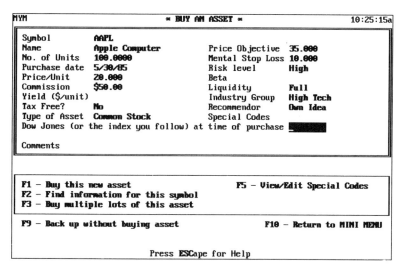

Figure 12-1. Bob fills out the Buy an Asset form.

INVESTMENT WATCHING

Bob likes to watch over his investments closely, so he uses the portfolio manager at least once a week. He first chooses the Update Prices option from the Chapter 7 mini menu. He then looks up the new price of each of his investments in the stock pages of the daily newspaper and enters the new prices in the program. The price of Apple stock one day in 1986 was $37.

Bob recorded the new prices for all the assets in all his portfolios. He was then able to check each asset individually to see how it had grown or shrunk since the last time he updated the prices by choosing Work With Portfolio Pointed To from the Portfolio Accounts screen.

For once-a-week updates, the daily paper is an adequate source of information. But if Bob becomes a more active investor, he may consider getting up-to-the-minute quotes automatically from an on-line service such as Dow Jones News/Retrieval and using the program Managing The Market. (See ''Managing The Market'' in Chapter 7.)

A FINANCIAL REMINDER

Before he turned to his list of unsold assets, Bob checked his financial reminders, which indicated all the assets that had reached either the price objective or the mental stop-loss amount that Bob had entered when he first recorded the asset. (See Figure 12-2.)

Because Bob had set a price objective of $35 for Apple, when he entered the new price of $37, AAPL was listed on the Financial Reminders screen with the message ''Reached your Objective of $35.00.'' When he saw this message, he knew it was time to consider selling. He reviewed the information that he originally recorded for his Apple stock by displaying the asset from the Financial Reminders screen. He confirmed his price objective and returned to the mini menu.

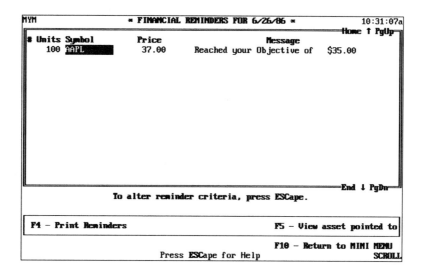

Figure 12-2. *Bob checks his financial reminders.*

ANALYZING APPLE

Before he made a decision, Bob decided to analyze his assets. He chose Portfolio Analysis from the Chapter 7 mini menu, and the program displayed a list of his portfolios. Because his Apple stock was listed in his "Fidelity" portfolio, he typed an X next to that portfolio and chose the first analysis tool, Analyze Selected Portfolios.

The Fidelity portfolio contained several other assets. Because Bob wanted to consider only the Apple stock, he chose the Select Specific Assets to Analyze option and typed an X next to the Apple stock symbol. He then checked the amount his Apple stock had appreciated by selecting the Appreciation Display. (See Figure 12-3 on the following page.) Here he saw that his 100 shares had appreciated by about 81 percent and earned a total of $1,700. Because he has held this stock for a little more than a year, the annual appreciation—the amount that the stock appreciated in the course of one year—was about 73 percent. Bob compared how Apple had performed against the market on the Performance Versus Index Display and decided to sell his shares of Apple.

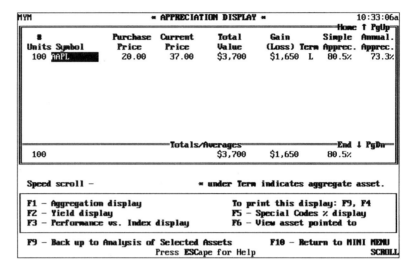

Figure 12-3. *Bob checks his stock's appreciation.*

**SELLING
A STOCK**

After instructing Fidelity to sell his shares in Apple, Bob recorded the sale in the portfolio manager. Returning to the Chapter 7 mini menu, he chose Portfolio Accounts and displayed the Apple stock listing. There he highlighted the Apple stock and indicated he wanted to sell it.

The program recapped the stock's performance in the Sell an Asset screen, which noted the portfolio in which the Apple stock was held, the number of shares, the date it was purchased, and the price. It also noted that the stock had increased in value by $1,700 and displayed exactly how many days Bob held it. Because Bob had already told Fidelity to sell the whole lot of Apple stock, he recorded the sale of all his shares. The Apple stock was then listed in the Sold Assets screen and no longer appeared in the Unsold Assets screen. The information also was recorded automatically in the tax estimator in Chapter 4.

To finish his record keeping, Bob turned to Chapter 3 of the program to make a note of a $1,700 deposit in his electronic checkbook.

TAX TIME

At tax time Bob prepared to fill out his tax forms and report his income for the past year. He reported the $1,700 from the sale of Apple stock and other capital-gains income by using the Portfolio Archives feature of Chapter 7. With this feature, he created a facsimile of a Schedule D—the tax schedule used to report all gains and losses incurred from the sale of investments.

To produce his Schedule D, Bob first had to convert the information about his sold assets, including his Apple stock, into a format that the Portfolio Archives feature of Chapter 7 could understand. From the Portfolio Archives screen, he selected T to temporarily archive information about the sold Apple stock. From the Report Generator screen, Bob indicated that temporarily archived information should be included. Skipping over the other options on this Report Generator screen, Bob told the program to print a Schedule D. The program provided information about capital gains from sales of Apple stock and other assets. But Schedule D also required information not available in the Chapter 7 archived records. Bob used the next two screens to provide this information.

On these screens, he entered capital gains and losses. He also carried forward losses from previous years. After he filled in all the necessary blanks in both screens, Bob printed his Schedule D, which listed $1,700 worth of Apple shares under capital gains. Bob used the totals from this Schedule D for the appropriate line on his Form 1040. When he sent his tax forms to the IRS, he attached this printed Schedule D to his other forms.

IT'S BOB'S DECISION

Managing Your Money helped Bob to decide which stocks to sell when. Of course, it didn't actually tell him to sell his stock, but it helped him understand the impact of selling various assets in his portfolio. And with this information, he made a decision.

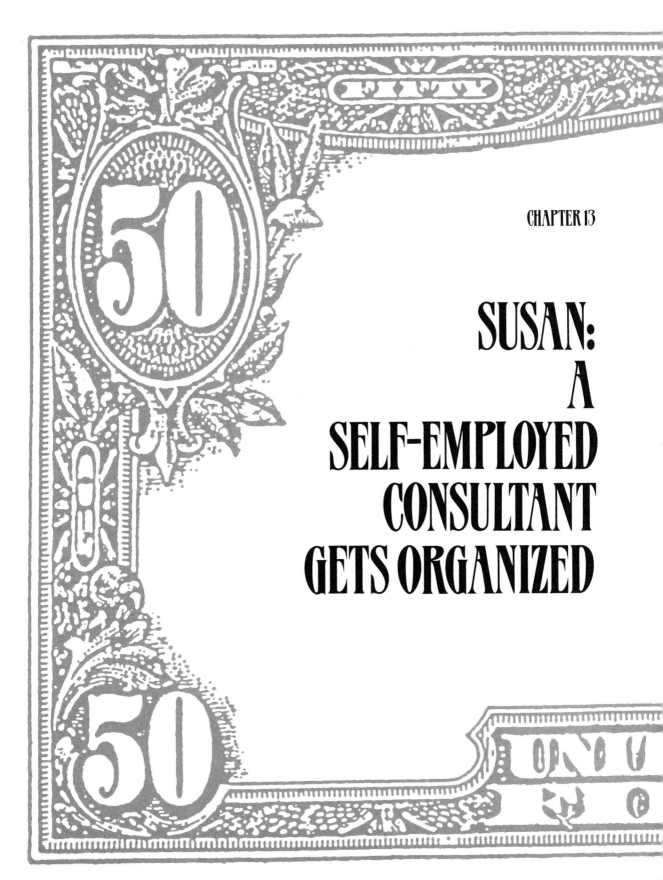

CHAPTER 13

SUSAN: A SELF-EMPLOYED CONSULTANT GETS ORGANIZED

Susan was perfectly happy at her job with a large corporation. As a marketing executive, she was responsible for training new employees in marketing the company's products. Her friends thought she was crazy when she resigned her $60,000-a-year position, but Susan wants to open her own business and become a marketing training consultant to several large and small companies. Having considered this for several years, Susan has saved enough money to fall back on in case the business doesn't succeed.

Knowing that she can return to a corporate job if she wants to, Susan has set a one-year goal for herself. If she doesn't earn at least half her former salary after one year and have prospects for earning at least as much as her full $60,000 salary in the second year, Susan will give up independent consulting and return to a full-time corporate job.

Susan's first task is to get organized. She doesn't want to set up her business with a full-blown accounting package yet, but she does want to track her accounts payable and accounts receivable—that is, her expenses and income. She also wants to project her income and expenses so that she can check her actual spending and receipts each month to determine if she will meet her year-end financial goal. Finally, she needs a way to track her schedule and her client contacts, both of which will be more varied than at her corporate job.

To meet these needs, Susan will use Managing Your Money every day. Using the Accounts Payable and Accounts Receivable features of Chapter 3, she will manage her business much as she manages her home finances. She can set up a budget for her business and allocate each income and expense check to a category in that budget. She can pay her business expenses with the program's check-printing facility and can print invoices to her clients.

To help her schedule appointments, Susan can use the reminder pad in Chapter 2 as an electronic daily planning calendar. The card file in Chapter 9 can help her keep track of her clients as well as save time because she can use it to dial directly through her computer's modem with the touch of a key.

A BUSINESS MAY USE A FISCAL YEAR THAT DIFFERS FROM THE STANDARD JANUARY-TO-DECEMBER CALENDAR YEAR.

Chapter 3 has several special options that are useful for running a small business. Susan plans to make good use of these options, but first she creates a second set of the Managing Your Money data files in a new subdirectory on her hard disk so that she can keep her business records separate from her home finances. Then she starts the program and turns to the Chapter 3 mini menu, where she chooses Optional Features.

At the Optional Features screen, Susan tells the program that she wants to use the Accounts Payable and Accounts Receivable options and she wants to change the fiscal year. Susan is beginning her new business in early April, so she types MAR in the blank for the last month of the fiscal year. Because she is using a separate set of data files and accounts, Susan doesn't need to worry about accidentally affecting her personal financial data, for which she uses a standard calendar year.

SUSAN'S BUSINESS BUDGET

Susan now sets up a business budget in the same way she set up her home budget. She chooses Budget Categories from the Chapter 3 mini menu. The first budget items she creates are those she can be sure of—her expenses.

Susan begins by creating a budget category for medical-insurance expenses, because it is one monthly expense she always pays. She allocates it to the Insurance category of the Schedule C tax category. Any business expenses and income that Susan incurs must be reported on Schedule C, so all the business expenses in her budget are allocated to subcategories in that tax category.

Next, Susan needs to record her projected budget for medical-insurance bills in the Budgets and Actuals screen. When she turns to this screen, she notices that the first month is April instead of January because she changed the program to use her April-to-March fiscal year. Medical insurance is a fairly stable expense, so Susan allocates $150 for each month of the year in the "Budget" column. As she pays her medical-insurance bills, the program automatically fills in the "Actual" column of her budget.

BUSINESS EXPENSES AND INCOME ARE REPORTED ON SCHEDULE C AT TAX TIME.

293

Because she's working out of the study in her home, her office expenses are minimal. However, she knows that she will incur telephone costs and mailing costs as well as bills for her office supplies. For each of these expenses, Susan creates a separate budget category, assigns it to a Schedule C tax category, and estimates some monthly budget figures for the Budgets and Actuals screen. Later, as Susan writes checks for these expenses, she can allocate the expenses to the appropriate budget category.

On the other side of the ledger, Susan creates only one budget income category: ''Consulting Income.'' In this category she will record her clients' payments. Like her expenses, her business income is reported on Schedule C, so she assigns this budget category to a Schedule C income category.

Now Susan must estimate her monthly income. She knows that she needs to project a monthly income of about $3,000 in order to achieve her $30,000 goal for her annual salary and still cover her operating costs. Susan enters $3,000 in the ''Budget'' column next to each month of the year. As she records the checks she receives from her clients, she will be able to track how close she comes to reaching her goal for her first year's pay.

CREATING A BUSINESS LEDGER: PAYABLES

After she creates her budget, Susan returns to the Chapter 3 mini menu and chooses Money Accounts. Her first task is to add a new account. To do this, she enters information about the checking account she opened to manage her business accounts, including the name of the bank, the account number, the type of account, and the initial balance of $5,000 that Susan loaned herself for start-up costs.

The new Metro Bank account appears on the Money Accounts screen, which looks a little different from the Money Accounts screen for Susan's personal finances. Susan can select two new options: Payables and Receivables. To record her initial accounts payable—her bills— Susan chooses the Payables option.

The screen for adding an account payable looks like a check. Here Susan adds her first bill, which is from her medical-insurance provider, Eastern Life Company. When adding a payable in the Add Account Payable screen, Susan enters the date of the invoice and the date on which the payment is actually due. Then she types the company name, its address, and the amount of the check she will eventually write. Susan must also allocate the payment to a budget category, so she chooses Allocate to Budget Categories and assigns the $150 payment to the Medical Insurance budget category. She then repeats this procedure for her other expenses.

Adding a payable and allocating it to a budget category is not the same as spending money out of the electronic checkbook in Chapter 3. Although Susan might not be able to pay all her bills immediately, she wants a record of bills and when they are due. The Accounts Payable screen provides this record. Susan then adds bills to the Accounts Payable screen as they come in, but pays them only when she decides the time is right. In addition to the ledger in the Accounts Payable screen, Susan also has the standard list of unreconciled transactions as a record of the bills already paid.

ACCOUNTS PAYABLE ARE BILLS THAT THE COMPANY OWES.

To pay Eastern Life from the Accounts Payable screen, Susan types an X next to the Eastern Life payable and tells the program to subtract the payment amount. As far as Susan's checkbook and budget are concerned, the bill is now paid.

If she wants to print the check on her printer, Susan must go to the Print Checks screen of the Metro Bank account. She included Eastern Life's address on the check so she can sign it and slip it into a window envelope for easy mailing.

CREATING A BUSINESS LEDGER: RECEIVABLES

After two weeks, Susan completes her first consulting assignment with Cogswell, Inc. Now it's time to record a receivable in her Accounts Receivable ledger. Susan chooses the Receivables option from the Money Accounts screen. Then she adds a receivable by filling out the Add Account Receivable screen, which looks like a deposit slip. Here

ACCOUNTS
RECEIVABLE
REPRESENT
MONEY THAT
CUSTOMERS OR
CLIENTS OWE
THE COMPANY.

she enters the invoice date, the date on which she wants to be paid, the amount ($1,500), and the company name and address. She then allocates the $1,500 to her "Consulting Income" budget category.

Returning to the Accounts Receivable screen, Susan sees her first receivable listed with the amount due her. (See Figure 13-1.) Obviously, Susan won't be paid until she bills Cogswell, Inc. To create an invoice, she types an X next to the Cogswell receivable and tells the program to print the selected invoice.

The invoice includes Cogswell's company name and address, the amount owed, the invoice date, and the due date. Also, if Susan enters her own name, company, and address in the System Setup portion of Chapter 1, the program prints this information on her invoice. (See Figure 13-2.)

After a few weeks, Cogswell pays Susan's bill. She returns to the Accounts Receivable screen, types an X next to the Cogswell receivable, and selects the Receive Marked Receivables option. The program records the payment in the budget and in the list of unreconciled transactions for the Metro Bank account.

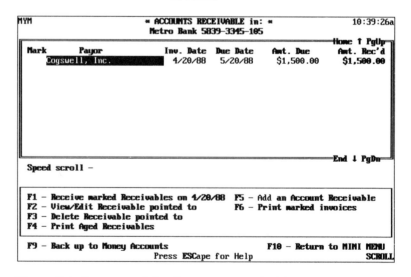

Figure 13-1. *Susan records her first account receivable.*

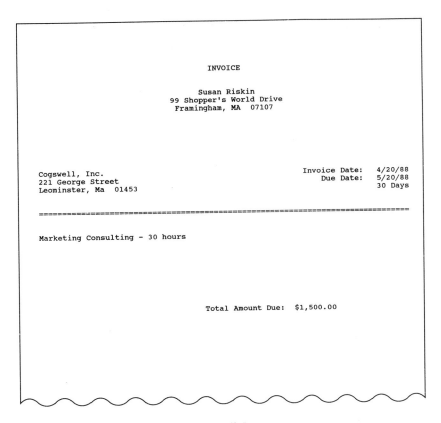

```
                                  INVOICE

                              Susan Riskin
                          99 Shopper's World Drive
                           Framingham, MA  07107




Cogswell, Inc.                                    Invoice Date:   4/20/88
221 George Street                                     Due Date:   5/20/88
Leominster, Ma   01453                                           30 Days


==========================================================================


Marketing Consulting - 30 hours




                            Total Amount Due:  $1,500.00
```

Figure 13-2. *A printed invoice to Cogswell, Inc.*

After a few more weeks, Susan has another important person to pay—herself. She needs to make a payment to her personal account with money from her business accounts, so that she can keep accurate records of her costs and income. Susan plans to make $30,000 annually, so she will pay herself $2,500 per month.

Rather than create a payable bill to herself, pay it to herself, and cash the check, Susan decides she will simply transfer the money from her business account to her personal account at the bank.

To record this transaction in her Managing Your Money accounts, she uses the Transfer Money feature. She returns to the Money Accounts screen and selects Transfer Money Between Accounts.

At the Transfer Money Between Accounts screen, Susan marks the Metro Bank listing with the FROM symbol and her personal account with the TO symbol. She enters $2,500 in the F1 field along with the date, method of transfer, and check number.

When Susan presses F1, the $2,500 is transferred from her business account to her personal account. The debit appears in the Metro Bank listing of Unreconciled Transactions and the income appears in her personal checking account.

But the Transfer Money feature does not allocate transactions to budget categories automatically, so Susan must visit the Unreconciled Transactions screens for both accounts and allocate the transfers to the proper budget categories. She can then reconcile the transactions in both accounts when she receives her bank statements.

Susan is now building up a healthy list of bills she paid and payments she earned. Her Accounts Payable and Accounts Receivable screens serve as a ledger of accounts, and the list of unreconciled transactions serves as her business checkbook. As Susan must reconcile her personal checkbook, she must also reconcile her business checkbook to the statements that Metro Bank sends her.

Susan returns to the Unreconciled Transactions screen and tells the program to reconcile her checkbook. The program displays the transactions to be reconciled, and Susan marks the checks and deposits that appear on the bank statement. She then enters the statement balance. Her electronic balance matches the bank's balance, so all the marked transactions can now be archived for later use with the Budget Archives feature of Chapter 3.

TRACKING BUSINESS GROWTH

After six months, Susan has worked for and billed several clients. She has also been able to pay her own monthly bills. Her bank account has grown, but she is unsure exactly how successfully she is meeting her original projected business budget.

To get an idea of how she is doing, Susan turns to the Chapter 3 mini menu and again chooses Budget Categories. This time she chooses the View Summary Graphs option, and a pie chart appears on the screen. (See Figure 13-3.) This chart segments her income according to the budget categories she set up. Susan has only two income budget categories: one for consulting income and a new one she created for interest on her business's savings account, which the pie chart includes.

Susan then displays the pie chart for her expenses. This one is more useful. Susan can see, for example, that her telephone bills account for a bigger piece of the pie than she anticipated. (See Figure 13-4 on the following page.)

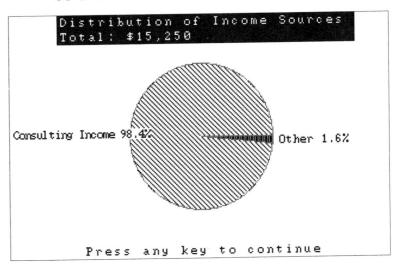

Figure 13-3. *Susan's income pie chart.*

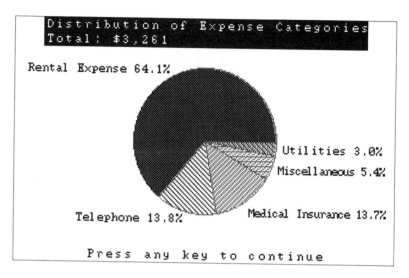

Figure 13-4. *Susan's expense pie chart.*

To investigate her telephone budget more closely, Susan returns to the Budget Categories screen, highlights the Telephone category, and displays the View or Edit screen. It shows that Susan has budgeted $50 per month, but her actual spending per month is more than she thought. A graph of this screen confirms that Susan is spending about $75 per month in this category. (See Figure 13-5.)

When Susan returns to the Budget Categories screen and indicates that she wants to view the "Consulting Income" category, she finds that she is earning about $3,500 a month—$500 more than she projected. At this rate, Susan will not only earn a salary of $30,000, but she will also compensate for the telephone and other expense categories that she originally underestimated.

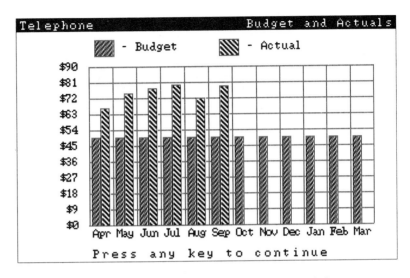

Figure 13-5. *Graph of Susan's telephone budget and actuals figures.*

AUTOMATING SUSAN'S SCHEDULE

In the six months that Susan has been consulting, she has not only used Chapter 3 to manage her accounts, but she has also used the reminder pad in Chapter 2 to manage her schedule. The reminder pad appears automatically the first time she enters the program on any day. Susan uses it to list her appointments, projects, and other tasks. She prints the reminder list at the start of each day and then checks off the tasks as she completes them.

Today, for example, the reminder pad indicates that she has an appointment with John Cogswell at 2:30 at the Cogswell offices. (See Figure 13-6 on the following page.) It also reminds her to call Spacely Inc. about their overdue bill. The rest of the day is open for her to write marketing reports, which are due in the coming weeks to other clients.

After she prints her reminders, she can check the amount of the Spacely bill by reviewing her accounts payable in Chapter 3. While there, she can take care of any other record-keeping tasks, or she can leave the program.

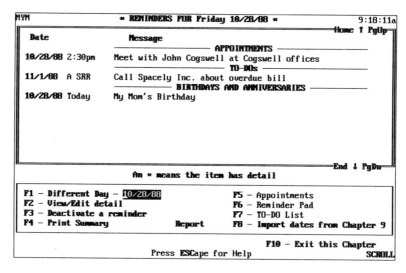

```
MYM                    * REMINDERS FOR Friday 10/28/88 *                    9:18:11a
                                                                     Home ↑ PgUp
  Date                     Message
  ─────────────────────────── APPOINTMENTS ───────────────
  10/28/88 2:30pm    Meet with John Cogswell at Cogswell offices
                                        ───── TO-DOs ─────
  11/1/88  A SRR     Call Spacely Inc. about overdue bill
                     ─────── BIRTHDAYS AND ANNIVERSARIES ───────
  10/28/88 Today     My Mom's Birthday



                                                                     End ↓ PgDn
                         An * means the item has detail

  F1 - Different Day - 10/28/88              F5 - Appointments
  F2 - View/Edit detail                     F6 - Reminder Pad
  F3 - Deactivate a reminder                F7 - TO-DO List
  F4 - Print Summary            Report      F8 - Import dates from Chapter 9

                                            F10 - Exit this Chapter
                         Press ESCape for Help                        SCROLL
```

Figure 13-6. *Susan views her Today's Reminders screen.*

At the end of the day, Susan returns to the reminder pad. Now she creates reminders for tomorrow and future dates. She forgot to call Spacely today, so she leaves that to-do item on the screen so that the program will remind her again. Also, because she always forgets to mark down the daily mileage she puts on her car for business purposes, she decides to create a reminder for this task. She needs this information on a daily basis if she wants to deduct this expense from her business income at tax time. So Susan creates a reminder that says "Record car mileage." The program then reminds her each day to mark down her business mileage.

Susan also creates weekly and monthly reminders to help her remember regularly scheduled client meetings and monthly billing cycles. She creates each reminder simply by entering the date and message on the Reminder Pad screen. When she creates a reminder to pay her monthly bills, Susan enters 10 in the Warning Days blank so that she will be reminded every day for the 10 days prior to the date the bill is due. In this way, she can be sure in advance that she has in stock enough form-feed checks, window envelopes, and stamps.

AUTOMATING SUSAN'S PHONE DIRECTORY

Susan has also found the card file in Chapter 9 of Managing Your Money to be a useful tool in running her consulting practice. Whenever she has several phone calls to make, Susan chooses Card File from the Main menu. The program then lists all her business contacts in alphabetic order by last name. Also listed on this screen are her contacts' first names, her relationship to each of them, and their telephone numbers.

Today Susan needs to telephone John Johnson, so she highlights Johnson's name and tells the program to dial. Using the automatic-dialing capability of Susan's modem, the program dials Johnson and tells Susan to pick up the phone. When Susan hears the phone ringing through her modem's speaker, she picks up the handset and presses the spacebar to open the phone line. If Johnson doesn't answer, Susan simply moves on to her next call and calls Johnson later.

A HAYES-COMPATIBLE MODEM IS NECESSARY FOR AUTOMATIC DIALING.

Of course, organizing the card file took some work. First, she had to connect her telephone to the output jack of her modem, and then she had to use the System Setup section of Chapter 1 to tell the Managing Your Money program that she was using a Hayes-compatible modem. The biggest task was entering the names and telephone numbers of all her contacts, who number more than 75. She had to record each file card separately with the Add a New Record option. Susan typically lists the names of her contacts, their titles, company names, telephone numbers, and their relationship to her. Whenever she dials someone, she can refer to the card to refresh her memory about the background and needs of the person she is calling.

A YEAR LATER

After a year of managing her schedule, telephone directory, and accounts with Managing Your Money, Susan earns $31,250 and decides to stick with her consulting business for another year. Next year, though, she hopes to earn almost twice as much. As a new fiscal year begins, she returns to her budget and increases her projections for the coming year.

INDEX

Page numbers for figures appear in italic.

JIM BARTIMO

Jim Bartimo is a business writer for the *San Jose Mercury News*. He has covered computing and the computer industry for *Personal Computing, InfoWorld,* and *Computerworld.* Bartimo has used Managing Your Money for five years to manage his investments.

OTHER TITLES FROM MICROSOFT PRESS

RUNNING MS-DOS®, 4th ed.
Van Wolverton

"This book is simply the definitive handbook of PC-/MS-DOS."
BYTE magazine

Join the more than one million PC and PS/2 users—from novice to expert—who use RUNNING MS-DOS, a richly informative overview of the PC-DOS and MS-DOS operating systems. Updated for version 4.0, RUNNING MS-DOS now includes information on the DOS Shell, the new graphical user interface. Wolverton shows you how to manage files and directories on a floppy-disk or hard-disk system; work with printers, monitors, and modems; automate frequently performed tasks with batch files; and use the built-in text editor and database. Novice computer users will value this book for Wolverton's clear writing style and the scores of easy-to-understand examples. Experienced PC users will find the command reference section in RUNNING MS-DOS an unmatched source of complete, up-to-date information.
560 pages, softcover $22.95   Order Code: 86-96965

SUPERCHARGING MS-DOS®, 2nd ed.
The Microsoft® Guide to High Performance Computing for the Experienced PC User
Van Wolverton

"If you want to make DOS jump through the hoops, this is probably where you want to start." *MicroTimes*

When you're ready for more, this updated sequel to RUNNING MS-DOS provides tips for intermediate to advanced business users on maximizing the power of MS-DOS through version 4.0. You'll find new material on the additions and changes to DOS commands, device driver updates, memory management, and printer control sequences. With SUPERCHARGING MS-DOS you get expert advice, reliable techniques, and short, effective programs to help you control the screen and keyboard with ANSI.SYS; create, examine, and change any file; personalize the CONFIG.SYS file; and construct a customized menu system.
352 pages, softcover $19.95   Order Code: 86-96973

SUPERCHARGING MS-DOS®, 2nd ed. (SOFTWARE VERSION)
Van Wolverton

SUPERCHARGING MS-DOS is also available with a handy 5.25-inch companion disk that contains all the batch files, script files, and programs in the book, and will save you time required to type them in. Used in conjunction with the book, the companion disk is a valuable, timesaving tool.
352 pages, softcover with one 5.25-inch disk $34.95   Order Code: 86-97013

QUICK REFERENCE GUIDE TO MS-DOS® COMMANDS, revised ed.
Van Wolverton

Need instant answers to DOS questions? Don't have much space at your workstation? The QUICK REFERENCE GUIDE TO MS-DOS COMMANDS will fill your needs. It's a handy, alphabetically arranged guide to all DOS, batch, configuration, and Edlin commands. A new section is devoted to the DOS Shell, and all the new and revised DOS commands are listed and explained. This is the perfect complement to RUNNING MS-DOS—invaluable to anyone with a DOS-based computer.
112 pages, softcover 4³/₈ x 8 $5.95   Order Code: 86-97047

LEARN WORD NOW

Janet Rampa

With little or no computer experience, you can easily follow this tutorial for Microsoft Word version 5. The liberal use of illustrations and step-by-step examples in LEARN WORD NOW makes this a welcome and nonthreatening introduction to Microsoft Word and word processing. The first section of the book addresses the 20 percent of Word that a novice must know to get started: entering and editing text, saving files, and printing. The second section addresses Word's more advanced features: glossaries, formatting, macros, and style sheets. In addition, easy-to-use appendixes include command summaries, keyboard and mouse shortcuts, and a primer on manipulating the AUTOEXEC.BAT and CONFIG.SYS files. You'll quickly find that LEARN WORD NOW will help you produce quality documents in no time at all.

416 pages, softcover $19.95   Order Code: 86-96445

RUNNING MICROSOFT® EXCEL
The Complete Reference to Microsoft Excel on the IBM® PC, PS/2™ and Compatibles

The Cobb Group: Douglas Cobb and Judy Mynhier

This is your tutorial and reference guide to Microsoft Excel on the IBM PC, PS/2, and compatibles. RUNNING MICROSOFT EXCEL covers every significant function and command of the spreadsheet, database, and charting environments. You will find examples of the major features of Microsoft Excel: worksheet auditing, file linking and sharing (with Microsoft Excel for the Macintosh and with Lotus 1-2-3), presentation-style formatting, and the built-in functions and macro commands. This combination reference and how-to book will be your primary source of information on Microsoft Excel.

736 pages, softcover $24.95   Order Code: 86-96197

RUNNING WINDOWS
The Microsoft® Guide to Windows 2.0, Windows/286, and Windows/386

Nancy Andrews and Craig Stinson

If you want a hands-on introduction to Windows 2.0, Windows/286, or Windows/386, turn to RUNNING WINDOWS. Here is all the current information you need to fully understand and successfully use Windows' built-in desk accessories and applications. And you'll learn to switch between applications, transfer information, and keep several tasks ready and open to work on. Additional sections show you how to tailor your Windows systems to your preferences and even use Windows in color. Dozens of examples are included.

368 pages, softcover $19.95   Order Code: 86-96346

Microsoft Press books are available wherever fine books are sold, or credit card orders can be placed by calling 1-800-638-3030 (in Maryland call collect 824-7300).

The manuscript for this book was prepared and submitted to Microsoft Press in electronic form. Text files were processed and formatted using Microsoft Word.

Cover design by Greg Hickman
Interior text design by Darcie S. Furlan and Rikki Conrad Design
Principal typography by Rodney Cook

Text and display composition by Microsoft Press in Times Roman, using the Magna composition system and the Linotronic 300 laser imagesetter.